SLOVAKIA SINCE INDEPENDENCE

A Struggle for Democracy

Minton F. Goldman

Westport, Connecticut
London

Library of Congress Cataloging-in-Publication Data

Goldman, Minton F.
    Slovakia since independence : a struggle for democracy / Minton F.
    Goldman.
        p.   cm.
    Includes bibliographical references (p.   ) and index.
    ISBN 0-275-96189-3 (alk. paper)
    1. Slovakia—Politics and government—1993– 2.   Slovakia—Foreign
relations—1993– I. Title
DB2848.G65 1999
    327.4373—dc21   98-15656

British Library Cataloguing in Publication Data is available.

Library of Congress Catalog Card Number: 98-15656
ISBN: 0-275-96189-3

First published in 1999

Praeger Publishers, 88 Post Road West, Westport, CT 06881
An imprint of Greenwood Publishing Group, Inc.

Printed in the United States of America

∞™

The paper used in this book complies with the
Permanent Paper Standard issued by the National
Information Standards Organization (Z39.48-1984).

10 9 8 7 6 5 4 3 2 1

Contents

To Maureen

for her thoughtful, imaginative, and invaluable assistance
as well as for her continuous encouragement and patience

Introduction

Since becoming an independent country after its split from Czechoslovakia on January 1, 1993, Slovakia's development from communism to political and economic democracy, underway when it was part of post-Communist Czechoslovakia, has been difficult and halting. Of all of the ex-Communist countries in central and Eastern Europe, Slovakia has been among the slowest to change. This book discusses this phenomenon, showing how Slovakia's political conservatism, economic poverty, multinational society, and desire for international recognition have shaped its development since independence.

The book is divided into eight chapters. The first chapter explores Slovak relations with Czechs from the establishment of the new Czechoslovak state in 1918 through the interwar years, World War II, and the years of Communist rule until its collapse in 1989, focusing on the growth of Slovak nationalism. The second chapter explains how this Slovak nationalism gave rise to Slovak separatism and led eventually, and inevitably, to the breakaway from Czechoslovakia at the end of 1992 and the creation of an independent Slovak state.

The theme of the next three chapters is the price the Slovaks paid for this independence. The book examines the political, economic, and sociocultural problems the new Slovak state experienced as it tried to establish its national identity, develop a democratic political system, move toward a more prosperous free market economy, and maintain societal unity and cohesion.

In the context of this theme, chapter 3 explains how and why Slovak society supported the authoritarian leadership of Prime Minister Vladimir Meciar. It discusses Meciar's authoritarian approach, in particular his government's efforts to influence the media and discourage opposition. This chapter shows how Meciar's behavior raised questions about Slovakia's capacity to fulfill the expectations of its people and those of its friends abroad in central/Eastern Europe and in the West that it could achieve a viable democratic political system.

Chapter 4 looks at Slovak efforts in the 1990s to introduce a free market economy and shows why the Bratislava government has moved only in the most halting way toward a dismantling of the centralized, state-controlled economy inherited from the Communist past. It focuses on a key aspect of Slovak free market reform, privatization, explaining why Slovakia could not accept the kind of rapid change advocated by Western governments (in contrast with the faster pace by Slovakia's neighbors in central Europe, notably Poland, Hungary, and the Czech Republic). Slovakia experienced punishing inflation, unemployment, and social anxiety, which bred a popular skepticism about economic liberalization and insistence that the government keep in place a costly social safety net regardless of the country's capacity to pay for it. While pointing out that Slovakia's gross national product is growing, this chapter shows that Slovakia still has a long way to go before its living standards match those of neighboring countries in central Europe and lags way behind the societies of Western Europe with which Slovaks like to compare themselves.

Chapter 5 discusses how Slovak leaders have wrestled with the problem of governing minorities, especially the country's large Hungarian minority, which constitutes 10 percent of its total population. The repressive nature of Slovak policies under Prime Minister Meciar toward Hungarian-speaking Slovak citizens violates the spirit and even the letter of the country's constitution, which guarantees minority rights. Moreover, these policies, intended to unify and assimilate the Hungarian minority and to strengthen national unity, have come at a price. At the very least, they have undermined the credibility of Slovak democracy not only with many Slovaks but also with the West, especially the European Union, of which Slovak leaders of all ideological persuasions would like Slovakia to be a member. They also have made for bad diplomatic blood with neighboring Hungary. This chapter also explores the predicament of other minorities, in particular Ruthenians and Roma. The Bratislava government's treatment of these smaller minorities, often given scant attention in books about contemporary Slovakia, is important because it reveals much about the country's values and development. Chapter 5 looks at other threats to social peace and harmony, in particular the predicament of women and a resurgence of anti-Semitism.

Chapters 6 and 7 examine post-independence Slovak foreign policy, explaining how in the mid and late 1990s Slovakia is trying to find its proper international role. In particular they show how and why Slovak leaders fear the isolation of their country and have worked hard to avoid it by developing new relationships with areas of strategic as well as economic importance to Slovakia's well-being as an independent state.

Chapter 6 argues that post-independence Slovak leaders seek a balance of Slovak interests in good relations with both Russia and other countries to the east, in particular Romania, with which it has had close ties in the immediate post-independence era, and in strengthened links to the West, of which all Slovaks in the post-Communist era of all political persuasions believe their country should be an integral part. The chapter looks at Slovakia's interest in joining the European Union, its ambivalent attitude toward NATO, and the difficulties it has had developing strong ties to the United States, which believes that Slovakia should go further and faster away from the old Communist autocratic political and socioeconomic order than it has under Prime Minister Meciar's leadership. This chapter shows that Meciar's strong role has been key. He has had personal interest in cultivating Slovakia's ties with post-Soviet Russia to balance relations with the West. Reflecting old Communist political realities, he wants to use friendship with Moscow as a lever in dealing with the European Union and the United States on trade and security issues.

Chapter 7 looks closely at Slovakia's relations with neighbors with which it has had some serious problems, notably the Czech Republic and Hungary. This chapter explores post-independence Slovakia's problems with the Czech Republic in the areas of citizenship, trade, and the shared boundary and suggests sources of potential confrontation between the two peoples who only a few years ago lived under a common administrative roof. Chapter 7 also shows how the minorities issue and the controversy over the way in which the Gabcikovo-Nagymoros dam project, which threatened the Danubian environment shared by both countries, strained Slovak-Hungarian relations. Slovak differences with Hungary also have complicated Slovak relations with the European Union, which often has expressed its concern about explosions of anger in both countries against each other that complicate their efforts to integrate with the West.

All through the book the theme of nationalism is emphasized. The book shows how a strong Slovak nationalism rooted in recent history has had an impact on policy-making in almost every sphere of national life. Shaped by a popular conviction that they had not been well served by Hungarian rule or by the more recent union with Czechs, this nationalism, the book argues, allows the Slovak leaders to disregard liberal principles in political, economic, and sociocultural spheres of policy-making when issues of national pride are involved. Thus,

Meciar's strong authoritarian tendencies, his conservative approach to privatization and other policies involving the curtailment and elimination of state control over Slovakia's economic life, his repressive treatment of the country's minorities, especially the Hungarian community, and much of his foreign policy—in particular his special interest in cultivating Russia despite the liabilities for his commitment to good relations with Western Europe—all have a logic born of Slovak nationalism, of which he is his country's chief and most persuasive spokesman.

But, as the book also shows in every chapter, there are other ingredients of post-independence Slovak development besides nationalism. Chapter 3 identifies obstacles to democratic development, which include Slovakia's multiparty system, the weakness of political groups with liberal democratic ideology, a nostalgia for the predictability and psychosocial security of the Communist past, a revival of interest in the fascist government of President Jozef Tiso during World War II, when Slovakia enjoyed a brief period of administrative independence as a satellite of Nazi Germany, and a popular penchant for the kind of strong, directive, and charismatic leadership provided by Prime Minister Meciar. Chapter 4 suggests that Slovakia's efforts to move toward a free market economy and raise living standards at least to a level enjoyed elsewhere in central Europe were complicated by overall economic underdevelopment that were far worse than that of the Czech Republic, Poland, and Hungary. This chapter shows how corruption of political leaders who saw in free market reform opportunities for the enhancement of personal wealth helped to undermine and slow the rate of economic change. Chapter 5 shows how a lack of an understanding of and sympathy for minority rights and the perceived need to maintain order in a multicultural, ethnically diverse social setting help explain the Bratislava government's difficulty conciliating its Hungarian minority. The chapters on foreign policy show how the intrusive concern of outsiders with Slovak domestic behavior, especially Slovakia's central European neighbors and the established Western democracies, nurtured a degree of defensiveness in the development of new foreign policy orientations.

This book shows why post-independence Slovak development contrasts with more successful patterns of development elsewhere in the region, notably in the Czech Republic, Poland, and Hungary. It is also clear why post-independence Slovakia has much in common in overall development with Balkan countries, in particular Romania, Bulgaria, Serbia, and Albania. As the decade of the 1990s draws to a close, however, these countries, with the exception of Albania, have been moving more rapidly than Slovakia toward democratic norms in the political and economic spheres. It is one of the purposes of this book to explain this phenomenon and to show that policies of the recent past could leave Slovakia poor and isolated from the democracies of central and Eastern Europe with which it most wants to be associated.

This consequence is not inevitable. Slovakia may be moving slowly, but despite the pain of transformation, Slovakia *is* moving toward a more liberal political system than it had under Communist rule and that will satisfy its own internal needs. While it is too soon to tell if it will succeed, there are strengths and resiliency in the country that give cause for hope. For example, Slovak politicians of all ideological persuasions seem willing to play according to the rules of parliamentary government, in particular the one that guards against dictatorship, namely, the requirement of a surrender of power when voters demand it in parliamentary and other elections. Also, the Slovak parliamentary system seems resilient despite the authoritarian behavior of the Meciar leadership, the burden of coping with still-severe economic problems, and the sociocultural problems arising out of the multiethnic character of the population.

As most of the other formerly Communist-ruled states of central and Eastern Europe move forward with their transformation to achieve some variant of democracy, Slovakia moves as well. However, its much slower pace is an intriguing subject for study and provides further insight into the problems of developing a variant of Western-style democracy in countries ruled by Communism and subjected to Soviet control for over 40 years.

The book tries to argue that Slovakia is more likely to go forward rather than backward given its historical and cultural makeup and eventually follow in the path of the West European democracies, ridding itself of authoritarian styles of political behavior when they become outmoded. Showing that a commitment to democratic government is strong among Slovak voters and leaders and arguing that the country can address the pressing socioeconomic problems inherited from the Communist era, the book concludes that Slovak democracy can succeed as most of its people and leaders earnestly hope.

Background to Independence

Slovaks and Czechs, 1918–1989

Within three years of the 1989 fall of Communist rule, the Czechoslovak state split into two separate and sovereign entities, the Czech Republic and Slovakia. The breakup of the country, which had been unified since 1918, came quickly and took politicians, voters, and concerned outsiders by surprise. A closer look at how the split occurred shows that the division of Czechoslovakia grew out of a long period of tension between the Czech and Slovak peoples and offers some lessons about the difficulty of controlling the growth of ethnocultural nationalism, especially its corrosive impact on otherwise stable and secure political communities.

HISTORIC DIFFERENCES AMONG SLOVAKS AND CZECHS

Though sharing a common Slavic heritage, Czechs and Slovaks had different political, economic, and cultural characteristics. Before World War I, Hungary had ruled the Slovaks; for the most part, its regime was direct, centralized, and repressive, especially regarding Slovak culture. Indeed, it is possible to speak of a "Magyarization" of Slovak language and culture, especially after the creation of the "Dual Monarchy," sometimes called the *Ausgleich* (compromise), in 1867, which gave the Hungarian government in Budapest direct control over territory inhabited predominantly by Slovaks.[1]

Austria in this same period administered territory inhabited by Czechs, notably Bohemia and Moravia. Having granted Czechs a measure of political rights and self-rule in the aftermath of the revolution of 1848 in Prague, Austria's rule of the Czech lands was much more benign than Hungary's administration of the Slovaks.

By the end of the nineteenth century the Slovaks had few political ties to the Czechs. While developing their own national identity, Czech nationalists paid little attention to the Slovaks. They assumed that Slovakia eventually would become part of Hungary and that they had no control over this eventuality.[2] Meanwhile, Slovaks were pulled closer to Hungary, with much less sociocultural interaction with the West and far less experience with self-government than Czechs had. By the beginning of the twentieth century Slovaks also had an economy much less developed than that of the Czechs, depending mostly on agriculture, while the Czechs under Austria had developed a solid transportation and communication infrastructure. By 1914, the Slovaks had a significantly lower standard of living than the Czechs. They were also less politically experienced than the Czechs, who had gained substantial, practical experience with self-government, including the universal male franchise introduced in 1906. By contrast most Slovaks remained outside of politics, lacking opportunities to participate because Hungary maintained stiff property and other qualifications for the right to vote.[3]

In addition, even though Czechs and Slovaks were predominantly Roman Catholic, the religious behavior of the two communities was different. Czech Catholics, like French Catholics, had a distinct anticlerical tradition, in contrast with the Slovak Catholics, for whom religion was an all-encompassing part of daily existence.[4]

THE 1918 CZECH-SLOVAK POLITICAL UNION

Despite these differences, Czech and Slovak nationalists, driven by a wave of nationalism sweeping Europe as World War I drew to a close, believed their common Slavic heritage offered a basis for union. Slovak nationalists were sympathetic to a union because they resented Hungary's attempts to Magyarize the Slovak people and because they believed Slovaks would benefit from close links to their Czech neighbors, both culturally and economically.[5]

Unfulfilled Slovak Expectations

Leaders of the two communities had different expectations of a union. T. G. Masaryk and other Czech nationalists dreamed of a great Czech-led Slavic nation in west central Europe, with its capital in Prague. Therefore they supported an agreement signed in May 1918 in

Pittsburgh, Pennsylvania, by Masaryk with Czech and Slovak emigres in the United States, uniting the two communities and assuring fair and equitable treatment of Slovaks in a new state of Czechoslovakia.[6]

For their part, Slovak leaders expected that Slovaks would be equal partners with the Czechs in the new state, not in any way subordinate to or overshadowed by them as they had been by the Hungarians. They expected that Czechoslovakia's national wealth and progress would be shared equally between the two Slavic peoples and therefore would benefit materially from the union.[7]

Their expectations were not unreasonable. Masaryk was sensitive to Slovak national feelings and to a degree did consider Slovaks partners with the Czechs in developing a Slavic-dominated country that had, in addition to the Czechs and Slovaks, a substantial German minority living in the Sudetenland. Masaryk also believed that the Czech-Slovak alliance was essential to offset the influence of the German minority the new Czechoslovak Republic must include.[8] Moreover, the Pittsburgh agreement itself contained a clause stipulating that Slovakia should have its own courts, administration, and assembly, which led Slovaks to feel confident about their equal role in the governance of the country.[9]

At the same time, however, there was skepticism among some Czechs about union with the Slovaks, who were seen as a potential drain on Czech resources. Indeed, many Czechs, because they were much better off economically and more politically advanced than the Slovaks, felt that Slovaks needed Czechs more than Czechs needed Slovaks.[10] Meanwhile, some Slovak nationalists also were resistant to a union. They distrusted Masaryk because of his agnosticism and liberalism. But, more important, they worried that in a union with the Czechs the Slovak national culture would be subsumed and lost. According to these people the similarity between Slovak and Czech culture made union with the Czechs more dangerous to the survival of a distinct Slovak culture than Magyarization, which was an obvious threat and therefore easy to resist.[11]

Czech Dominance

As matters turned out, Slovaks had far less influence than they had expected over how the new state was to work. The 1920 Czechoslovak Constitution, while liberal and democratic, did not recognize a separate Slovak identity; rather, it identified Slovaks with Czechs under the label "Czechoslovaks." [12] The Czechs had over 60 percent of the population of this new state, and with Prague, a Czech city, as its capital the Czechs soon dominated the new state. Czech dominance brought discrimination with it. Czechs were more numerous and better paid than Slovaks in the national government. In the early years of the Czechoslovak state, only 17 percent of ministerial assignments went to Slovaks. Czechs dominated the Czechoslovak Army leadership (out of 139 generals, only 1 was a Slovak); and of the 1246 officials in the Czechoslovak Ministry of Foreign Affairs, only 33 were Slovak. When Czech officials were appointed in Slovak-dominated areas, Slovaks were resentful and felt inadequate, because they did not have enough trained personnel to fill the vacancies. Even when trained Slovaks became available, Czech officials stayed on.[13]

Prague's economic policy was Czech oriented, with Slovakia's agriculture neglected. In addition, little was done to upgrade Slovakia's inferior technology, which made competition with Czech firms difficult and often impossible.[14] Slovak industry was already in a slump when the Depression hit in the early 1930s. As a result, the Slovak economy remained stagnant for most of the interwar period, and Slovaks became increasingly resentful of Prague's unwillingness to pay more attention to Slovakia.[15]

To some extent Czech dominance was driven by international conditions. The Czech leaders, Prime Minister Masaryk and President Benes, wanted a tight Czech-Slovak relationship to keep the new state unified. Together the Czechs and Slovaks could fend off possible claims on their territory by Germany, seeking the Sudetenland, and Hungary, having similar ambitions in southeastern Slovakia. Czech fears were justified. In the 1930s, both Germany and Hungary pursued an irredentist foreign policy that endangered Czechoslovakia's territorial integrity and independence. In particular Czech leaders believed that only by tightly controlling Slovakia could they keep it safe from a Hungarian effort to regain territory lost to Czechoslovakia after World War I.

Under these circumstances Czech dominance, at least for Czech nationalists, had an "iron logic."[16] Indeed, in 1932, Benes, then foreign minister, argued that greater autonomy for Slovakia would "mean for this state the slogan Slovakia to the Slovaks, German regions to the Germans, Magyar regions to the Magyars."[17]

Czech dominance of Czechoslovakia in the interwar period was driven also by cultural ideology. For example, in 1921, Masaryk said there was no Slovak nation or separate Slovak culture. "Cultural differences" between the two communities resulted from the way in which the pre–World War I Hungarian overlordship of Slovakia had kept the Slovaks down politically. Benes agreed, saying that Slovaks were a small population, insufficient to create a "national culture" of their own.[18]

These views underlie policies of "Czechoslovakism" or of a Czechoslovakian version of *La Mission Civilatrice* that had inspired the centralizing tendencies of French colonial policy in some portions of North and West Africa controlled by France in the nineteenth century. Czech leaders in the early history of the Czechoslovak state fancied they had a moral responsibility to improve the level of development of their ethnic Slavic brothers, making it equal to that of their own. This belief and the integrative policies that sprang from it, by precluding autonomy for Slovakia, met the security needs of the new state by fostering unity and cohesion based on one common, though Czech-dominated, polity.

Slovak Reactions. While some Slovak nationalists, notably Vavro Srobar, saw advantages in accepting Czech dominance, which they believed could strengthen Slovak society politically and economically until it could be ready for self-assertion at a later date, other Slovaks thought differently. Indeed, Srobar was in many respects what could be called a "Czechoslovak Slovak," that is, one with faith in the unity of Slovaks and Czechs. For Srobar, Czechs did not speak a foreign language or practice an alien religion that set them off from the Slovaks. However, from the vantage point of a disillusioned, angered, and radicalized group of Slovak nationalists, in particular the Roman Catholic priest Andrej Hlinka, founder of the Christian Slovak People's Party, who combined Slovak nationalism with strong anti-Semitism and anti-communism, Czech dominance was not so materially beneficent. In his view Czech dominance denied Slovaks their fair share of political power and national wealth. The Czechs, he believed, had violated the spirit, if not the letter, of promises made in 1918. Some Slovak political and intellectual leaders also believed that the Czechs were bent on eventually assimilating the Slovak community.[19]

Czech dominance in the interwar period provoked deep resentment among many thoughtful Slovaks. As Ferdis Juriga, a Slovak deputy in the federal parliament, put it:

> The Slovak region has only the right to be able to ask and only receives what the ministry approves, and therefore cannot decide anything without the approval of . . . Prague. I hope and believe that the Slovak nation will grow in culture, education, and economic capacity, and in the struggle for the rights of the Slovak nation, so that we need not say to Prague, "pretty please," but "I require."[20]

The Nazi Threat

Slovak distrust of the Czechs increased in the late 1930s. Germany annexed the Sudetenland in the fall of 1938 and invaded Prague in March 1939; throughout this aggression the Czechoslovak government offered little resistance, hoping that powerful friends abroad like France and Russia would come forward with diplomatic and military help. These outsiders never did. The successful invasion of Prague in March 1939 convinced some Slovaks that the Czechs were weak and that the Slovak community would be better off as an independent nation.[21]

On October 6, 1939, less than a week after German troops had forcefully entered the Sudetenland, the Czechoslovak government approved an accord granting autonomy to Slovakia. It was a move to nudge the Slovaks closer to the Czechs in this moment of crisis by responding to concerns of the Slovaks for more control over their local affairs. This Zilina Accord granted the Slovak community substantial administrative autonomy, resembling what many Slovaks believed the Pittsburgh agreement had promised but never delivered. According to the Zilina Accord, Slovakia was to have at long last a regional parliament and regional ministries. The Zilina Accord implemented the Pittsburgh agreement. The name of the state was changed to "Czecho-Slovak Republic" to take into account the new and extensive administrative autonomy Slovakia now enjoyed. Although the Zilina Accord was never implemented by Prague, it still symbolized what Slovakia wanted and would demand in the future as the price of unity with the Czechs. Benes, however, never recognized the Zilina Accord, considering it in the same category as the Munich agreement, that is, as conditions forced on Czechoslovakia against its will at gunpoint.[22]

By the eve of World War II, many Slovaks had a strong feeling of hostility toward Czechoslovakia. Father Hlinka was typical of Slovaks who resented and disliked Czechs. His party reportedly greeted the October, 1938, German annexation of the Sudetenland with a laconic "Adieu, Prague."[23]

NAZI GERMANY AND SLOVAK–CZECH RELATIONS

In early 1939, Berlin proposed Slovak independence in return for an alliance against the Soviet Union. Slovak leaders, despite strong anti-Czech nationalist leanings, had reservations about German policy. But, they agreed on March 14, 1939, to the German proposition, and Slovakia declared independence.[24] In June 1941, Slovakia joined Germany in declaring war on the Soviet Union. Germany's alliance with the new Slovak state along with its occupation of Bohemia and the conversion of Moravia into a German protectorate extinguished the Czechoslovak state.[25]

Slovakia's Controversial Independence

During World War II the independent Slovak state was led by Monsignor Jozef Tiso, a conservative Catholic cleric. He reenforced Slovakia's national identity, increasing educational opportunities for Slovak youth and creating the Slovak Academy of Arts and Sciences. He also encouraged economic growth and development. The Germans had a large hand in the Slovak economic system during the war, helping Slovak banks, agriculture, and export industries to thrive. With the help of German investment Tiso's government expanded the country's transportation and communications infrastructure. By the end of the war there was no doubt that the Slovaks had managed their affairs quite efficiently and had made a success of limited self-rule despite their intimacy with Germany.[26]

Of course, as a German political satellite, Slovakia had to meet German expectations to become an example of the "New Order" Hitler intended for allies in southeastern Europe. Initially, there was little German interference in the day-to-day operation of the Slovak administration, although Hitler insisted that the Tiso regime display in all its behavior a positive and friendly attitude toward Germany. But before long, Hitler was insisting that Slovakia in fact become a Nazi state. Berlin made sure that everything the government in Bratislava did was in accordance with German wishes. German government agencies assigned large "advisory missions" to all Slovak ministries to assure complete coordination of policy between Slovakia and Germany. The Slovak economy was harnessed to the German war effort, with production determined by German needs. To assure abject Slovak loyalty, German troops were stationed in the Vah valley outside of Budapest and on Austrian territory across the Danube; and German diplomats in Bratislava kept a vigilant eye on local politics, ready to advise Berlin of the slightest anti-German gesture. Finally, top positions of the Slovak government, including the Foreign Ministry, were led by Slovak "Hitlerites."[27]

Throughout World War II, as a German satellite, Slovakia cooperated with Nazi anti-Jewish policies. The Tiso government enacted laws restricting Jewish participation in the political and economic life of the country and eventually helped in the deportation of Slovak Jews to Nazi-occupied Poland. Though he knew better—he was warned by Slovak rabbis that deported Jews would be exterminated—Tiso chose not to refute the Nazi fiction that European Jews were to be concentrated in one place and allowed to develop their own life.[28]

Those who defended Tiso, and accepted a view that it was in Slovakia's best interests to accommodate the Nazis, also believed him when he said that when he learned Slovak Jews were being murdered in Poland by the Nazis, he tried to save as many as he could from transit. Moreover, Tiso, a conservative Catholic, seemed at times uneasy over aggressive Nazi policy toward the Church, and tried to make out that he was not a Slovak "Hitlerite," as were some other Slovak politicians like Bela Tuka. Tuka achieved lasting fame in the history of this period for having been instructed, presumably by Hitler, to declare Slovakia's commitment to National Socialism on July 30, 1940.[29]

Slovakia's World War II alliance with Germany encouraged many in both Slovakia and abroad to associate Slovak nationalism with Nazi fascism and anti-Semitism. This was not entirely justified. For example, Minister of the Interior Jan D'urcansky, thought to be pro-German, in fact had changed his mind about the virtue of German power in Slovakia. Early on in the new era, he suspected that Hitler would eventually be defeated by the Western powers. He tried to delay the expansion of German influence over the Slovak administration and economy and to protect Slovak Jews in an effort to dissociate Slovakia from Germany's anti-Semitic policies and to enhance the Tiso government's image in the West. He tried as best he could to push his country in the direction of neutrality, which was out of the question. Indeed, the Germans came quickly to suspect D'urcansky's loyalty and had him dismissed.[30]

Furthermore, by 1943, many Slovaks had begun to organize resistance to the Tiso government. In December 1943, in what came to be known as the Christmas agreement, several resistance groups including the communists pledged cooperation against the Tiso regime and its Nazi patron. The Resistance pledged that after the war the Slovak and Czech nations should reconstitute Czechoslovakia on the basis of national equality and should ally itself in foreign policy and military affairs with the Soviet Union. With Soviet encouragement and support and with the acquiescence of exiled Czechoslovak President Benes, Slovak Communists steadily increased their influence over the Slovak antifascist resistance, positioning themselves to play a leading role in postwar Slovak politics.[31]

In the summer of 1944, the resistance prepared for a major uprising against the Tiso regime. It occurred in August of 1944. Among its leaders were influential Slovak Communists like Gustav Husak and Aleksandr Dubcek, who had participated with the approval of the Kremlin in the Christmas agreement. Although the nucleus of the uprising was the Slovak Army, the Communists eventually took control of it. The uprising turned out to be a disaster for the Slovaks. The Germans brought in reinforcements from other fronts and quickly got the upper hand. They decisively crushed the uprising by October. The Germans then punished the resistance, killing civilians as well as partisans and deporting 30,000 people to German concentration camps.[32]

The whole episode, by suggesting that many Slovaks hated the Tiso regime and were willing to risk their lives to rid the country of fascism and the Nazi overlordship, helped cleanse the somewhat tarnished image of this first Slovak experience with independence. It also gave rise to a degree of schizophrenia in Slovak nationalism, which henceforth reflected both antifascist and fascist tendencies.

Czech Reactions to Slovak Independence. The 1944 uprising did little to mitigate Czech hostility toward the Slovaks for their "desertion" and closeness to Hitler. The Czech community saw the independent pro-Nazi Slovak state during World War II as a betrayal of Czechoslovakia, of which they had been an integral part. In 1939 Benes told Milan Hodza, a former Czechoslovak prime minister, that Slovaks could not possibly be ignorant of the significance of their behavior, saying, "No Czech will forget this. For twenty years we did everything for the Slovaks . . . When things were at their worst for us, the Slovaks stabbed us in the back."[33] Benes also chastised the Slovaks directly, saying in a radio broadcast in 1943 from exile, "Do you realize the moral horror of the situation? Do you see how the dates of March 14–15, 1939, will appear in the history of Slovakia?"[34]

Benes thought he had the only plausible explanation of Slovak treachery, given the kindness he believed Czech leaders had always shown Slovaks. He said that they got their disloyalty from the Hungarians, who in their long rule of Slovak lands had "corroded" the Slovak soul.[35] It was probably more true that Benes's harsh words for the Slovaks were simply a reflection of his own demoralization over having had to capitulate to the Germans and stand by helplessly as they destroyed his young country. Slovak leaders deeply resented Benes's view, which implied that Slovakia should have risked the wrath of Hitler, defied him, and fought against the Germans. Dr. Stefan Osusky, in his critical study of Benes and Slovakia, called attention to the way tens of thousands of Czechs worked in factories producing goods for Germany. Was this not a kind of "treason," he wondered?[36]

Slovaks and Czechs at the End of World War II

When World War II came to an end in 1945, the Tiso government collapsed. The Allies saw to it that the Slovaks were reunited with Czechs in a reconstituted Czechoslovak state that had never really disappeared. Certainly, this was the Czech point of view. Moreover, in the view of the Allies the only legitimate Czechoslovak government in the war years was the one in exile in London under the leadership of President Benes. Slovaks were told that their continued independence in the postwar period was unacceptable to the Allies, that reunion was the only alternative, and that they had the Czechs to thank for not being treated by the Allies as an enemy state. Many Slovaks, in particular Slovak Communists, accepted the restoration of Czechoslovakia's prewar unity but on the understanding, expressed in the so-called Kosice Agreement in 1945, that the new state would provide for Slovak equality and autonomy.[37]

As events demonstrated, Slovak politicians had very little bargaining power with their Czech counterparts. Though Benes spoke of some administrative decentralization in the new Czechoslovakia, he gave no details.[38] For example, he told the opening session of the Czechoslovak National Assembly on October 28, 1945, that "if we have no Germans and Hungarians among us, decentralization will not only be possible but will be absolutely essential for the whole population of the Republic." But, he never made clear what he meant by "decentralization."[39]

It made no difference for Slovak-Czech relations that the country did indeed rid itself of most of the German minority, who were blamed for the German invasion and destruction of Czechoslovakia. The Czechoslovak Government expelled most of the Sudeten Germans, who settled in Germany, which for many of them was a foreign country. The expulsion seemed to undermine an argument made in the past that concessions to the Slovak community also would have to be made to other minorities endangering the country's fragile unity. Henceforth, the Czechoslovak National Socialist Party led by Benes sought the total assimilation of the Slovak people, by whatever means necessary.[40]

An influential Slovak politician at the end of the war summed up the Slovak reaction to these developments: "(Benes) did not recognize for us any national rights. In fact he did not even recognize us as a nation."[41] Further to this point were comments attributed by Karol Sidor to Karel Kramar, Czechoslovakia's first prime minister, in a book on Slovak politics in the interwar period and published in Bratislava in 1943. Kramer allegedly remarked that Slovaks should be given the independence they craved to show them how truly dependent they were for their survival on the Czechs. According to Sidor, Kramar said, "I am strongly convinced that you (soon)...would be on your knees for us to take you back." Implicit in this kind of thinking was the perception that Slovaks were indebted to Czechs but stubbornly refused to acknowledge their indebtedness and, worse, that Slovaks showed ingratitude by demanding that Czechs bequeath them self-rule. Needless to say, this kind of thinking, quite pervasive among Czechs in this era, infuriated Slovaks.[42]

By the post–World War II era, many Slovaks had become convinced that Czechs never did and never would understand Slovaks and that they viewed Slovak demands for autonomy as unrealistic, even boorish and provincial. To Slovaks this Czech point of view was quite unacceptable because it seemed to imply an all-too-easy dismissiveness of sentiments strongly held by Slovaks. Despite the many cultural similarities that were readily apparent, Slovaks really did see themselves as different from Czechs and deserving of recognition, by Czechs as well as by others, of their distinctive identity including aspirations for genuine and extensive self-rule, perhaps even independence.[43]

Another wedge in the Slovak-Czech relationship came when, in the spring of 1947, the Allies brought ex–Slovak president Tiso to trial for treason. The trial of Tiso, who remained a popular figure after the war, provoked a social crisis. His apologists in Slovakia insisted that he should not be condemned because he did what was "expedient" to preserve some Slovak autonomy in the face of German domination. Communists in both the Czech and Slovak parts of the country, however, held him responsible for Slovak participation in the German invasion of the Soviet Union. The government in Prague, led by Klement Gottwald, a Communist, also wanted to use the trial as a cautionary example to would-be Slovak separatists. Communists who controlled several key ministerial posts had no use for Tiso as a priest and considered him a traitor. The trial opened on December 3, 1946, and ended in March 1947, with a sentence of death.[44] Benes supported the verdict, rejecting requests for a stay from the Vatican. He viewed the punishment as well deserved and a necessary catharsis for the Slovak treason. Needless to say, it was another episode that strengthened Slovak resentment of Czechs and poisoned interethnic relations.[45]

SLOVAK-CZECH RELATIONS UNDER COMMUNISM

In the late 1940s, Czechoslovakia, like its neighbors Poland and Hungary and the rest of Eastern Europe, came under Communist rule and Soviet influence.[46] By the early 1950s post–World War II Czechoslovakia had become a satellite of Moscow, with a Soviet-style monolithic dictatorship committed to the introduction of economic and social policies developed by Stalin in the Soviet Union.[47]

More Czech Dominance

Initially, Czechoslovakia's Communist leadership gave the Slovaks at least the appearance of equality with the Czech community. The

Communist government recognized Slovakia's separate cultural identity and gave the Slovaks their own local government institutions. These were located in Bratislava.[48] The Communist leadership in Prague acted with the approval of the Kremlin, which saw an advantage for Marxism and Soviet influence in postwar Czechoslovakia in a balance between the conservative Slovaks and the pragmatic Czechs, who in 1947 had been interested in obtaining Marshall Plan aid but demurred when Stalin objected.[49]

Administrative Dominance. Nevertheless there still was substantial Czech influence over the central government in Prague. For example, the new Czechoslovak Constitution drafted and promulgated by the Czechoslovak Communist leadership made sure that the central government could act in any of the policy areas assigned to Slovak organs, leaving virtually no policy area where the local Slovak administration in Bratislava had exclusive jurisdiction. In addition, the 1948 constitution required the Czechoslovak prime minister's countersignature of all measures passed by the Slovak administration in Bratislava and gave the Czechoslovak cabinet in Prague a veto over Slovak decisionmaking in Bratislava.[50] Finally, given the Communist Party's unity and discipline, it was very difficult for Slovak members of the government in Prague to lobby narrowly Slovak interests. Nor could they question the concentration of power in Prague that was at the expense of local Slovak administration.

A slight but telling procedural change reinforced the subservience of local Slovak governmental organs to the central authorities in Prague. An earlier constitutional act had provided that no constitutional law affecting the status of Slovakia could be enacted without "the majority of the present members of the constituent assembly elected in Slovakia." The 1948 constitution, however, allowed an amendment to be enacted into law by a simple three-fifths vote of the national parliament. The Czech-dominated central leadership conceivably could abolish Slovak local organs entirely, without Slovak approval.[51]

Czechs also dominated the diplomatic corps and staffed Czechoslovak embassies abroad. As of May 1968, of 585 appointees to Czechoslovakia's *corps diplomatique*, only 82 were Slovak; and over half of all missions abroad had no Slovak representation at all. The story goes that the man in the garb of a Slovak shepherd at the Expo 67 in Montreal was a Czech.[52] Furthermore, of 181 appointments to head state agencies from 1948 to 1967, only 40, or 22 percent went to Slovaks.[53]

Although Slovaks occasionally held high ministerial positions, such as the prime ministership, which was held by Slovak Communists without interruption from 1953 through 1968, their power to further the interests of the Slovak part of Czechoslovakia was always limited. Ministerial posts in the Communist era were far less influential than in the pre–World War II democratic era because ultimate decisionmaking rested with the Czech-dominated leadership of the Communist party. In addition, under the Communists Slovaks were never allowed control of the security agencies.[54]

Slovaks were grossly underrepresented in the central bureaucracy in Prague, where only 3.7 percent of personnel were Slovak, only 3.4 percent of department heads were Slovak, and only 8.8 percent of division heads were Slovak. An argument that these low figures were the result of a small reservoir of well-trained Slovak government officials and possibly even of some qualms about living in Prague is not credible. The disproportionate number of Slovak officials in the Prague administration was the product of discrimination. While it can be said that the Communist regime was more willing to promote Slovaks to high government positions, it was only marginally better in this regard than its democratic predecessor.[55]

Also, Slovaks were put off by the fact that while Prague was designated the capital of Czechoslovakia, Bratislava had no formal status as a Slovak political center. Whether this was intentional or not is of less importance than the reality for Slovaks that as far as the Czechs were concerned Bratislava had no special significance and, worse, that the political center of the country remained a Czech city even though it was impossible to conduct all of the state's business there.[56]

Political Dominance. The Czechs restricted Slovak participation in the upper echelons of the Czechoslovak Communist Party. While not excluding Slovaks from the Communist Party's leading bodies, the Czechs limited Slovak influence to avoid challenges to their decisionmaking. Enough Slovaks served in the national organs of the Party to demonstrate at least to the satisfaction of the Czechs the interethnic character of the Communist Party's *apparat*. Thus, the percentage of Slovaks in the Politburo and Central Committee, while substantial, lagged behind the percentage of Slovaks in the Czechoslovak population. Many Slovak Communists, in fact, did double duty, holding two posts at the same time so that more Slovaks would not have to be admitted to membership in the party's leading bodies.[57]

Though Slovaks also had their own branch of the Communist party headquartered in Bratislava, this machinery was at all times subordinate to the Party's leading bodies in Prague. The weak influence of the Slovak membership on the Czech-dominated leadership was underscored at the end of July 1948, when the Party's Central Committee passed several resolutions effectively depriving the Slovak branch of autonomy of the central leadership. The Central Committee of the Slovak branch was administratively subordinated to the Central Committee of the Czechoslovak Party and obliged to carry out its policies in Slovakia. The Czechoslovak Communist Party's practice of democratic centralism gave force to these resolutions.[58]

Novotny's Role. Czech Communists throughout the 1950s, and especially after Antonin Novotny, a rigid Stalinist, became Party First Secretary in 1954, steadily concentrated power in Prague at the expense of the Slovaks, and did so with the approval of the Kremlin, which, once assured of Czechoslovakia's subservience to the Kremlin, favored development of a strong centralized regime to assure Prague's loyalty to Moscow. Novotny was also suspicious of Slovak comrades who had protested fascism in 1944. One of his first acts as Party chief was to purge Slovaks in the Party such as Gustav Husak, one of the leaders of the 1944 uprising, whom he labeled "bourgeois-nationalists," a term meant to imply an excessive concern with nationalism, unacceptable to true Marxist-Leninists, that could inspire Slovak calls for autonomy and threaten both the unity of the state and the integrity of his Soviet-style dictatorship.[59]

Indeed, Novotny was angered by Slovak grumbling, especially in the early 1960s, about the need for decentralization. He saw this grumbling as just another form of dissidence. His perceived anti-Slovak policy antagonized Slovak colleagues, who considered him with some justice almost totally insensitive to their interests. Novotny rarely visited Slovak lands.

In 1960, the Novotny leadership promulgated a new constitution known as the "Charter," increasing Slovak subservience to Prague. The 1960 Charter, reducing the powers of the Slovak parliament in Bratislava and strengthening the authority of Prague over Slovakia, effectively relegated Slovaks to a subordinate role in the Czechoslovak socialist system.[60]

Slovaks, understandably, had little use for the leadership of Novotny. In their view he embodied the historic Czech indifference to Slovak problems and to the concept of interethnic equality. With his ill-concealed discrimination against Slovaks, Novotny antagonized Slovak party leaders, who campaigned to oust him from power. The beginnings of this campaign in the 1960s can be seen in subtle efforts by Slovak Communist leaders to rid their local organization of Novotny conservatives like Karol Bacilek, first secretary of the Slovak branch of the Party. In 1963, Bacilek was replaced by Aleksandr Dubcek. Novotny acquiesced in this change despite his own misgivings to discourage friction with his Slovak lieutenants. Moreover, at that time, Dubcek was hardly considered a liberal reformer; he was seen as just the opposite, a shrewd disciplinarian. Novotny's effort to "head off at the pass," so to speak, incipient Slovak discontent turned out to be nothing more than a temporary palliative, inasmuch as it hardly transformed the Czech-dominated power structure. The campaign in the Slovak *apparat* to replace Novotny continued.[61]

The "Prague Spring" and Slovak-Czech Relations

In early 1968, the Slovak opposition together with sympathetic Czechs formed a coalition of reformers to force Novotny to resign. The coalition replaced him with Slovak party leader Aleksandr Dubcek.[62]

Under Dubcek's leadership, the coalition now worked together to bring about economic and political reforms, which became known as the "Prague Spring."[63] An important component of the Prague Spring was the so-called Action Program of May 1968, which provided for an unprecedented liberalization of the Czechoslovak system, reducing censorship and opening the way for political party pluralism and eventually an end to the Czechoslovak Communist Party's political monopoly. Slovak and Czech reformers also agreed on a new administrative system to correct the "asymmetry" of the existing system, which Slovaks had criticized as "lopsided" because many of the same people who ran the republic-level government also were in charge of the central government. There was no equivalent of this situation for the Slovaks, whose government in Bratislava was in no way identical to the central government in Prague. Consequently, Czech influence over the national government was far greater than the influence of the Slovaks. This setup reinforced a feeling of many Slovaks after World War II of having a secondary and subordinate role in national policy-making that did not allow them adequate opportunity to protect their local interests.[64]

Soviet Interference. But Czechs and Slovaks were not allowed to proceed with their reform efforts. The Brezhnevian Kremlin opposed political liberalization, fearing it would inevitably undermine both Communist control and Soviet influence in Czechoslovakia. To prevent implementation of the "Action Program," a Soviet-led multinational Warsaw Pact military force made up primarily of Soviet troops invaded Prague in mid-August of 1968. The Soviets ousted Dubcek as head of the Czechoslovak Communist Party, replacing him with another Slovak leader, Gustav Husak, a neo-Stalinist. While rejecting political liberalization, Husak, with Moscow's blessing, introduced a new constitution on January 1, 1969, which gave Slovaks and Czechs their own local republic governments. Together they made up the Czechoslovak Federal Socialist Republic, with a central government in Prague responsible for defense, foreign relations, economic and financial regulation, citizenship, and currency. The republics had the right of self-determination, including secession. These arrangements for parity were the closest the Slovaks had come in the history of their union with the Czechs to equality.[65]

Differences over Democratization. Although local Slovak Communist leaders in 1968 had accepted the democratic reforms contained in Dubcek's "Action Program," Slovak society did not seem to share the enthusiasm of many Czech reformers for liberalization. The Slovak Catholic Church, although it spoke out on behalf of religious freedom, was critical of other democratic ideas. Many Slovak newspapers, such as *Smena*, the youth paper, and *Praca*, a trade-union daily, were far less enthusiastic about democratic values than the Czech reformers. In the proceedings of the Slovak Communist party's Central Committee in the spring months of 1968, there was no "ringing endorsement" of the liberalization measures Dubcek had called for.

The Slovak Communist Party leadership apparently had made a critical tactical decision to give priority in the reform process to federation rather than democratization to assure the vitality of Slovak influence over Czechoslovak political development. The party leadership was therefore in no hurry to replace conservatives with liberals. Indeed, in January 1968, when Dubcek became Czechoslovak party leader, he was replaced as head of the Slovak party by Vacil Bilak, a conservative who would become a stalwart opponent of *perestroika*-style reforms in Czechoslovakia in the late 1980s.[66] There was other evidence that the Slovak public was more interested in equality for Slovakia than in democratization of the Communist system. Whereas 91 percent of Czechs approved the National Assembly resolution abolishing government censorship, only 74 percent of Slovaks did so.[67]

Many Czechs indeed believed that in the 1968 Prague Spring the Slovaks had been more interested in their own narrow interests than in the overall well-being of Czechoslovakia. In their view, democracy was important for all of Czechoslovakia, while federation was of interest primarily to the Slovaks. To get the federation of 1969, the Slovaks, in the Czech view, had tolerated Soviet "normalization," namely a restoration of neo-Stalinistic authoritarianism. It was not difficult for Czechs to compare Slovak behavior in 1968 with that of 1938, which got Slovaks the Zilina accord.[68]

If Czechs were critical of Slovak caution on the issue of democratization, Slovaks were critical of perceived Czech indifference to what was close to their hearts: equality and self-rule. Slovaks complained that in the early months of 1968, when so much reform was being discussed and implemented, Czechs were insufficiently responsive. For example, in opinion polls Czechs showed little enthusiasm for reforming the constitutional relationship between the two communities defined in the 1960 constitution. In the Slovak view Czechs had little interest in changing a situation in which they had had the upper hand, which many Czechs presumably thought was natural and inevitable.[69]

Limits of Slovak Autonomy. Beyond the achievement of a revised federation that seemed to be favorable to Slovak aspirations, the Prague Spring did less for improving Slovak-Czech relations than both Slovaks and Czechs had hoped. In both the governmental/constitutional and the political spheres, Slovaks obtained little relief from the Czech dominance that pervaded most aspects of Czechoslovak public life under Communist rule. It could not be otherwise as long as Czechoslovakia remained a Communist dictatorship. The Communist Party's continuing monopoly of power, its adherence to central planning, and its intolerance of criticism and opposition precluded genuine self-rule.[70] Moreover, the parity principle of equal Czech and Slovak representation established in the new constitution was devalued by the weaknesses under Communist rule of the two government institutions where it was applied—the national parliament and the constitutional court—both of which were under Party influence. Elsewhere in the national government, notably the ministries, Czechs continued to outnumber Slovaks. For the 1969 federal system to have given the Slovaks the equality they wanted, Czechoslovakia would have had to be a Western-style liberal democracy, which it certainly wasn't under Soviet-imposed "normalization."[71]

From a Slovak point of view and despite Slovak leadership of the Czechoslovak Communist Party from January 1968 to the end of 1987 (Aleksandr Dubcek in 1968 and Gustav Husak from 1969 to 1987), the government in Prague was considered anti-Slovak in the sense of fostering a united Czechoslovak state that denied the Slovak community full recognition of its separate identity. Some Slovaks saw the whole Communist experience in Slovakia as an instrument of "Czechoslovakism," or the fusing of two peoples into one at the expense of the Slovak identity.[72]

This was not an unreasonable view. Czech leaders in 1968 were not sympathetic to Slovak advocacy of equality. Agreeing to the 1969 federal arrangement simply because Slovak colleagues insisted on it,

Czech political leaders rather displayed a certain condescension toward the Slovaks. Czech commentators acknowledged a degree of scorn for Slovak culture, as did Czech politicians and voters. Many Czechs considered the Slovaks politically immature.[73]

The Party's Asymmetrical Internal Organization. At the same time, plans to federalize the Czechoslovak Communist Party by dividing it into Czech and Slovak branches topped by a federal leadership structure in Prague never materialized. The Czechoslovak Party remained what it had always been, a Czech-dominated organization with an influential but by no means dominant Slovak branch barely able to protect Slovak local interests despite having a veto over decisionmaking in Prague. Slovaks never did gain their fair share of influence over national party policies. To the dismay of Slovak nationalists, newly installed party leader Husak, despite his nationalist past, endorsed continuation of the asymmetrical character of Czechoslovak party organization, categorically telling a Central Committee plenum in May 1969 that "the party is not federalized, on the contrary, it is unified."[74]

Slovak Political and Economic Advantages after 1968

Although the Slovaks never got the political parity they craved, they did gain other advantages in the aftermath of the Prague Spring. In this period the conservatism of Slovak leaders served them well. The Slovaks were more supportive of the status quo than were the Czechs, and the conservative central Party leadership saw them as more reliable on political and economic issues than Czechs, many of whom never did give up hope of the kind of systemic reform of the Czechoslovak Communist system that had provoked the Kremlin in the summer of 1968.

Political Advantages. In the 1970s and 1980s there was a striking rise in Slovak representation on the federal ministerial level. Between 1969 and 1983, one third of ministerial portfolios were given to Slovaks. In part this reflected an increase in the reservoir of Slovaks with requisite expertise, as more Slovaks obtained advanced academic training and replaced Czechs in administrative positions in Slovakia. At times the proportion of Slovaks in the federal cabinet reached 40 percent. Slovaks were in charge of a variety of public policy areas, though Czechs still were in control of security positions.[75]

Slovak appointees also enjoyed job security. Once appointed, they tended to keep their jobs because of the extraordinary stability of leadership, a characteristic of most other Communist-ruled systems in central and Eastern Europe. There was little turnover; when there was a change, Slovaks were replaced with Slovaks.

Economic Advantages. Despite the harsh political environment of Communist rule, Slovakia benefited economically, at least relative to the Czech Republic. Responding to Soviet demands, Husak promoted a weapons-producing industry in eastern Slovakia, far from NATO bases. These weapons had a ready market in the Eastern Bloc and the Third World. Located mainly in Kosice, the large weapons-manufacturing enterprises and steel mills employed thousands of Slovak workers, helping to expand industrialization in the region and improve living conditions. According to the Slovak economist, Eduard Sarmir, by 1974 "Slovakia had overcome her economic, social, and cultural backwardness and become a country with a developed economy and was well on the way to reaching equalization with the Czech lands." Not all Slovaks agreed with this generous view. Nevertheless, the overall standard of living for Slovaks when compared with Czechs improved. While Slovak wage levels remained somewhat below those prevalent in the Czech part of the country, the standard of living for Slovaks was almost the same as that for Czechs by the end of 1980. Slovaks had achieved a level of creature comforts, including ownership of an automobile, comparable to Czechs.[76]

The Slovaks seemed not to have done that badly under the Soviet imposed post-1968 "normalization," and Czechs may have held that against them. In particular, there was a degree of Czech resentment over the influx of Slovaks into the central ministries in Prague. Nor did it do the Slovak image with the Czechs any good that Husak, a Slovak, was the instrument of the oppressive normalization that killed any chances of democratic reform in Czechoslovakia for 20 years. As the Communist era was drawing to a close, relations between Slovaks and Czechs remained strained.

SLOVAKS AND CZECHS AT THE
END OF COMMUNIST RULE

It really cannot be said that Slovaks were partners or even soulmates of the Czechs in forcing the Communist regime to embrace democratic reform and, failing that, in forcing it out of power. In the steadily increasing dissident activity inaugurated by the promulgation of Charter 77, in January 1977, and encouraged in no small way by the refusal of the conservative party leadership to liberalize the country's Soviet-style repressive dictatorship, Czechs, not Slovaks, played the leading role.

Slovaks and Charter 77

In January of 1977, Czechoslovak dissidents made the first telling assault on the Communist dictatorship since Dubcek's "Action Program" of April 1968. They signed Charter 77, a statement accusing the Husak leadership of extensive violations of the human rights of Czechoslovak citizens considered critics or opponents of regime policies. The Charter called attention to widespread regime discrimination in education, employment, and other sectors of national life against citizens who had spoken out against the regime. Charter 77 inspired a growing popular opposition to communist rule.

Only eight of the early Charter 77 signatories were Slovaks, and some of these lived in Prague. The development of Charter 77 was almost an exclusively Czech affair, with little Slovak involvement. No formal Slovak input into the formulation of Charter 77 was sought, and none was apparently received by its predominantly Czech authors.

It almost seemed as if in this period Slovaks lived geographically and culturally distant from their Czech neighbors. While the Czech Republic chafed under Husak's conservative leadership, there was little anti-government dissidence in Slovakia. As protests against the Husak regime escalated in the late 1980s, the Slovaks were largely silent. Moreover, Slovaks had virtually no contact with dissidents in neighboring countries; there were few underground protest publications or *samizdat*, and hardly any public letters condemning the regime's political excesses appeared in the Slovak press. In sum, there was little Slovak agitation on human rights issues when compared with the behavior of Czechs, in particular dissidents such as the poet and playwright Vaclav Havel. Slovak antiregime demonstrations that did occur, such as Hana Ponicka's dramatic protest against censorship at the 1977 Slovak Writers' Congress, were the exception, not the rule.[77]

Slovaks and Czechs in the Fall of 1989

The upheaval in the fall of 1989 that brought down the Communist regime and its Czech leader, Milos Jakes, who had succeeded Husak as head of the Communist Party the previous year, centered in Prague, where the Czechs directed it. Havel eloquently and passionately captured its spirit, which was mostly Czech. Nevertheless, Slovaks, especially through the newly organized Public against Violence Party (PAV), did participate with Czechs in bringing down the last Communist leadership of Czechoslovakia. Aleksandr Dubcek returned to political prominence and was elected Chairman of the Federal Parliament in December 1989, in recognition of his early effort to liberalize the Communist system. Slovak party leader Marian Calfa became Czechoslovak prime minister. These events, however, were not the center of change.

Czechs rather than Slovaks were at the helm, steering the transition to a new political system. From a Slovak point of view the Czechs were doing what they had been doing since 1918: playing the leading role in the political development and evolution of the Czechoslovak state.

CONCLUSIONS

Throughout most of the period 1918–1989, Slovaks and Czechs had co-existed peacefully and to their mutual benefit even though the Slovak minority was kept in its place, so to speak, by the Czech majority. By the end of this 70-year period, one could speak of Czechoslovakia as a true nation state with its own unique national identity despite the substantial and frequently divisive political, economic, and sociocultural differences between Slovaks and Czechs. Indeed, many other states in continental Europe had survived with far greater interethnic and intercultural differences. Moreover, Czech leaders, who always had more influence over the management of the Czechoslovak state, from time to time did show an understanding of and sympathy for Slovak concerns and a willingness for the sake of equity as well as expediency to address them. Indeed, it may well be that the Communist leaders bent on assuring the success of their socialist experiment tried harder than the leaders of democratic Czechoslovakia in the interwar period to improve the relationship between Czechs and Slovaks and thereby strengthen the unity of the state.

Nevertheless, when the Communist era came to an end, many Slovaks had deep misgivings about their relationship with the Czechs. Sources of Slovak unhappiness and dissatisfaction were deep, numerous, and long-standing. However, what was most troubling to Slovak leaders was their sense that the Czechs had undermined every political agreement designed to assure Slovaks their political autonomy to assure their dominance of Czechoslovakia. Behind this thinking was the conviction that Slovakia, as a national community, was entitled to coequality with the Czechs in running the Czechoslovak state and to complete autonomy in managing their local affairs. Despite administrative reforms, such as the federation established in January 1969, many Slovaks were dissatisfied. They wanted a devolution of administrative authority that would give them the coequality and autonomy they craved.

With the collapse of Communist authoritarianism and the emergence of a Western-style pluralistic parliamentary democracy, Slovaks saw an opportunity to adjust their historic relationship with the Czechs. As succeeding chapter shows, the Slovaks were prepared to use the new democratic system to obtain the coequality and autonomy they deserved and were determined to have. Their efforts presented post-Communist Czechoslovakia with a serious challenge to its stability and survival.

NOTES

1. Frederick G. Heymann, *Poland and Czechoslovakia* (Englewood Cliffs, N.J.: Prentice Hall, 1966), pp. 116–117; Carol Skalnick Leff, *National Conflict in Czechoslovakia: The Making and Remaking of a State 1918–1987* (Princeton, N.J.: Princeton University Press, 1988), p. 20; Otto Ulc, "Czechoslovakia's Velvet Divorce," *East European Quarterly*, vol. 30, no. 3 (Fall 1996), p. 332.

2. Stanislaw Kirschbaum, *A History of Slovakia: The Struggle for Survival* (New York: St. Martin's Press, 1995), pp. 136–144, 153–157.

3. Ibid.; see also Leff, *National Conflict in Czechoslovakia*, p. 35.

4. Heymann, *Poland and Czechoslovakia*, p. 140.

5. For a brief but detailed discussion of the circumstances surrounding the establishment of the Republic of Czechoslovakia in 1918 see Victor S. Mamatey, "The Establishment of the Republic," in Victor S. Mamatey and Radmir Luza (eds.), *A History of the Czechoslovak Republic 1918–1948* (Princeton, N.J.: Princeton University Press, 1975), pp. 3–38; for a discussion of how Czechs and Slovaks viewed the interwar government in the 1960s, see Sharon Wolchik, "Democratization and Political Participation in Slovakia," in Karen Dawisha and Bruce Parrot (eds.), *The Consolidation of Democracy in East-Central Europe* (Cambridge, U.K.: Cambridge University Press, 1997), pp. 200-201.

6. Vaclav Benes, "Czechoslovak Democracy and Its Problems 1918–1920," in Mamatey and Luza (eds.), *History of the Czechoslovak Republic 1918–1948*, p. 84.

7. Kirschbaum, *History of Slovakia*, pp. 156–163; Heymann, *Poland and Czechoslovakia*, pp. 132–133; Ulc, "Czechoslovakia's Velvet Divorce," p. 332.

8. Leff, *National Conflict in Czechoslovakia*, pp. 34–35.

9. Ibid., p. 152; see also Benes, "Democracy and Its Problems 1918–1920," p. 95; Thomas G. Masaryk, *The Making of a State: Memories and Observations 1914–1918* (New York: Frederick A. Stokes, 1927), p. 220.

10. Leff, *National Conflict in Czechoslovakia*, p. 36.

11. Ibid., pp. 38–39; for a detailed discussion of how Slovak nationalists viewed a union with Czechs in the late nineteenth and early twentieth centuries see Mamatey, "The Establishment of the Republic," in Mamatey and Luza (eds.), *History of the Czechoslovak Republic 1918-1948*, pp. 8-11.

12. Benes, "Democracy and Its Problems, 1918–1920," p. 97.

13. Leff, *National Conflict in Czechoslovakia*, p. 221; Ulc, "Czechoslovakia's Velvet Divorce," p. 333.

14. Victor S. Mamatey, "The Development of Czechoslovak Democracy, 1920–1938," in Mamatey and Luza (eds.), *History of the Czechoslovak Republic 1918–1948*, p. 117.

15. Leff, *National Conflict in Czechoslovakia*, pp. 160, 175; Heymann, *Poland and Czechoslovakia*, p. 142; Zdenek Suda, *The Czechoslovak Socialist Republic* (Baltimore: Johns Hopkins Press, 1969), pp. 8–9.

16. Leff, *National Conflict in Czechoslovakia*, p. 136.

17. Ibid., p. 137.

18. Ibid., p. 138.

19. Ibid., pp. 203–204; for additional detail on Hlinka's advocacy of Slovak autonomy in the interwar years see Benes, "Democracy and Its Problems 1918–1920," pp. 82–84; Mamatey, "Development of Democracy 1920–1938," pp. 120–121, 134.

20. Leff, *National Conflict in Czechoslovakia*, p. 79.

21. Kirschbaum, *History of Slovakia*, p. 181; John Morison, "The Road to Separation: Nationalism in Czechoslovakia," in Paul Latawski (ed.), *Contemporary Nationalism in East-Central Europe* (New York: St. Martin's Press, 1993), pp. 73–75; H. Gordon Skilling, *Czechoslovakia's Interrupted Revolution* (Princeton, N.J.: Princeton University Press, 1976), p. 9.

22. Leff, *National Conflict in Czechoslovakia*, p. 153; for more detail on the development of Slovak autonomy in the weeks and months following the German annexation of the Sudetenland, see Theodor Prochazka, "The Second Republic 1938–1939," in Mamatey and Luza (eds.), *History of the Czechoslovak Republic*, pp. 260–261.

23. Ulc, "Czechoslovakia's Velvet Divorce," p. 332.

24. Jorg K. Hoensch, "The Slovak Republic 1939–1945," in Mamatey and Luza (eds.), *History of the Czechoslovak Republic*, p. 275.

25. A brief account of events leading to the establishment of the pro-German independent Slovak state is in Heymann, *Poland and Czechoslovakia*, pp. 151–154; a more detailed analysis appears in Hoensch, "Slovak Republic 1939–1945," pp. 271–295.

26. Kirschbaum, *History of Slovakia*, pp. 201–203; see also Wolchik, "Democracy and Political Participation in Slovakia," pp.201-202.

27. Hoensch, "Slovak Republic 1939–1945," pp. 277, 287.

28. Ibid., pp. 290–291.

29. Kirschbaum, *History of Slovakia*, pp. 198–200; Morison, "Road to Separation," pp. 73–75; Hoensch, "Slovak Republic 1939–1945," pp. 283–284, 290.

30. Hoensch, "Slovak Republic 1939–1945," pp. 280–281.

31. Anna Josko, "The Slovak Resistance Movement," in Mamatey and Luza (eds.), *History of the Czechoslovak Republic 1918–1948*, pp. 370–372.

32. Ibid., pp. 378–380, 382–383; see also Tad Szulc, *Czechoslovakia since World War II* (New York: Grosset and Dunlap, 1971), pp. 243–244; Suda, *Czechoslovak Socialist Republic*, pp. 22–23; Wolchik, "Democratization and Political Participation in Slovakia," p. 202.

33. Leff, *National Conflict in Czechoslovakia*, p. 164.

34. Ibid.

35. Ibid.

36. Ibid., pp. 164–165.

37. Skilling, *Czechoslovakia's Interrupted Revolution*, p. 9; Wolchik, "Democratization and Political Participation in Slovakia," p. 203.

38. Kirschbaum, *History of Slovakia*, p. 209.

39. Leff, *National Conflict in Czechoslovakia*, p. 94.

40. Kirschbaum, *History of Slovakia*, p. 228.

41. Ibid., p. 218.

42. Leff, *National Conflict in Czechoslovakia*, p. 157.

43. Ibid., pp. 156–157.

44. Radomir Luza, "Czechoslovakia between Democracy and Communism," in Mamatey and Luza (eds.), *History of the Czechoslovak Republic 1918–1948*, p. 407.

45. Leff, *National Conflict in Czechoslovakia*, p. 166; Hugh Seton-Watson, *The East European Revolution* (New York: Frederick A. Praeger, 1956), pp. 184–185.

46. Seton-Watson, *East European Revolution*, pp. 179–180.

47. The satellization of Czechoslovakia and its East European neighbors is described at length in Brzezinski, *The Soviet Bloc: Unity and Conflict*, revised and enlarged ed., (Cambridge, Mass.: Harvard University Press, 1971), pp. 84–129.

48. Skilling, *Czechoslovakia's Interrupted Revolution*, pp. 9–10.

49. Szulc, *Czechoslovakia since World War II*, pp. 33–34; Seton-Watson, *East European Revolution*, pp. 183–184.

50. Leff, *National Conflict in Czechoslovakia*, pp. 100–101.

51. Ibid, p. 101.

52. Ulc, "Czechoslovakia's Velvet Divorce," p. 335.

53. Leff, *National Conflict in Czechoslovakia*, p. 221.

54. Ibid., p. 222.

55. Ibid., p. 224.

56. Ibid., p. 107.

57. Ibid., p. 223.

58. Ibid., p. 100.

59. Ibid., pp. 168–169.

60. Ibid., p. 101; Skilling, *Czechoslovakia's Interrupted Revolution*, p. 10.

61. Leff, *National Conflict in Czechoslovakia*, p. 110.

62. Skilling, *Czechoslovakia's Interrupted Revolution*, pp. 49–51.

63. Szulc, *Czechoslovakia since World War II*, pp. 183, 244–246.

64. Leff, *National Conflict in Czechoslovakia*, pp. 122–123.

65. Kirschbaum, *History of Slovakia*, pp. 243–244; Morison, "Road to Separation," pp. 77–78; Suda, *Czechoslovak Socialist Republic*, pp. 120–121; Skilling, *Czechoslovakia's Interrupted Revolution*, pp. 220–221, 241–242.

66. Skilling, *Czechoslovakia's Interrupted Revolution*, pp. 241–244; Leff, *National Conflict in Czechoslovakia*, pp. 170–171.

67. Jaroslaw Piekalkiewicz, *Public Opinion Polling in Czechoslovakia 1968–1969* (New York: Praeger, 1972), p. 84, cited in Leff, *National Conflict in Czechoslovakia*, p. 171.

68. Leff, *National Conflict in Czechoslovakia*, pp. 174–175.

69. Ibid., p. 175.

70. The late Harvard University professor Carl J. Friedrich argued the impossibility of genuine federalism in an authoritarian dictatorship of the kind that governed Czechoslovakia in the Communist era. See Carl J. Friedrich, "Federalism and Opposition," *Government and Opposition*, vol. 1 (May 1966), pp. 286–288, cited in Leff, *National Conflict in Czechoslovakia*, p. 250.

71. Leff, *National Conflict in Czechoslovakia*, p. 245.

72. Kirschbaum, *History of Slovakia*, p. 252; Wolchik, "Democratization and Political Participation in Slovakia," p. 205.

73. See the citations of Czech commentators in 1968 in Skilling, *Czechoslovakia's Interrupted Revolution*, p. 463, footnotes 52, 53, and 54.

74. Leff, *National Conflict in Czechoslovakia*, pp. 245–246.

75. Ibid., p. 253.

76. Kirschbaum, *History of Czechoslovakia*, p. 246; Wolchik, "Democratization and Political Participation in Slovakia," p. 207.

77. Leff, *National Conflict in Czechoslovakia*, pp. 264–267.

2

Post-Communist Slovakia Becomes Independent

The lifting of censorship, the proliferation of new political parties, and the democratization of national and local governments following the collapse of Communist rule at the end of 1989 created opportunities for Slovak political leaders to promote issues in limbo under Communist rule, in particular those having to do with Slovak nationalism and Slovak grievances against the Czechs. Indeed, open, free, and competitive elections for parliament allowed Slovak politicians to develop a power base they could use to defend their interests.

From 1990 onward, Slovak nationalist sentiment surfaced dramatically and expressed itself directly in discontent with the Czechoslovak political system. Slovak political leaders believed that the new post-Communist democratic system perpetuated many of the faults of the past, continuing Czech dominance of the national government in Prague. They wanted equality with the Czechs through a transformation of the Czechoslovak state into a confederation. But, Czechs and Slovaks could never agree on the constitutional makeup of a post-Communist Czechoslovak state. At the end of 1992, the Republic of Czechoslovakia split into two separate and sovereign independent administrative entities: the Czech Republic and Slovakia.

SLOVAK GRIEVANCES

In the early 1990s, Slovak political leaders believed that the national government in Prague did not adequately recognize the Slovak national identity. In addition Prague's free market reforms, in their view, did not take adequate account of Slovak needs and problems, in particular the inferiority of Slovak living standards when compared with those in the Czech Republic. Slovak interests abroad also were neglected, they believed, because Czechs dominated the Ministry of Foreign Affairs in Prague.

Concerns about the Slovak Identity

Slovak leaders wanted increased recognition of their cultural identity. They opposed what they called "Czechoslovakisation" or use by Czechs of the national political system to further their interests at the expense of other ethnic groups. In the Slovak view even the name of the country, Czechoslovakia, symbolized this Czech bias. The Slovaks considered the term "Czechoslovak" an artificial concept implying Czech-inspired centralism and domination. In the spring of 1990, Slovak politicians in the Federal Assembly in Prague wanted a new name for Czechoslovakia to emphasize Slovak equality with the Czechs. They insisted that the word "Czechoslovak" be dropped in favor of "Czech" and "Slovak."

The Federal Assembly responded with a highly emotional debate over the wording of a new name for the state. President Havel proposed "the Czech-Slovak Republic" with a hyphen between Czech and Slovak. While Slovak deputies liked Havel's proposal, some Czechs denounced the new name, saying it "maligned Czechoslovakism" and calling the hyphen "an insult to a significant part of the Czech nation." Eventually, the Federal Assembly agreed on a somewhat awkward compromise. On April 19, 1990, the Assembly voted that Czechoslovakia would now be called the "Czech and Slovak Federative Republic." Omission of the hyphen satisfied the Czechs without provoking the supersensitive Slovaks, many of whom viewed the Czech position on the hyphen issue as further evidence of Czech determination to keep them "number two" in the Czechoslovak state.[1]

Criticism of Free Market Reform

Slovak leaders saw an anti-Slovak bias in the federal government's handling of the economy. They were critical of federal Finance Minister Vaclav Klaus, a Czech, who advocated "shock therapy," or rapid and extensive movement of Czechoslovakia to a free market economy, which included privatization of most state-owned industries and a sharp curtailment of state management of the country's economic processes, especially the areas of pricing, banking, and foreign trade. As "shock therapy" went into effect and state control over the country's economic life diminished, Slovakia's economy suffered and workers experienced unemployment and inflation simultaneously.

Slovak leaders argued that the Prague government needed to have in place an extensive social net to soften the hardships of such economic dislocation. They reflected a deep concern of Slovak voters about the future well-being of Slovakia as the Prague government's free market reforms went forward. In April 1992, the Bratislava Institute for Social Analysis, in a study titled "Profiles of Supporters of Political Parties," reported that 50 percent of the supporters of the new populist Slovak political party Movement for a Democratic Slovakia (MDS), led by Slovak Republic Prime Minister Vladimir Meciar, which attracted a substantial plurality of the Slovak electorate, favored a large amount of state control of the economy. In poll after poll the Slovak public displayed less and less support for free market reform and increased interest in a mixed economy with something like the "cradle to grave" social welfare system of the Communist era.[2]

In the early 1990s, Slovak leaders told their Czech counterparts in the Federal Assembly that Slovakia was not ready for the free market reforms of Prague. Slovakia, they said, was poorer than the Czech lands and more vulnerable than they were to economic dislocation and social trauma. The facts supported their argument. For example, Slovak industrial enterprises, especially those producing armaments, were large and inefficient, as was the case in most Communist-ruled countries that imitated the highly centralized and regimented Soviet model of economic organization and, therefore, were extremely vulnerable to the disruptive effects of free market reform. Furthermore, in the early 1990s, Slovak annual unemployment rates remained well over 10 percent while the rates in the Czech Republic were consistently below this figure. Czech unemployment tended to be one-third to one-fifth that of Slovakia, with Slovakia suffering from a higher percentage of chronic unemployment. While the Czech budget in these years had a surplus, the Slovak budget was consistently running a deficit.[3]

The economic contrasts between the Czech Republic and Slovakia were especially dramatic in the area of foreign trade. While Czech exports to the West increased and the Czech Republic's annual unemployment rate was below 10 percent, Slovak unemployment skyrocketed to double digits as the giant energy-consuming and polluting smelting, chemical, and weapons-producing industries built by the Husak regime after 1968 were closed down because they were inefficient, unprofitable, and a drain on national wealth. Slovak industrial exports, dependent on two buyers—the Soviet Union and East Germany—suffered when these markets almost completely disappeared with the collapse of communist rule in these and other Eastern Europe countries.[4]

Finally, Slovakia also lagged behind the Czech Republic in the area of foreign investment. Of 3,000 joint ventures with Western companies, only 600 were located in Slovakia by the fall of 1991. Of the $8.98 billion worth of foreign investment committed to the Visegrad countries (Poland, Hungary, and Czechoslovakia) from 1990 to 1994, only some $366 million came to Slovakia, about 4 percent of the total. Aggravating this economic gap was the fact that, as Slovak leaders contended, this trade imbalance reflected discrimination by Western investors against Slovakia in favor of the Czech lands.[5]

Slovak politicians also worried that the gap in living standards between Czechs and Slovaks would worsen for Slovaks, given the growing political influence of Klaus, with his strong free market views at the expense of the more moderate President Vaclav Havel, who favored gradualism in the transition to a free market. When, in February 1991, the differences between Klaus and Havel caused a rift in the leading political party, the Civic Forum (CF), and it subsequently split into two independent factions, a rump CF and a new party, the Civic Democratic Party led by Klaus, the Slovaks could see only more unwelcome Czech domination.[6]

Complaints about Foreign Policy

Nowhere was Slovak sensitivity to Czech influence more evident than in the area of foreign policy, where Slovak nationalism carried great emotional power. Slovak political leaders craved an internationally recognized Slovak identity abroad. They believed that all too often Slovakia was seen as an appendage of the Czech lands, an attitude made worse by the widespread habit of the Western media of referring to Czechoslovak citizens as Czechs. Furthermore, in the early 1990s, with little influence on foreign policy-making, Slovakia had no way of protecting its interests abroad. Jan Carnogursky, leader of Slovakia's Christian Democratic Movement (CDM), complained about the Slovak government's "weak global standing," remarking that Slovakia needs to be able "to speak for itself."[7]

In the Slovak view, the policy of Czechoslovak foreign minister Jiri Dienstbier did not, and could not, take into adequate account Slovak interests. Czechoslovak foreign policy was determined by the needs of the country as a whole, not just of the Slovak population. In the Slovak view, a good example of this perceived Czech indifference to Slovak interests was the decision by Prague to halt all Czechoslovak arms exports to accommodate pressures from the West, despite the fact that the arms industry was a mainstay of the Slovak economy. Slovaks also pointed out their low representation in the federal diplomatic service. When Slovak nationalists called for their own foreign policy-making machinery and separate Slovak representation in the United Nations and other international organizations, the Slovak Republic government in the fall of 1991 created a Slovak Ministry of International Relations.[8] This move was intended to project Slovakia's national identity abroad while furthering its international economic and other interests when those interests, such as maintaining arms exports, were in conflict with Czech perceptions of what was best for the entire country.[9]

SLOVAKS PROPOSE POWERSHARING

To address their grievances against the Federal government in Prague, Slovak leaders proposed a change in the Czechoslovak constitution that would transform the state from a centralized union into a decentralized federation based upon a system of powersharing in which the two large ethnic communities would have parity. In this proposal, the federal government in Prague would have limited powers, with the bulk of administrative authority reserved to the republic governments. The Slovak Republic would have equality with the Czechs in critical law-making areas such as the economy, finance, and foreign policy.[10] At this time most Slovak leaders, including Vladimir Meciar and Jan Carnogursky, did not have in mind the extinction of the 1918 union. In fact, Carnogursky argued that a breakup of the Czecho/Slovak state would hurt Slovakia. It would interfere with the critical economic links between the east and west of the country. It might also contribute to a revival of nationalist sentiments among Slovakia's 600,000 Hungarians, who might themselves demand autonomy or union with the Hungarian republic.[11]

In October 1991, a motion supported by radical nationalists in the Slovak republic parliament, the Slovak National Council (SNC), in Bratislava, to consider a declaration of Slovak sovereignty failed. The view of moderates in the SNC that Slovak leaders should still try to reform the Czechoslovak state from within prevailed.[12] But when Slovak leaders proposed a powersharing agreement in the form of a treaty between the Czech and Slovak republics based on the principle that ultimate sovereignty rested in each of them,[13] the Czechs objected. Federal Prime Minister Marian Calfa, himself a Slovak and supportive of a new powersharing arrangement that would give Slovakia parity with the Czechs in a common state, rejected a state treaty "because there are no states that can conclude it." For most Czechs who favored a unified Czecho/Slovak state, the idea of a treaty was unacceptable "because it would inject a corrosive 'confederate element' into the structure."[14]

For its part, the Slovak National Party (SNP), which represented a strongly nationalist minority of the Slovak electorate, called for Slovakia's separation from and independence of the Czechs. Slovak separatists blamed the Czechs for having denied Slovakia the opportunity to fulfill its nationalist aspirations and accused them of having taken possession of Slovak territory without giving anything in return. They complained that historically Czechs had failed to understand and to accommodate Slovak feelings and thoughts. Jozef Salak, the deputy minister of finance in the Slovak Republic, captured these views when he said the Slovak nation should be on the international stage as Slovakia. He faulted the Czechs for not having absorbed "Slovakism" into their collective conscience.[15]

SLOVAK-CZECH NEGOTIATIONS, 1990–1992

In 1990, Slovak and Czech leaders tried to come to grips with Slovak concerns. While Czech negotiators sympathized with Slovak complaints, they opposed the kind of powersharing sought by the Slovak side. Czech leaders resisted Slovak proposals for administrative decentralization to allow the Slovak republic government to determine its own pace of economic change and in particular to avoid privatization and other steps to the free market reforms. In the view of Federal Finance Minister Klaus, a successful economic transition in Czechoslovakia required a strong central government setting policy for the entire country.[16]

Inclined to conciliate the Slovaks for the sake of preserving the political union, Czech leaders agreed to a devolution of limited administrative power from the center to the republics. Czechoslovak Prime Minister Calfa and Czech Republic Prime Minister Peter Pithart in meetings with Slovak Prime Minister Meciar agreed to a substantial grant of autonomy to Slovakia, leaving foreign policy, foreign trade, the central bank, taxation and foreign policies to the federal Government in Prague. In December 1990, the Federal Assembly in Prague passed a new law giving each of the two republics responsibility for its own economy except in the areas of budgetmaking, taxation, and foreign policy. The Federal Assembly refused to allow Slovakia to establish its own ministry of international relations. While the new law emphasized the common state and the single internal market, it stipulated the "inalienable right" of the two republics to self-determination "up to separation." The law also embodied the idea championed by Slovak leaders that both the Czech and Slovak republic governments were the creators of the Czecho-Slovak state.[17]

In the Slovak view, however, this new arrangement did not go far enough in granting Slovakia extensive control over local affairs. Aleksandr Dubcek called for stronger republic governments and a weaker central government. He spoke of an "alliance of republics with equality of the 'nations,' rights, and citizens."[18]

Meciar, who became prime minister in early 1990, for his part, called for the old Czechoslovakia to be a loose association of states sovereign at home and abroad but with a common market.[19] He insisted on the right of Slovaks to chart their own slower pace of free market reform, especially in the area of privatization in a Czech/Slovak state in which the Czech and Slovak republics would have parity. Though denying he favored it, Meciar and other Slovak politicians, especially the SNP, began to contemplate Slovak separation in the event the Czechs refused to agree to transform the country into a confederation with a generous grant of autonomy to the two constituent republics.

Prospects of Separation

Some Czechs, notably Klaus, despite their past defense of a united Czechoslovak state, also started thinking about an administrative separation of the two Republics which would involve a dissolution of the 1918 Czechoslovak union. By mid-1992, Klaus was convinced that differences with the Slovaks over the constitutional makeup of post-Communist Czechoslovakia were irreconcilable.[20]

In the Czech view, administrative separation made a lot of economic sense. Bratislava was reluctant to privatize the state sector as the Czechs were doing in their part of the country. As Slovak economic development languished, Klaus and his supporters worried about how the more prosperous Czech community might have to subsidize the less developed Slovak part of the country. Without the Slovaks, they could proceed expeditiously with the introduction of free enterprise that Klaus believed essential to Czech prosperity and integration with Western Europe.

Czech liberals also were disturbed by authoritarian tendencies in Slovak political life, in particular a nostalgia for the country's fascist past evident in a renewal of popular interest in the World War II leadership of Monsignor Tiso. Especially striking was the degree of popular support in Slovakia for Prime Minister Meciar, despite his strong authoritarian instincts. Meciar was blatant in expanding his personal influence over the Slovak bureaucracy, installing personal cronies and party loyalists in the universities, the health service, and the bureaucracy.[21] Supersensitive to any kind of criticism, Meciar was heavy-handed in his dealings with the Slovak media. He resented the media's charges that he had abused his positions in 1990 and 1991 to cover up his past links with the Communist party, to promote his friends, and to destroy the careers of his foes.[22] He said these charges were false and part of a plan to discredit him. Frequently showing anger at press conferences, he upbraided reporters who were critical of him, accusing them of "disloyalty" and "disrespect."[23]

Resentment toward the press led Meciar to a systematic campaign to intimidate journalists to gain as much control over the media as possible. In his view, the state had a right and an obligation to regulate the media.[24] Annoyed when Slovak journalists broadcast Slovakia's faults abroad, Meciar encouraged the formation in 1992 of a rival union of journalists, as he put it, "for a truthful picture of Slovakia."[25] Meciar also used the state-controlled media against political rivals and critics, encouraging them to attack independent politicians, writers, and journalists who opposed him.[26]

In 1990 and 1991, Czech political leaders could hardly ignore Meciar's efforts to impede the free flow of information from Czech media into Slovakia. For example, programs of Czech radio and television were occasionally not broadcast in large areas of Slovakia; Slovak contributions to federal broadcasts were kept at a minimum; and some of President Havel's interviews and statements taped in Slovakia were of such poor technical quality that they were barely usable. Slovak officials tried to make light of such incidents, frequently dismissing them as technical problems and pleading no intent to censor. These excuses had little credibility. It soon became clear that the Bratislava government had undertaken an ill-concealed campaign against Slovak journalists working for federal media institutions considered anti-Slovak, telling them that their job with the federal authorities significantly reduced their chances for employment in the Slovak media.[27]

The political image of Slovakia was tarnished further in the Czech view by a revival of anti-Semitism. Some local Slovak groups had contacts with the extremely anti-Semitic World Congress of Slovaks, an influential separatist organization based mainly in the United States and Canada. In addition, many Slovak nationalists, reflecting feelings of injured pride, as well as a tinge of jealousy of Czech economic well-being, fell back on traditional anti-Semitism to console themselves. They said that Czech leaders either were Jewish or under Jewish control and out to dominate Slovakia. They attacked the Slovak democratic politician, Fedor Gal, a Jew born in a Nazi concentration camp and now chairman of the Public against Violence (PAV), a moderate Slovak party in coalition with the Civic Forum. Anti-Semites sent him numerous threatening letters, forced him to seek police protection, and ultimately drove him out of Slovakia. Beyond that, a whole range of grotesquely anti-Semitic literature appeared in print, with little official recrimination.[28] Moderate Slovaks were threatened with lynching and accused of "not speaking Slovak but Hebrew." Even Havel was dragged through this mud, characterized as a "swinish Jew." [29]

Klaus and other Czech leaders considered Meciar's autocratic behavior an embarrassing liability for Czechoslovakia's integration with the West, in particular membership in NATO and the European Union, which insisted on adherence to democratic principles of all its members. In light of the fact that Meciar had the support of more than 30 percent of the Slovak population, many Czechs saw separation as a desirable step.

Havel Opposes Separation

Although Havel himself was disturbed by the increasingly anti-democratic character of Slovak political life and by Slovak reluctance to move forward with free market reform, he was not ready for a break and was more willing than Klaus to address Slovak complaints for the sake of preserving the unity of the country. He also became alarmed by the rapid growth of Slovak sentiment favoring separation. In November 1990, Slovak nationalists got the SNC to pass legislation declaring republic laws paramount over those of the federal government.[30] By 1991, nationalist agitation for Slovak independence was evident in the mass media. Nationalist politicians called for Slovak separation from Czechoslovakia if Slovak demands for confederation and the recognition of Slovak sovereignty were not met.[31]

In early 1991, to deal with the growth of Slovak separatism, Havel sought emergency powers to bypass parliament. He also asked for the establishment of a constitutional court to resolve problems of the kind arising out of the controversy between Czechs and Slovaks over powersharing.[32] In the summer of 1991, he asked the Federal Assembly for a referendum on the separation issue.[33] While denying Havel's request for emergency powers and a constitutional court, the Federal Assembly did pass a law allowing the president to call a referendum if it were proposed by either the parliament in Prague or by one or both of the two republic parliaments.[34]

Both Meciar and Klaus, however, opposed a referendum on the separation issue.[35] Meciar did not want a referendum because he did not want a possible public gesture of support for unity to push him to compromise on issues of administrative centralization, autonomy, and Slovak independence. Certainly, Meciar would have an unprecedented opportunity with an independent Slovakia to be leader of the new state.[36] Klaus also had no interest in a referendum on the future of the country, that, given popular sympathy for preservation of the unified state, would strengthen the hand of Czech moderates like Havel, whose willingness to make concessions to the Slovaks would only delay an event he now viewed as not only politically inevitable but also economically desirable for the Czech community.[37]

Finally, although smaller parties in the Prague parliament believed that only the voters through a referendum could decide on separation, they were hesitant to oppose and thereby provoke Meciar and Klaus. Above all else, they wanted to avoid a chaotic disintegration that could produce a long-lasting antagonism between the two communities.[38]

Chances of a referendum diminished in September 1991, when responsibility for negotiating an agreement on constitutional issues was transferred from the Federal Assembly to the governments of each of the two republics. Heavily influenced by Klaus and Meciar, the Czech and Slovak republic legislatures soon showed interest in a separation of the republics and had little sympathy for the referendum, which was never called.[39]

In November 1991, alarmed by the prospect of national breakup as leading Slovak and Czech politicians seemed unable to agree on constitutional reform, Havel tried to arouse public support. In a nationally televised address on November 17, he spoke of a crisis that threatened the country's survival. He asked voters to pressure the federal parliament in Prague through letter-writing campaigns, political clubs, and rallies to grant him special powers to dissolve the parliament and rule by decree until a new parliament more sympathetic to his conciliatory approach could be elected.[40] In this address Havel criticized the view of people such as Klaus that the Czechs should "let them (the Slovaks) go." He astutely observed that this attitude "revealed a particular Czech historic inclination, whenever someone complicates our lives—we say let him go. In this way we got rid of three million of our fellow (German) citizens after World War II."[41]

Unfortunately for Havel and for a united Czechoslovak state, Czechs responded only mildly and Slovaks not at all to his appeal. The popular response to Havel was sluggish not because Czechs and Slovaks had no interest in the unity of their country. Public opinion polls indicated otherwise. It was rather, as local politicians understood, the reflection of a national inclination to passivity. Also, here was evidence of a beginning of a decline in Havel's popularity since its high point in November and December 1989, during the resistance to Communist rule. As some have suggested, Havel's popularity had begun to decline as he settled into the less exciting job of managing the country on a day-to-day basis. Moreover, some Slovak leaders such as Peter Weiss, head of the Slovak Party of the Democratic Left, many of whose members were ex-Communists, saw in Havel's bid for increased authority evidence of the centralistic and unitarian tendencies Slovak nationalists always had attributed to the Czechs.[42]

Slovak-Czech Stalemate

In the early months of 1992, Slovak-Czech negotiations on the constitutional relationship between the two communities resumed. The Slovak side again insisted on a formal treaty defining the powers of the central government and those of the two republics. This treaty, to be ratified by the legislatures of both republics and with approval of the federal parliament in Prague, would serve as the basis of a new constitution for the Czecho/Slovak Republic. In the Slovak view such a treaty was needed in light of their historic experience, described as one "of broken understandings with the Czechs."[43] Slovak leaders also insisted that the treaty identify the two republics as the signatory parties, emphasizing the sovereignty and equality of each, and that each should formally ratify the agreed-upon arrangements.

In early 1992, Czech negotiators still could not accept the notion that the two republics were sovereign entities, any more than they could accept a confederative Czecho/Slovak state in which the central government would be a weak entity with much of its policy-making authority left to the governments of the constituent republics. Nor could they accept the Slovak position that the treaty arrangements should be ratified by each republic's legislature, as if it were the government of a completely independent state. When in mid-February 1992 the Czechs came up with a draft agreement that made no mention of the two republics as parties to it and that preserved traditional central control of foreign affairs, internal security, customs regulation, and banking, the Slovak leadership rejected it.[44]

THE INEVITABILITY OF SEPARATION

In the second half of 1992, circumstances converged to make the division of Czechoslovakia into two separate states at the end of the year inevitable. They included (1) the June 1992 parliamentary elections; (2) the Slovak declaration of sovereignty immediately following the elections; (3) the failure of further Slovak-Czech negotiations undertaken in June, July, and August; (4) the promulgation of a new Slovak constitution in September; and (5) Havel's resignation. Additional circumstances that served as catalysts for the breakup of the country were the peculiar character of Czechoslovak ethnocultural demography and the passivity of the West.

The June 1992 Parliamentary Elections

On the eve of the elections, Meciar, whose MDS party was very popular in Slovakia, made no secret of what he would do to enhance Slovak autonomy of Prague should he succeed Jan Carnogursky as republic prime minister. In talks with Havel, Meciar said he would ask the Slovak parliament to pass a declaration of sovereignty, though he assured the president that this gesture would not end the common state; he would seek a referendum on Czech-Slovak coexistence, which he presumed he would win if voters supported his party in the upcoming parliamentary elections; he would work for a new Slovak constitution, which would replace the existing federal constitution in Slovakia but retain Slovak membership in the Czecho/Slovak state and respect what he termed "valid" federal legislation. He reminded Havel that both federal economic reforms and a law calling for the removal from public office of ex-Communists and known Soviet sympathizers "did not fit Slovak needs."[45]

Havel was deeply disturbed by Meciar's views. While sympathetic to his insistence on constitutional change, Havel criticized Meciar's plans for a declaration of sovereignty and a new Slovak constitution, calling them" controversial, not thought out, and dangerous."[46] Although Havel and other Czech leaders were tempted to denounce Meciar, they held back lest they increase his already substantial popularity. In addition, Havel was aware that in the Czech Republic Meciar's position tended to strengthen the hand of nationalists like Klaus, who now suggested a readiness to let the Slovaks go.

In the elections on both the federal and republic levels held in early June 1992, candidates loyal to Klaus and Meciar and sympathetic to separation made substantial gains. In the Czech Republic, Klaus's Czech-based Civic Democratic Party, which was committed to free enterprise and a strong Czechoslovak federal state, won 33 percent of the ballots for the federal parliament. In Slovakia, Meciar's MDS, which had called for equality of Slovaks with Czechs in a confederative Czecho/Slovak state, also won 33 percent of the ballots cast for the federal parliament and 37 percent of the ballots cast for the Slovak republic parliament. The liberal Civic Democratic Union, successor to the moderate antiseparatist Slovak PAV, won only 4 percent of the popular vote and therefore was no longer a factor in Slovak national politics. Carnogursky's CDM, which was nationalistic but more sympathetic to continuation of a united Czecho/Slovak state than Meciar and his MDS, did only slightly better than the PAV with 8 percent of the popular vote, entitling it to a small foothold in the SNC.[47]

Voter support for the SNP, which had called for the independence of Slovakia if the traditional Czechoslovak state could not be transformed in a confederation, dropped in both the federal and Slovak republic parliamentary contests. The decline in popular support for the SNP suggested that although Slovak voters favored greater administrative and cultural autonomy for the Slovak republic, they were not sympathetic to separation and hoped that Slovak and Czech political leaders could eventually reach a compromise.[48] A new dissident ultranationalist pro-independence breakaway branch of the CDM, calling itself the Slovak Christian Democratic Movement, received only 3 percent of the popular vote, additional evidence of voter sympathy for preserving the united Czechoslovak state.[49]

Electoral results also indicated that the Hungarian community in Slovakia opposed separation and favored a strong central government in Prague as a counterweight to their minority status. Together, the Hungarian parties garnered 7 percent of the popular vote, which meant a very strong showing among Hungarian voters in Slovakia. The Hungarian opposition to separation undoubtedly strengthened the commitment of most Slovak politicians to back a loose confederation that would allow Bratislava to control non-Slovak minorities as it saw fit.[50]

The results of the elections also suggested very striking contrasts between Slovaks and Czechs. Czech voters had voted for candidates supportive of further movement toward the market economy, while Slovaks had elected leaders who wanted to go slowly. On the other hand, both Czechs and Slovaks overwhelmingly supported parties with strong leaders determined to do what they thought best for the country and, arguably, for themselves, regardless of controversy. These leaders had a certain toughness, self-confidence, pertinacity, and independence of mind and were highly nationalistic.

Czech and Slovak voters gave their leaders in the June 1992 parliamentary elections an ambiguous or perhaps impossible mandate on the issue of Czechoslovak unity, given their strong personalities unaccustomed to flexibility and compromise. They were asked to strike a proper balance between statehood and economic reform. Indeed, voters, like the politicians they had just elected, arguably had little idea how to reach such a compromise. They may not in fact have had a clear idea of what "unity" meant nor a particular affinity for the Czechoslovak ideal.

It may also have been true that Czech voters were less sympathetic to living in a common state with Slovaks than they appeared. Czechs always had thought that Czechoslovakia was a good deal for Slovaks, better than Slovaks were willing to admit, while Slovaks always had thought Czechoslovakia was a better deal for Czechs and that Slovaks had never received their promised and deserved recognition in the state. This may well have meant that both Czech and Slovak voters in the June 1992 parliamentary elections were less committed to the idea of a unified Czechoslovakia than they said they were and that their political leaders well understood this thinking.[51]

Slovak Declaration of Sovereignty

Influenced in part by declarations of sovereignty on the part of the constituent republics of the former Soviet Union and the former Yugoslavia in 1991, some Slovak politicians in May 1992 proposed a Slovak declaration of sovereignty. At first there was much opposition to this gesture, which Slovak Prime Minister Carnogursky called "the height of political primitivism" and "a criminal daredevil game in the fate of the citizen."[52] The SNC decided not to act on the proposal.

After the June elections, which brought Meciar to power, the SNC promptly passed a declaration of Slovak sovereignty, emphasizing, however, that it was only a symbolic move with no legal consequences. Havel and others saw it as another step toward the disintegration of Czechoslovakia. They were not far off the mark. While short and not very specific, the declaration did state that the Slovak nation had a natural right to self-determination. An overwhelming majority of the Slovak republic parliament approved it.[53]

Although the declaration of sovereignty included a pledge to respect the rights of all minorities and ethnic groups, members of the Hungarian delegation in the Bratislava parliament, who were distrustful of Slovak power and against Slovak separation from Czechoslovakia, opposed the declaration.[54] Carnogursky's CDM also opposed the declaration, warning that it and a proposed adoption of a constitution giving the country attributes of an independent state would result in early independence for which Slovakia was ill prepared. The CDM also said that the public should be given the chance to voice its opinion in a referendum, especially given the fact that the MDS had received the support of only 37 percent of Slovak voters.[55]

Further Slovak-Czech Negotiations

After the June 1992 parliamentary elections Czech and Slovak leaders tried once again to reach a mutually acceptable agreement on the constitutional structure of Czecho/Slovakia. During June, July, and August, Meciar and Klaus held several rounds of discussion. From the outset it looked as if neither side had changed its position.

Meciar still called for a loose economic and defense union between Czechs and Slovaks, with each republic having its own banking and credit system and separate membership in international organizations like the United Nations and the European Union. Meciar insisted that this plan did not amount to a breakup of Czechoslovakia, but he reiterated his view that the pace of Czechoslovakia's movement to a market economy needed to be slower, pointing out that Klaus' free market reforms hurt Slovakia unfairly, producing unemployment four times greater than in the Czech part of the country.[56]

For his part, Klaus, now Czech Republic prime minister, rehearsed familiar arguments. He still rejected the Slovak proposal of confederation, saying that only a strong central government was capable of implementing reforms for the entire country. He said once again that the looser federation that Meciar proposed would interfere with Czechoslovakia's development of a free market economy, would delay indefinitely membership in the European Union, and would compromise the achievement of prosperity.[57]

Klaus tried to persuade Meciar to accept the highly centralized Czech version of the common state, offering Slovakia a large program of economic assistance and parity for Slovaks in a ten-member federal cabinet. Meciar countered with demands for Slovak control of the powerful ministries of Foreign Affairs and Defense. Klaus refused. He suspected Meciar of wanting to use Federal money to build up the Slovak military establishment and questioned Meciar's protestations of loyalty to a common state. Convinced that the Slovak side was determined eventually to achieve independence, Klaus concluded it was better to break up the state sooner rather than later.[58]

After what seemed like an endless debate between the two leaders over the meaning of federation, confederation, union, and independent state, Klaus said he saw no point in continuing the negotiations, which would only prolong the insecurity of the public and damage economic development.[59] Klaus and Meciar finally agreed in late June 1992 that the issue of separation and independence should be decided no later than September 30, by the two republic-level parliaments and by the federal parliament in Prague, that is to say, by the politicians and not the people.[60]

Meciar's "Second Thoughts." Sometime in June Meciar seems to have had "second thoughts" about the separation that now seemed inevitable. He was aware that many Slovak voters did not support a total break with the Czechs and a dissolution of the federation. A poll conducted the preceding April by Bratislava's Center for Social Analysis had shown that only 19 percent of the people in Slovakia favored an independent Slovak state.[61] Moreover, Meciar may never have wanted a definitive and complete separation of Czechs and Slovaks. He realized that Slovakia needed Czech resources to finance a smooth transition to the free market. He also may have assumed, wrongly as it turned out, that eventually he could persuade Klaus to make concessions on intergovernmental relations by threatening separation to someone he was convinced was a unitarist.[62]

Meciar and his followers were surprised by and, arguably, unprepared for Klaus's willingness to accept separation. The Slovak side may well have underestimated Klaus's willingness to sacrifice the union for the sake of Czech material interests he considered threatened by Slovak opposition to his "shock-therapy" reformism. By the summer of 1992, the Slovak side could see that many Czech deputies in the federal parliament had also bought Klaus's arguments that the Czech Republic would be better off without Slovakia.[63]

Meciar also was aware that the Slovak economy might not be ready to cope with the economic ramifications of separation, in particular an abrupt termination of federal (meaning Czech) subsidies to Slovakia.[64] His fears were confirmed in a report by a Slovak delegation visiting the IMF and the World Bank in mid-August. The report stated among other things that the Slovak population should be told in no uncertain terms that the economic price of independence would be high and that with separation the population of Slovakia must expect another drop in living standards over the next three years.[65]

Finally, for Meciar there was a political "upside" to preservation of a common state. If he failed to get the Czechs to agree to confederation, he still could curry favor with the Slovak electorate by perennially complaining about a "Prago centered bully" pressing Slovakia to adopt a potentially disastrous reformism that he was ordained to resist.[66]

During July and August, Meciar tried to move closer to the Czech position on powersharing and confederation. He withdrew the demand for a separate Slovak banking and currency system and backed off on previous demands that Slovakia be given its own seat at the United Nations.[67] But, these concessions did not move Klaus. He insisted that the Slovaks accept either the federation in its present form, with a strong central government in Prague and with the present federal commitment to a rapid introduction of free enterprise, or separation.

Agreement to Separate. Meeting on July 22 and 23 in Bratislava, Klaus and Meciar decided they had no alternative but to divide the Czecho-slovak state into two sovereign entities, the Czech Republic and

Slovakia. They agreed that the Federal Assembly in Prague would determine the details of separation based on the following principles: (1) the rights of citizens of either republic would be equally protected in the other; (2) the two new states would coordinate their foreign and defense policies, while dividing the armed forces without disruptive movement of troops from one republic to another; (3) there would be a smooth adjustment of federal institutions involving the abolition of some, like the Czechoslovak Academy of Sciences, and the transformation of others, notably federal broadcasting and press institutions; and (4) the Federal Security and Intelligence Service would be divided. Klaus and Meciar also agreed that the two new states should form a customs union and establish a zone for the free movement of goods, services, labor, and capital. They could not agree in the summer of 1992 on monetary, fiscal, and currency questions, which would have to be settled later, as in fact they were.[68]

The New Slovak Constitution

In October 1992, the Slovak government promulgated a new constitution, a decisive gesture toward independence. In section 1 of the constitution Slovakia defined itself as a sovereign democratic state. Article 7 gave the Slovak republic the right to unite with another state or to secede from a common state. The constitution did say that annexation or secession must be approved by both parliament, in the form of a constitutional law, and by the people through a referendum, though nothing was said about which process was to come first. In addition, section 3 gave the Slovak republic the right to set up its own central bank and to create its own currency. Section 4 gave the Slovak Parliament, officially identified as the "National Council of the Slovak Republic," exclusive constituent and lawmaking prerogatives, provisions that violated the constitution of the Czechoslovak federation to which Slovakia still legally belonged.[69]

Havel's Resignation

In the face of these events, President Vaclav Havel could do little to save the Czechoslovak union. He ran for reelection in July 1992 and was not returned to office. Given the rules governing presidential elections whereby either the Slovak or Czech parliamentary group could block any candidate (with a 60 percent majority of parliament needed for election of the president), Slovak nationalists loyal to Meciar helped to deny Havel the presidency. They worried that the election of Havel would strengthen Klaus's hand in pressuring them to accept the centralized state he wanted. But Czech deputies also were responsible for the defeat of Havel. The far-right Republican Party and the small Communist Party voted against him. Support from Klaus's followers, now committed to separation, was lukewarm. In their hasty scheduling of a second, runoff ballot, Czech deputies, many of whom were members of Klaus's Civic Democratic Party, did not leave Havel and his backers enough time to mobilize the support absent in the first round of voting.[70]

In July, Havel resigned the presidency. He felt personally humiliated by his defeat. It didn't help Havel that his rival, Miroslav Sladek, leader of the extreme rightist Republican Party, had won almost as much parliamentary support as Havel had. In Havel's view Sladek had not earned and did not deserve this support.[71] Moreover, Havel was demoralized by the Slovak Parliament's declaration of sovereignty in mid-July 1992, which he took to mean that the Slovak leadership was bent on independence. This was the beginning of the end of Czechoslovakia. Havel allegedly said that he did not want to preside over the liquidation of the Czechoslovak state.[72]

In a televised speech on the day he announced his resignation, Havel declared that to remain in office meant betraying his conscience and the presidential oath that bound him to defend the federation. He also expressed dismay over the failure of Klaus and Meciar to find the compromise needed to preserve historic Czechoslovakia. He also regretted the unwillingness of the politicians to allow the people to determine the fate of their country in a referendum.[73]

At the same time, in leaving office when he did, Havel was probably also trying to preserve his credibility with Czech politicians, whose support he might want later on were he to run for the presidency of a newly independent Czech republic. He was encouraged in this thinking by Klaus, who told reporters on July 20 that he was counting "on Havel's reemerging as an important personality at the level of the Czech Republic."[74]

Constitutional Limits and Political Constraints. Havel's role in trying to keep his country united was undercut by the Czechoslovak constitution, which intended the federal presidency to be little more than a figurehead chief executive, without real power, which was reserved for the prime minister and the cabinet. Havel frequently complained that the Czechoslovak presidency was too ceremonial. He had sought more authority to keep the country together, and his failure to get it troubled him. The Federal Assembly in Prague had denied him decree power and rejected his request for a popular referendum on revising the Czechoslovak constitution.

Moreover, whatever influence Havel may have had because of his immense popularity was compromised by a unique feature of the post-Communist Czechoslovak political system whereby the two constituent republics gradually overshadowed the federal government in Prague. This was seen clearly in the debate over the future configuration of Czechoslovakia. When the Slovak republic government declared sovereignty in July 1992 and drafted a separate constitution in September, Bratislava became the center of the debate, weakening Havel's influence.[75]

Havel also was frustrated by the difficulty of mobilizing a majority of support in the Federal Assembly, which was frequently paralyzed by a divisive party factionalism. A cumbersome voting procedure that required three-fifths of the total membership of each of the two houses of the federal parliament to support an amendment before it could become law complicated matters further. Because the upper house, the so-called House of Nations, was divided equally between Czech and Slovak deputies, a handful of either could and did block constitutional legislation. As one expert put it, "from the old mortifying pattern of totalitarian unanimity, the parliament moved to stubborn fragmentation, unwillingness to compromise, and a fairly low civility." Another deputy made this telling remark: "My dream is to witness a big fist fight here—all three hundred of us taking part."[76]

By contrast, the unicameral republic-level parliaments, where sentiment for separation was quite pronounced, were less conflict ridden, more cohesive, and better able than the national parliament in Prague to transact business. The federal president's influence in these bodies was minimal.

Making matters worse for Havel's leadership was the weakness of Civic Movement (CM), an offshoot of the Civic Forum founded by Federal Foreign Minister Dienstbier and Federal Prime Minister Peter Pithart and supportive of Havel. The CM was never able to provide him with a cohesive and disciplined parliamentary following. To a degree Havel himself was to blame. He had made little effort to mobilize voters and transform the CM into a presidential party. Indeed, the idealistic Havel tried to keep himself above politics to be the president of all voters, not just those who supported his party in the federal- and republic-level legislatures. In addition, because the Civic Movement had a mostly Czech base, it had difficulty mobilizing support among Slovak voters, who gravitated primarily toward Slovak-based parties.[77]

Without presidential inspiration, Havel's followers in the CM, which actually was managed by former foreign minister Jiri Dienstbier, seemed listless and lackluster. Hardly anybody attended CM rallies, which in earlier years would have attracted hundreds of thousands of supporters. It could never capitalize on the undercurrent of popular sympathy for a united Czechoslovak state.[78]

Another political problem for Havel was Klaus, a tough, stubborn hardball player, who was in many ways the opposite of the conciliatory and scholarly Havel. Klaus was an aggressive policy wonk, a skillful and persistent advocate of "shock therapy" in developing the free market system in Czechoslovakia. He was respected and admired in the Czech republic, where his political base was solid and reliable. Quite unlike Havel, Klaus understood the importance of creating a loyal and disciplined political party organization, which is what he did with his Civic Democratic Party. Moreover, Havel and Klaus, despite many shared values and ideas, did not work well together even in areas where they agreed, such as economic reform. Their different political style and an occasional sense of rivalry for the support of Czech voters were a liability for Havel's leadership of Czechoslovakia in the Slovak-Czech crisis.[79]

Finally, Havel's personality was a liability for his leadership. While certainly a man of admirable moral quality, inclined to conciliate and unite, both at home and abroad, Havel's idealism, which helped him resist the Communists, ill-suited him for the task of holding his country together in the face of strong divisive forces working for its dissolution. As president in a democracy, Havel needed a hard-knuckled political pragmatism. Leaders such as Klaus and Meciar, who were less interested in consensus and more sharply confrontational in pursuing their agendas, often prevailed over the indulgent Havel.

Demography

The peculiar character of Czechoslovakia's demography seems to have favored separation. Unlike other multiethnic ex-Communist societies, Czechoslovakia's large ethnic groups were relatively self-contained geographically. Czechs and Slovaks were not dispersed on each other's territories. The overwhelming majority of Czechs lived in Bohemia and Moravia, and the overwhelming majority of Slovaks lived in Slovakia. Of course, some Czechs resided and were employed in Slovakia, and the same was true for some Slovaks in the Czech republic. But the size of these Czech and Slovak "minorities" living outside their home regions was very small. Ultimately this situation weakened the incentive for unity.[80]

One could argue that a distinct Czechoslovak cultural identity never developed. Sympathy for Czechoslovak unity seems to have been mainly political, not cultural or psychological, with many Czechs and Slovaks giving priority to their regional identity over their national identity. Though the national Czechoslovak identity was strong, and though many Czechs and Slovaks wanted to preserve the Czechoslovak state, in the end their regional identity had a stronger influence over their thinking than their sense of being "Czechoslovak." In 1992, Czech and Slovak political leaders who favored separation clearly understood this priority and played to it.

The Role of the West

Western democratic governments watching the Slovak-Czech controversy unfold in the early 1990s refused to get involved. While investing substantially in Czechoslovakia, they did not respond to Slovak complaints that Western money was flowing disproportionately into the Czech part of the country. Ignoring the political need to target increased economic assistance and financial investment to the depressed Slovak regions and instead favoring the more prosperous Czech area, Western countries tended to aggravate the Slovak economic crisis and thereby intensify Slovak nationalism.

The West did have an interest in preserving Czechoslovak unity. It was certainly clear to outsiders, if not to Slovak nationalists in Bratislava, that the separation of Slovaks from the Czechs would weaken Slovakia economically and slow its move away from the state-controlled economy. With the growing economic hardship caused by their isolation, the Slovaks might also have difficulty developing a liberal democratic political and social order favored by the West. They might also gravitate toward Russia.

Political leaders in the European Union and the United States probably took for granted the permanence of Czechoslovak unity, especially given President Havel's popularity and his strong commitment to keeping the country together. Western governments also were distracted by the disintegration of the Soviet Union and Yugoslavia in 1991 and the outbreak of the civil war in Bosnia-Herzegovina in early 1992. The political conflict in Czechoslovakia by comparison struck Western leaders as a mild disagreement and one that could be resolved by the politically astute Czechoslovak population without perturbing the international community.

The United States in particular was preoccupied with many pressing concerns: the Persian Gulf War in early 1991, the onset of a serious domestic recession, and a presidential election campaign in which the voters made clear that national leadership must pay more attention to domestic problems than to foreign policy issues. American officials in Prague believed that it was improper to interfere in Czechoslovakia's internal affairs to discourage the split.

FINALIZATION OF SEPARATION

During September 1992, as Meciar and Klaus discussed administrative problems posed by the separation, popular opposition to a breakup of the Czecho/Slovak state increased. Sensitive to a pervasive uneasiness in the Federal Assembly over the prospect of a breakup of Czechoslovakia, the unitarist Czech Communists called for mass demonstrations, against the breakup.[81] There also was some sympathy in the Federal Assembly on the part of both Slovak and Czech deputies for submitting the separation issue to the public in a referendum as an alternative to passing a law that simply dissolved the Czecho/Slovak state, the course preferred by Meciar and Klaus.

When the issue of separation was put to a vote in the Federal Assembly on October 1, it failed to get the majority of more than 60 percent needed to pass. Meciar may have been relieved, but Klaus was shocked. Making matters worse for him, opponents of separation with the backing of MDS deputies now requested a vote by the assembly on a resolution calling for the establishment of a commission that would prepare a constitutional law on the transformation of the Czecho/Slovak Federation into a confederative union along the lines proposed by Meciar in August. This union would coordinate economic, social, ecological, foreign, and defense policies while respecting the sovereignty of both republics and would be ratified by the republics. The Federal Assembly passed the resolution with support from MDS deputies, although a decisive factor was the absence of one Civic Democratic Party deputy who left the parliament just before the vote.[82]

If Meciar again was trying to induce a compromise with Klaus, his effort failed. Klaus, backed by Havel, now a private citizen, was reconciled to the inevitability of the breakup of Czechoslovakia. Perhaps even looking forward to it, as a means of ending once and for all the uncertainty about Czechoslovakia's future as a unified state, and clarifying his prospects of leading an independent Czech Republic, Havel was bent on finalizing the separation in accordance with the July 22 agreement. In more discussions Meciar and Klaus said they again would ask the Federal Assembly to pass a law extinguishing the 1918 Czechoslovak state. They agreed there was no possibility of an alternative administrative arrangement such as a federation, confederation, or union of the kind described in the union resolution recently approved by the Federal Assembly. They also agreed that each republic would have its own budget after that date.[83]

The October 29 Agreements

On October 29, 1992, Klaus and Meciar signed 16 agreements defining future relations between the Czech and Slovak republics worked out in numerous discussions throughout October.[84] They agreed that the Czechoslovak Republic should be dissolved on January 1, 1993. The October 29 agreements also called for the creation of a customs union between the Czech and Slovak successors; and for the signing of treaties on Czech-Slovak monetary arrangements, on border regulations, and on legal matters concerning personal documents like automobile registration, residency requirements for third-country nationals, visa requirements, cooperation in communications, social security and health care services, and cooperation in environmental protection.[85]

While the primary intent of these agreements was to assure that the separation would occur peacefully and efficiently, there were other considerations. The creation of a customs union was especially important for future Czech and Slovak membership in the European Union, which expected a high level of cooperation between the two new states. In a memorandum announcing the creation of the customs union to a meeting of the so-called Visegrad group of central European countries (Poland, Hungary, and Czechoslovakia) at the end of October 1992, Klaus and Meciar stipulated that the customs union was intended to create conditions "for the eventual integration of the two new states into the European Community," as the European Union was then known. They formally requested the extension of associate membership to both.[86]

The continuation of a common currency, to be managed by a joint committee of Czech and Slovak officials was intended to assure a period of monetary stability. Klaus and Meciar wanted to avoid disruptions to the country's economic life that could increase economic hardship and impede growth in the short term.[87] Given the divergent levels of material well-being and policy programs, both sides expected that the common currency agreement would be temporary and that each would adopt separate currencies sometime in 1993. They agreed that the details of implementing the agreements, especially in the areas of citizenship and division of federal assets, would have to be worked out by the governments of the two new states following their independence.

The Federal Assembly Legalizes Separation

On November 25, 1992, the Czechoslovak Federal Assembly in Prague adopted the provisions of the Meciar-Klaus agreement of October 29 and formally divided the country into two separate republics effective December 31, 1992. The assembly thus created a legal framework for the separation to reassure foreign investors. The law provided for a temporary joint currency until both republics had established their own monetary system; for the setting up of a customs union; and for the division of the armed forces into two separate organizations, one for the Czech Republic and one for Slovakia. The law authorized the legislatures of the two republics to function as sovereign entities even before the official end of the Czecho-Slovak state. The law also provided that members of the assembly elected in 1992 whose terms would be cut short at the end of the year were to join the legislatures of the newly independent republics—which were to decide on exactly how its membership would be determined.[88]

Persistence of Skepticism and Doubt. Many politicians on both the Slovak and the Czech sides in the Federal Assembly had reservations about the haste of Meciar and Klaus in dissolving the 1918 Czechoslovak union. They complained about the absence of popular input, which could have been made through a referendum. CDM leader Carnogursky and his party colleagues in the Federal Assembly had voted against the November 25 law because it failed to provide for a referendum, but they said they would support the new Slovak state. There also were complaints that the Federal Assembly had failed to implement the union resolution calling for the appointment of a commission to examine the possibility of transforming the Czecho-Slovak state into a confederative union. Other complaints involved the failure of the Slovak and Czech leaders to examine the economic consequences of separation. The harshest criticism came from the neofascist left, in particular Republican party leader Miroslav Sladek, who equated separation with "the spiritual genocide of the nation." Even Vaclav Havel was denounced for "having fled the sinking ship." In response Klaus declared that separation was necessary and inevitable to avoid chaos, saying, "this state would be uncontrollable, ungovernable" if the two republics did not separate. "The cost of dividing the state," he said, "must be set against the cost of not dividing it, the cost of the non-functioning of this country."[89]

A "Velvet" Divorce? Despite criticisms and complaints about the modalities of the separation, the event itself occurred without the trauma or violence seen in other ethnic confrontations and conflicts. In part this was because the Czech and Slovak peoples had little if any deep hostility toward one another; with no history of war, the two peoples had had a long period of peaceful coexistence in the modern Czechoslovak state. They also had a strong commitment to democratic processes and the rule of law and little will to confrontation. Moreover, Czech and Slovak political leaders, while determined to have their way, were willing and able to work out their differences within the political and administrative framework provided by the Czechoslovak national government. Indeed, these post-Communist Czechoslovak institutions, while certainly flawed, did provide a framework within which major disputes and controversies could be adjudicated without recourse to violence.

Irrevocability. The separation is permanent. The present Slovak political establishment, in particular Prime Minister Meciar, is convinced that economic and other problems arising out of the administrative separation of Slovaks and Czechs are worth enduring for the sake of Slovak sovereignty and independence. For their part, Czech Republic leaders, starting with Klaus, were convinced that the Czech lands would prosper without administrative links to less developed Slovakia.

Indeed, Czech leaders envisaged difficulties dealing with Slovakia even after separation because of its weak economy. On August 20, 1992, Czechoslovak federal prime minister Jan Starsky, a leader of Klaus's Civic Democratic Party who favored separation, said that a common market embracing both the Czech and Slovak republics after the breakup would be possible only if Slovakia remained committed to privatization and free market economics, presumably the Czech version, which Slovaks obviously had rejected.[90]

CONCLUSIONS

When democracy was restored in Czechoslovakia at the end of 1989, the conflicting interests and aspirations of the two peoples were obvious and profound. Traditional ethnocultural differences were exacerbated by sharp disagreements over economic policy, constitutional issues, and the personal political ambitions of both Slovak and Czech leaders, who had their own reasons for splitting the country. Moreover, the fragile democratic processes, having had only the briefest tenure while they confronted horrendous problems of post-Communist social and economic development, lacked the stability and strength needed to facilitate a compromise. The institution most likely to have undertaken such a task, the federal presidency, was weak, and so was its first occupant, Vaclav Havel, to the dismay of Czechoslovak citizens who greatly admired him and had extravagant expectations of his leadership.

The separation must be attributed also to the single-mindedness of Vladimir Meciar and Vaclav Klaus, who dominated the political process. For their own reasons, each leader worked for separation of the Slovak and Czech communities—though, in retrospect, Klaus was more determined than Meciar to bring it about. Klaus was obsessed with the notion that the Czechoslovak transformation to Western-style free enterprise was jeopardized by the Slovak preoccupation with equality and autonomy. Furthermore, Klaus seemed to be more inflexible and more stubborn than Meciar, who eventually showed some "give." Meciar, it turned out, had stronger incentives than Klaus not to separate Slovakia from the Czech lands, at least not in this early period of post-Communist development. Some Czechs wondered whether the common state might have been saved if someone less single-minded than Klaus had been leading their side.[91]

Could 1918 Czechoslovakia have been salvaged? The "velvet" character of the divorce in some ways suggests a positive response to this question. Slovaks never hated Czechs, and vice versa. At the same time, however, the two communities seemed to lack a "fervent Czechoslovak patriotism" that might have provided the incentive to do more than was done to preserve the 1918 union.[92]

NOTES

1. Stanislaw Kirschbaum, *A History of Slovakia: The Struggle for Survival* (New York: St. Martin's Press, 1995), p. 255; see also Eric Stein, *Czecho/Slovakia: Ethnic Conflict, Constitutional Fissure, Negotiated Breakup* (Ann Arbor: University of Michigan Press, 1997), pp. 30, 58–59; Milos Dokulil, "Ethnic Unity and Diversity," *International Social Science Review*, vol. 67 (Spring, 1992), pp. 76–86; Sabrina P. Ramet, *Whose Democracy? Nationalism, Religion, and the Doctrine of Collective Rights in post 1989 Eastern Europe* (Lanham, Md: Rowman and Littlefield, 1997) p. 115.

2. Peter Passell, "An Economic Wedge Divides Czechoslovakia," *New York Times* (hereafter cited as *NYT*) (April 19, 1992); Pavol Fric, "Slovakia on Its Way toward Another Misunderstanding?" *Sisyphus*, vol. 8, no. 2 (1992), p. 117; see also Otto Ulc, "The Right in Post-Communist Czechoslovakia," in Joseph Held (ed.), *Democracy and Right Wing Politics in Eastern Europe* (New York: Columbia University Press, 1993), pp. 94–95; Bernard Wheaton and Zdenek Kavan, *The Velvet Revolution* (Boulder, Colo.: Westview, 1992), p. 169; J. F. Brown, *Hopes and Shadows: Eastern Europe after Communism* (Durham: Duke University Press, 1994), p. 136; Carol Skalnik Leff, *The Czech and Slovak Republics: Nation versus State* (Boulder, Colo.: Westview Press, 1997), p. 185.

3. Leff, *Czech and Slovak Republics*, p. 185; Ramet, *Whose Democracy?*, pp. 117, 125; Sharon Wolchik, "Democratization and Political Participation in Slovakia," in Karen Dawisha and Bruce Parrott (eds.), *The Consolidation of Democracy in East-Central Europe* (Cambridge, U.K.: Cambridge University Press, 1997), pp. 216-217.

4. Leff, *Czech and Slovak Republics*, pp. 185–186.

5. Passell, "An Economic Wedge Divides Czechoslovakia"; Wheaton and Kavan, *Velvet Revolution*, p. 169; Brown, *Hopes and Shadows*, p. 137; Kirschbaum, *History of Slovakia*, p. 261; Leff, *Czech and Slovak Republics*, p. 262.

6. Judy Batt, *East Central Europe: From Reform to Transformation* (New York: Council on Foreign Relations, 1991), pp. 98, 100.

7. Stein, *Czecho/Slovakia*, p. 113.

8. Kirschbaum, *History of Slovakia*, pp. 263–264.

9. Ibid.; Jan Obrman, "Uncertain Prospects for Independent Slovakia," *Radio Free Europe/Radio Liberty Research Report* (hereafter cited as *RFE/RL*), vol. 1, no. 49 (December 11, 1992), p. 43.

10. Kirschbaum, *History of Slovakia*, p. 266; see also Jiri Pehe, "The Czech-Slovak Conflict Threatens State Unity," *RFE/RL*, vol. 1, no. 1 (January 3, 1992), pp. 83-84.

11. John Tagliabue, "Autonomy Issue Turns Slovak against Slovak," *NYT* (October 22, 1991).

12. "Slovak Council Rejects Bills Aimed at Sovereignty" (Prague, CSTK in English, October 8, 1991), United States Department of State, *Foreign Broadcast Information Service Daily Report Eastern Europe* (hereafter cited as *FBIS-EEU*), vol. 91, no. 198 (October 11, 1991), p. 12.

13. "Republican Presidiums Examine Power Sharing Bill" (Prague, CSTK in English, December 6, 1990), *FBIS-EEU*, vol. 90, no. 238 (December 11, 1990), p. 10; Otto Ulc, "The Bumpy Road of Czechoslovakia's Velvet Revolution," *Problems of Communism* (May-June 1992), p. 31; Stein, *Czecho/ Slovakia*, p. 107.

14. Stein, *Czecho/Slovakia*, pp. 110, 112.

15. Peter Martin, "Relations between the Czechs and the Slovaks," in Lyman H. Legters (ed.), *Eastern Europe Transformation and Revolution 1945–1991* (Lexington, Mass.: D. C. Heath, 1991), pp. 382–383; Ulc, "The Right in Post-Communist Czechoslovakia," p. 96.

16. Leff, *Czech and Slovak Republics*, p. 136; Ramet, *Whose Democracy?*, p. 118.

17. Stein, *Czecho/Slovakia*, pp. 72–74; Kirschbaum, *History of Slovakia*, p. 257; Gordon Wightman, "The Czech and Slovak Republics," in Stephen White, Judy Batt, and Paul G. Lewis (eds.), *Developments in East European Politics* (Durham, N. C.: Duke University Press, 1995), p. 57; Ramet, *Whose Democracy?*, p. 118.

18. Wightman, "Czech and Slovak Republics," p. 58.

19. Ibid.

20. As early as November 1991, Klaus's Civic Democratic Party had voted at its congress in favor of a strong federal union for Czechoslovakia or a split of the country into separate, sovereign, and independent states. Ibid., p. 62.

21. Paul Wilson, "Czechoslovakia: The Pain of Divorce," *New York Review of Books* (December 17, 1992), p. 72.

22. See Jan Obrman, "Slovak Politician Accused of Secret Police Ties," *RFE/RL Research Report*, vol. 1, no. 15 (April 12, 1992), pp. 13–17.

23. Jan Obrman, "The Slovak Government *versus* the Media," *RFE/RL Research Report*, vol. 2, no. 6 (February 1993), pp. 26–27.

24. "Meciar Seen to be 'Intimidating' Slovak Press" (Prague, *Mlada Fronta DNES* in Czech, December 30, 1991), *FBIS-EEU*, vol. 92, no. 002 (January 3, 1992), pp. 8–9; Obrman, "Slovak Government *versus* the Media," pp. 26–30.

25. "Meciar Asks for 'Truth Image of Slovakia'" (Bratislava, *Rozhlaszova Stanica Slovenska* Network in Slovak, July 10, 1992), *FBIS-EEU*, vol. 92, no. 134 (July 13, 1992), pp. 20–21; see also Obrman, "Slovak Government *versus* the Media," pp. 27–28; Leff, *Czech and Slovak Republics*, p. 115.

26. Wilson, "Czechoslovakia: The Pain of Divorce," p. 72; Stephen Engelberg, "Foes of Slovak Chief Fear He'll Resist Democracy," *NYT* (August 10, 1992).

27. Obrman, "Slovak Government *versus* the Media," p. 28.

28. Jeffrey Goldfarb, *After the Fall: The Pursuit of Democracy in Central Europe* (New York: Basic Books, 1992), pp. 104–105; "Former VPN Leader Gal Quits Active Politics" (Bratislava, *Verejnost*, in Slovak, January 2, 1992), *FBIS-EEU*, vol. 92, no. 007 (January 10, 1992), p. 15; Ulc, "The Right in Post Communist Czechoslovakia," in Joseph Held (ed.), *Democracy and Right Wing Politics in Eastern Europe in the 1990's* (New York: Columbia University Press, 1993), pp. 96–98.

29. Ulc, "Czechoslovakia's Velvet Divorce," p. 340.

30. *Yearbook of International Communist Affairs 1991* (Stanford, Calif.: Hoover Institution, 1992), p. 277; Batt, *East Central Europe: From Reform to Transformation*, p. 99; "Republican Presidiums Examine Powersharing Bill" (Prague, CSTK in English, December 6, 1990), *FBIS-EEU*, vol. 90, no. 238 (December 11, 1990), p. 10; "Meciar Speaks on Federation and Economic Reform" (Prague, Television Service in Slovak, December 9, 1990), *FBIS-EEU*, vol. 90, no. 239 (December 12, 1990), p. 20.

31. "Meciar Interviewed on Constitutional Position" (Bratislava, *Verejnost* in Slovak, January 24, 1992), *FBIS-EEU*, vol. 92, no. 024 (February 5, 1992), pp. 13–24.

32. Stein, *Czecho/Slovakia*, p. 108; see also "Havel Outlines Proposals to Solve Crisis" (Prague, Domestic Service in Czech, December 10, 1990), *FBIS-EEU*, vol. 90, no. 238 (December 11, 1990), p. 10.

33. Jiri Pehe, "The Referendum Controversy in Czechoslovakia," *RFE/RL Research Report*, vol. 1, no. 43 (October 30, 1992), pp. 35–36.

34. Ibid., p. 36; Stein, *Czecho/Slovakia*, p. 126.

35. By the end of October 1991, more than half a million Czechs and Slovaks had signed an appeal for an early referendum. In a nationwide poll, according to a report of the *CTK* news agency in mid-November, 78 percent of the Czech Republic and 66 percent in Slovakia supported a referendum. Stein, *Czecho/Slovakia*, p. 127.

36. "President Havel Comments on Klaus-Meciar Talks" (Prague Federal Television Network in Czech, June 17, 1992), *FBIS-EEU*, vol. 91, no. 118 (June 18, 1992), p. 5, "Havel Favors Same Referendum throughout Country" (Prague, *Mlada Frontadnes*, in Czech, June 13, 1992), *FBIS-EEU*, vol. 91, no. 119 (June 19, 1992), p. 3.

37. Wilson, "Czechoslovakia: The Pain of Divorce," p. 70; opinion polls in the spring of 1991 had confirmed that an overwhelming majority of Slovaks favored preservation of the Czechoslovak state. Jiri Pehe, "Growing Slovak Demands Seen as Threat to Federation," *RFE/RL Research Reports* (March 22, 1991), pp. 1, 2, cited in Stein, *Czecho/Slovakia*, p. 30, note 31.

38. Jiri Pehe, "Czechs and Slovaks Prepare to Part," *RFE/RL Research Report*, vol. 1, no. 37 (September 18, 1992), p. 13.

39. See Stein, *Czecho/Slovakia*, pp. 128–133.

40. "Havel Appeals for Support to Resolve Crisis" (Prague, Federal Television network in Czech, November 17, 1991), *FBIS-EEU*, vol. 91, no. 222 (November 18, 1991), pp. 7–8; see also Pehe, "Referendum Controversy," p. 36; Stein, *Czecho/Slovakia*, pp. 139–141; Ramet, *Whose Democracy?*, p. 123.

41. Stein, *Czecho/Slovakia*, p. 140.

42. Ibid., p. 143.

43. Ibid., p. 158.

44. Ibid., pp. 172–173.

45. Ibid., p. 180.

46. Ibid.

47. For the influence of ethnic issues on the campaign see "Meciar Addresses Rally on Slovak Sovereignty Agreement," "Civic Democratic Party Sets Terms for 'Reasonable Federation'" (Prague, CSTK in English, June 3, 1992), *FBIS-EEU*, vol. 92, no. 108 (June 4, 1992), p. 17; "Meciar, Klaus Score Electoral Victories" (Prague, CSTK in English, June 7, 1992), "Slovak Parliament Results" (Bratislava, *Stanica Slovenska* Network in Slovak, June 7, 1992) *FBIS-EEU*, vol. 92, no. 110 (June 8, 1992), pp. 14–17; see also Stein, *Czecho/Slovakia*, p. 184.

48. See Jan Obrman, "Czechoslovakia: Stage Set for Disintegration?" *RFE/RL Research Report*, vol. 1, no. 28 (July 10, 1992), p. 30; Ulc, "Czechoslovakia's Velvet Divorce," p. 342.

49. Stein, *Czecho/Slovakia*, p. 184.

50. Ibid., p. 185; Leff, *Czech and Slovak Republics*, pp. 138–139.; see also Alfred Reich, "Hungarian Coalition Succeeds in Czech Elections," *RFE/RL Research Report*, vol. 1, no. 26 (June 16,1992), pp. 20–22.

51. Leff, *Czech and Slovak Republics*, p. 139.

52. Stein, *Czecho/Slovakia*, p. 180.

53. Jan Obrman, "Slovakia Declares Sovereignty; President Havel Resigns," *RFE/RL Research Report*, vol. 1, no. 31 (July 31, 1992), p. 25; Stein, *Czecho/Slovakia*, p. 180.

54. Obrman, "Slovakia Declares Sovereignty; President Havel Resigns," p. 25.

55. Adele Kalniczky, "The Slovak Government's First Six Months in Office," *RFE/RL Research Report*, vol. 2, no. 6 (February 5, 1993), p. 21.

56. "Meciar Interviewed on Constitutional Position" (Bratislava, *Verejnost* in Slovak, January 24, 1992), *FBIS-EEU*, vol. 92, no. 024 (February 5, 1992), pp. 13–14, "Meciar, Other HZDS (Movement for a Democratic Slovakia) Leaders View Talks" (Bratislava, *Rozhlasova Stanica Slovenska* in Slovak, June 12, 1992), *FBIS-EEU*, vol. 92, no. 115 (June 15, 1992), p. 8; see also Marek Bankowicz, "Czechoslovakia from Masaryk to Havel," Sten Berglund and Jan Ake Dellenbrant (eds.), *The New Democracies in Eastern Europe: Party Systems and Political Cleavages*, 2nd ed. (Brookfield, Vt.: Edward Elgar, 1994), pp. 164–165.

57. "Slovak Press Comments in Klaus-Meciar Talks" (Prague, *CSTK* in English, June 12, 1992), *FBIS-EEU*, vol. 92, no. 117 (June 17, 1992), pp. 6–7, "Meciar Denies Provoking Breakup of Federation" (Vienna, *Der Standard* in German, June 17–18, 1992), *FBIS-EEU*, vol. 91, no. 119 (June 19, 1992), pp. 3–4.

58. Stein, *Czecho/Slovakia*, pp. 202–203.

59. Ibid., p. 200.

60. "Meciar, Klaus Announce Agreement to Split State" (Bratislava, *Rozhlasova Stanica Slovenska* Network in Slovak, June 19, 1992), *FBIS-EEU*, vol. 92, no. 120 (June 22, 1992), pp. 12–17; see also Stein, *Czecho/Slovakia*, pp. 197–198, 204–205.

61. "Study Examines Views of Meciar's Supporters" (Prague, *Mlada Fronta DNES* in Czech, June 5, 1992), *FBIS-EEU*, vol. 92, no. 113 (June 11, 1992), p. 11; see also the comments of Michele Kayal, news editor of the *Prague Post*, *NYT* (September 30, 1992).

62. Stein, *Czecho/Slovakia*, p. 222.

63. Mary Battiata, "Slovaks Softening Sovereignty Demand," *Washington Post* (hereafter cited as *WP*) (July 16, 1992); Henry Brandon, "Who Split Czechoslovakia?" *NYT* (September 24, 1992); Fric, "Slovakia on Its Way to Another Misunderstanding?" p. 118.

64. Pehe, "Czechs and Slovaks Prepare to Part," p. 13.

65. Ibid.

66. Stein, *Czecho/Slovakia*, p. 222.

67. Battiata, "Slovaks Softening Sovereignty Demand"; Brown, *Hopes and Shadows*, pp. 62–63.

68. Jan Obrman, "Czechoslovakia: Stage Set for Disintegration," *RFE/RL Research Report*, vol. 1, no. 28 (July 10, 1992), p. 32.

69. Pavel Mates, "The New Slovak Constitution," *RFE/RL Research Report*, vol. 1, no. 43 (October 30, 1992), pp. 39–40.

70. "HDZS (The Movement for a Democratic Slovakia) Refuses to Support Havel's Candidacy" (Prague, *CSTK* in English, June 9, 1992), *FBIS-EEU*, vol. 92, no. 112 (June 10, 1992), p. 17; see also Obrman, "Czechoslovakia: Stage Set for Disintegration?" pp. 28–29; Stephen Engelberg, "Slovakia Deputies Bloc Reelection of Vaclav Havel," "Slovaks Here, Czechs There," *NYT* (July 4, 5, 1992, respectively); Mary Battiata, "Slovaks Block Havel from Reelection," *WP* (July 4, 1992).

71. Obrman, "Slovakia Declares Sovereignty," p. 26.

72. Stein, *Czecho/Slovakia*, p. 209.

73. Obrman, "Slovakia Declares Sovereignty," p. 26.

74. Ibid.

75. David M. Olsen, "Federalism and Parliament in Czechoslovakia," in Thomas F. Remington (ed.), *Parliaments in Transition: The New Legislative Politics in the Former USSR and Eastern Europe* (Boulder, Colo.: Westview Press, 1994), p. 116; Wightman, "Czech and Slovak Republics," p. 60; Ulc, "Czechoslovakia's Velvet Divorce," p. 341.

76. Ulc, "Czechoslovakia's Velvet Divorce," p. 341.

77. Olsen, "Federalism and Parliament in Czechoslovakia," in Remington (ed.), *Parliaments in Transition*, pp. 104–105.

78. John Tagliabue, "Uncertain Days for Havel and Czechoslovakia," William E. Schmidt, "Where Did Czechoslovakia's Democrats Go?" *NYT* (March 8, June 4, 1992, respectively).

79. Jane Perlez, "The Fist in the Velvet Glove," *New York Times Magazine* (June 16, 1995); see also Obrman, "Slovakia Declares Sovereignty; President Havel Resigns," p. 28.

80. Carol Skalnik Leff, "Could This Marriage Have Been Saved? The Czechoslovak Divorce," *Current History* (March 1996), p. 132.

81. Stein, *Czecho/Slovakia*, pp. 229–231.

82. Ibid., pp. 233–235.

83. Ibid., pp. 238–239.

84. Ibid., pp. 244–250.

85. Ibid., pp. 251–256; Jiri Pehe, "Czechs and Slovaks Define Post-divorce Relations," *RFE/RL Research Report*, vol. 1, no. 45 (November 13, 1992), p. 8; for additional detail of the agreements see pp. 8–10.

86. Pehe, "Czechs and Slovaks Define Post-divorce Relations," pp. 8–10.

87. Ibid.

88. For a detailed discussion of the vote see Stein, *Czecho/Slovakia*, pp. 257–270, especially p. 261; see also "Politicians React to Breakup Law Approval" (Prague, *CSTK* in English November 25, 1992), *FBIS-EEU*, vol. 92, no. 230 (November 30, 1992), pp. 17–18.

89. Stein, *Czecho/Slovakia*, pp. 263–264; see also Karolyi Okolicsanyi, "Uncertain Prospects for Independent Slovakia," *RFE/RL Research Report*, vol. 1, no. 49 (December 11, 1992), pp. 43–48.

90. Battiata, "Slovaks Softening Sovereignty Demand"; Brown, *Hopes and Shadows*, pp. 62–63.

91. Stein, *Czecho/Slovakia*, p. 223.

92. Leff, "Could This Marriage Have Been Saved?" p. 132.

3

Democratic Political Development

Challenges and Achievements

When Slovakia became independent in the beginning of 1993, its constitution,[1] promulgated in October 1992, and its multiparty system provided for a Western-style parliamentary democracy. However, its leadership for most of the period since independence, in the person of Prime Minister Vladimir Meciar, has displayed strong authoritarian tendencies that raised doubts among some Slovak voters as well as the West about Slovakia's will and capacity to make a success of its new democratic system.

THE SLOVAK CONSTITUTION

The constitution makes the popularly elected legislature called the Slovak National Council (SNC), whose 150 members are chosen in free, open, competitive elections for a four-year term, the legal source of sovereignty. While the legislature must approve the budget and levies taxes, one of its most important functions is the selection and supervision of the national leadership, which is divided among the president of the republic and a cabinet chaired by the prime minister. The SNC elects the president of the republic for a five-year term. The president is commander in chief of the armed forces, appoints the prime minister, and on the latter's recommendation selects the membership of the cabinet. Normally the leader of the majority party or of a coalition of parties in the SNC is the obvious choice for prime minister. The prime minister and his cabinet colleagues are accountable to and can be removed by the SNC in a vote of no confidence that requires an absolute majority of its members. The legislature can require ministers to explain and justify their policies. The SNC, however, cannot censure the president, who holds office unless he is impeached for a legal wrongdoing. While the president is primarily a figurehead chief of state, he does have some opportunity to influence the government, namely, the prime minister and the cabinet. The president must approve all laws. If he refuses to sign a law, it cannot be promulgated. And, through speeches and other means of communication the president can try to use the symbolism of his high office to influence public opinion at home and abroad to support him when he disagrees with the government.

The constitution also provides for an independent judiciary. The court system consists of local and regional courts, a Supreme Court, and a Constitutional Court, which is the highest court of appeal in constitutional cases. Judges who sit on the Constitutional Court are nominated by parliament and appointed by the president. Other judges are nominated by the Ministry of Justice and elected by the parliament, which can remove them for misconduct. The constitution provides for civil rights, guaranteeing freedom of speech, religion, press, assembly and association, and the right to a fair trial. It prohibits arbitrary arrest, detention, and exile, and also prohibits cruel and unusual punishment.

SLOVAK POLITICAL PARTIES

Though not described in any detail in the nine sections of the 1992 constitution, Slovak political parties are arguably a critical aspect of the country's democratic system; it is hard to imagine how Slovak democracy could work without them. Indeed, it is impossible to discuss and assess Slovak democratic development without frequent reference to them.

Distinctive Features

From the beginning of independence Slovakia has had a multiparty system with no single party able to win more than a 37 percent plurality in parliamentary elections. To govern the country, Slovakia's prime ministers and cabinets have had to rely on a political majority in the parliament consisting of an alliance of parties which together have a majority of seats in what is commonly called a coalition.

Partly the multiparty system is the result of the new, open, and highly competitive political environmemt introduced in Slovakia and in the Czech Republic in the aftermath of the collapse of the Communist dictatorship. A long-pent-up demand for freedom of political expression led inevitably to a proliferation of parties. The electoral system is also responsible, providing an opportunity for small parties through proportional representation to win at least a few seats in the parliament and so deny a party with a large voter constituency, such as the Movement for a Democratic Slovakia (MDS), the opportunity to win the majority necessary to govern without a coalition. Finally, rules governing the threshold of voter support a party needed to seat its deputies in parliament tended to increase the proliferation of party groups. Normally a party needed to win at least 5 percent of the popular vote to participate in the parliament. But parties affiliated with a coalition could seat their deputies with less than the 5 percent minimum of voter support. This rule was very democratic in the sense of allowing voters a maximum amount of representation, producing only a minimum of the "lost" or "wasted" votes that result from the first-past-the-post or winner-take-all system of electing members of a legislature. But the practical effect of the system in Slovakia was to multiply the number of political groups that were eligible to seat deputies in the parliament, contributing to its fragmentation and weakness in dealing with an overbearing and quasi-authoritarian prime minister.

Although Slovak parties look and act like political parties in the Western democracies, they are quite different. Their internal structures and hierarchies are not fully developed, and they have had neither clear nor consistent platforms. As a result, it is difficult to place them in particular ideological positions on a left-right political spectrum. Some of them were founded in the early post-Communist era with one overriding purpose, such as the defense of Slovak political and economic interests against the Czechs or the defense of the interests of ethnic Hungarians in Slovakia. Slovak parties in fact are in a transitional phase, moving away from a predominantly nationalist agenda and, in some cases, from populist promises made before the June 1992 elections. In recent years they have seemed to be trying to develop programs that address in a constructive manner the new state's domestic and foreign policy needs. Most also are still concerned about political survival, and they too often sacrifice ideological principles for the sake of political expediency.

Programs and Policies[2]

In the mid-1990s, in describing the programs and policies of the Slovak parties it was possible to identify government and opposition parties. There is the government side, which since the October 1994 parliamentary elections has consisted of the Movement for a Democratic Slovakia (MDS), the Slovak National Party (SNP), and the Association of Slovak Workers (ASW). There are also parties that belong to the so-called opposition, including the Christian Democratic Movement (CDM), the Party of the Democratic Left (PDL), the Social Democratic Party of Slovakia (SDP), the Peasants' Movement (PM), and the Green Party (GP). The SDP and the GP worked closely with the PDL and in parliamentary elections held in September 1994 formed an electoral coalition known as "Common Choice." Three other parties that belonged to the opposition were the Hungarian minority party, Coexistence, the Hungarian Christian Democratic Movement, and the Hungarian Civic Party. They tended to work closely with one another in a "Magyar Coalition."

Government Parties. The leading government party, largely because it has been the most popular political party in the sense of commanding the support of about a third of the Slovak electorate in the mid-1990s, is Meciar's MDS, initially a center-left party committed to moderate reforms or "progress without pain." The MDS is difficult to categorize in Western terms. Meciar ousted critics of his policies, and transformed the MDS into a loyal instrument of his political leadership of the country. But occasionally MDS colleagues did criticize aspects of Meciar's behavior and refused to follow him, risking his wrath and inviting retribution. For example, Jozef Moravcik, a former Meciar ally, in 1994 bolted the MDS and formed a new organization in the parliament, the Democratic Union (DU), made up of other MDS deputies critical of the prime minister. At the same time, President Michal Kovac, a leading member of the MDS and a supporter of Meciar, became one of his severest critics, opposing several of his policies with whatever power he could muster as chief executive. Meciar and Kovac fought bitterly over economic, sociocultural, and foreign policy issues. Conflict within the leadership of the MDS hurt the party by dividing it, forcing some members to defect and start their own political organizations, and diminishing popular respect and support of it.

The SNP, with a much smaller popular base, having championed Slovak separation from the Czechs, after independence had to look for a new platform and favored rapid privatization and increased foreign investment to accelerate economic growth. It became a logical ally of the MDS on foreign policy issues, in which it was, like the MDS, highly nationalistic, suspicious of the West, and sympathetic to strong ties with post-Communist Russia. As a small party, whose voter constituency in fact declined significantly between the June 1992 and September 1994 parliamentary elections, it felt it had much to gain by supporting Meciar in a coalition with the MDS, especially as it agreed with important MDS policies, and even though Meciar refused to allow it much influence in Slovak policy-making. The SNP remained a fairly faithful ally of the

MDS despite occasional criticism of or disagreements with Meciar's policies, especially in the matter of how much influence—or, rather, how little influence—he allowed the SNP leadership over cabinet policy-making.

The ASW joined the MDS-SNP coalition following the September 1994 parliamentary elections. It is an offshoot of the PDL. ASW members are committed to socioeconomic reform but, like the PDL, to which most of its members originally belonged, it wanted preservation of a substantial social safety net to minimize hardships accompanying the movement away from the socialist to a free market economy. ASW members left the PDL over disagreement with PDL leader Weiss over the issue of cooperation with Meciar and the MDS. They did not share Weiss's personal hostility to Meciar and the populist reformism of the MDS. Rather, the ASW pragmatically opted for cooperation with the MDS under Meciar to get a chance to participate in government and avoid being permanently relegated to the political sidelines and marginalized.

The Opposition. The self-styled opposition parties cover a wide political spectrum stretching from Carnogursky's CDM to Weiss's PDL and the small parties that represented the Hungarian community. The most prominent member of the opposition was the CDM, a moderate party with perhaps a political program better defined than that of other parties. It advocated market reform and respect for human rights and was a strong critic of Meciar's authoritarian political style. In the mid-1990s the CDM had difficulty expanding its very modest voter constituency largely because it was blamed for the economic hardships caused by the free market reforms it has supported.

Despite a shared hostility to Meciar and many of his political, economic, and sociocultural policies, the opposition remained fragmented. It developed no common program. Parties that considered themselves in the opposition acted in unison mainly on an ad hoc basis when provoked by some action of Meciar, such as his controversial handling of the May 1997 NATO referendum. Throughout most of the 1990s the opposition parties never were able to offer voters an alternative to Meciar leadership because of divergent ideological perspectives. For example, the CDM was concerned primarily with the antidemocratic aspects of Meciar's leadership and favored rapid movement toward the free market economy, while the PDL at the other end of the spectrum advocated a very slow pace of reform although it shared the CDM's dislike of Meciar's frequently high-handed and illiberal management of power. At the same time the Hungarian parties tended to focus primarily on the well-being of the Hungarian community.

The opposition parties also seemed intimidated by Meciar, whose popularity and charismatic personality kept them on the defensive. For example, they took seriously MDS warnings against the pursuit of a "broad-based antigovernment coalition." Indeed, trying to act as the conscience of the country and the only group that knows what is best for it, the MDS and Meciar bullied the opposition into a kind of submission. There was always a hint in Meciar's dealings with the opposition that he considered its resistance to his policies akin to treason. He certainly said as much in response to President Kovac's frequent objections to his policies. He keeps the opposition parties on the defensive.[3]

A Political Center? The closest to a center in Slovak politics in the mid-1990s was the DU, which became a moderate reformist party in favor of the free market, a pro-West foreign policy, and minority rights. For a brief moment following Meciar's resignation in March 1994, the DU under the leadership of former foreign minister Jozef Moravcik ran the country. But, the DU's leadership was lackluster; and Moravcik, a relatively colorless and unexciting leader, was no match for Meciar in the September 1994 parliamentary elections, which brought the MDS back to power.

The Constitution and the political party system present the institutional framework of post-independence Slovak democracy. But to understand how it actually worked, one has to look closely at the leadership of Prime Minister Meciar, who governed Slovakia for most of the period since it gained independence on January 1, 1993. In the two phases of his leadership during these years—from June 1992 until March 1994 and from October 1994—Meciar demonstrated a remarkable political resiliency, despite mounting and occasionally very belligerent criticism of his leadership and calls for his ouster from power by angry opponents, including president Kovac.

MECIAR'S LEADERSHIP, JUNE 1992–MARCH 1994

Even as the Slovak constitution was being drafted and voted upon in the summer and fall of 1992, Meciar and his MDS were building a power base that would compromise Slovak democracy. Having won a substantial plurality of seats in the SNC in the June 1992 elections, Meciar formed a coalition with the SNP, but gave its leadership only one cabinet post, the economics ministry. This near-monolithic coalition, which played a major role in developing the new constitution promulgated in October 1992, led Slovakia to complete independence at the end of the year. By the time independence had been achieved, however, the coalition was already showing signs of having become a personal vehicle of Meciar's powerbuilding.

Meciar's Purging and Packing

Using his party's dominance of the cabinet, Meciar replaced ministerial leaders with personal friends and supporters; expanded government influence over the state-run radio and television; arbitrarily named members of the newly established constitutional court, a prerogative the constitution reserved for the Slovak president; and in the absence of a civil service law, replaced hundreds of national and local bureaucrats with MDS supporters. For Meciar, political loyalty counted as much as professional expertise and merit in the appointment of the Slovak bureaucracy. Throughout 1993, Meciar built a very effective political machine to strengthen his personal control over the levers of governmental power. The opposition parties and even members of his own party were critical. However, the more criticism came his way, the more sensitive and power-grabbing Meciar became—determined to establish a personal dominance over the Slovak government.[4]

Manipulation of the Presidential Election

Following independence, in January 1993, one of the first items of business on the SNC agenda was election of the country's first president. Meciar used the opportunity to try to insure his hold on the levers of political power. He used his influence with supporters in both his own party and the SNP to try to get the parliament to elect a crony, Roman Kovac, a former member of the Slovak Communist party. But the MDS parliamentary caucus, troubled by Meciar's aggressiveness, was critical of Roman Kovac. When Meciar tried to enforce party discipline to get his choice of candidate elected president by the SNC, Deputy Prime Minister and Foreign Minister Milan Knazko, and other members of the MDS parliamentary group, angry over of Meciar's overbearing behavior, suggested that it was reminiscent of Soviet-style communist intraparty authoritarianism, an unpleasant wrist-slap Meciar would neither forget or forgive.[5] During January 1993, in the preparation for a first ballot to elect the president, Knazko successfully mobilized opposition within the MDS parliamentary group to Roman Kovac's election. The SNP also opposed the election of Roman Kovac, fearing he would further strengthen Meciar's power at its expense. The SNP already had only a minimum of influence over government policy.

In a first ballot, none of four candidates was able to obtain the three-fifths majority needed to win the presidential office. In a second ballot on February 15, MDS deputies continued to defy the prime minister and, along with other political groups, elected Michal Kovac as president.[6] No relation to Roman Kovac, Michal Kovac, the deputy chairman of the MDS and former chairman of the Czechoslovak Federal Assembly, was a liberal and a reformer. He took office determined to defend the new democratic order against the authoritarian behavior of the prime minister and his backers in the cabinet and parliament.

Dismissal of Milan Knazko

In March 1993, Meciar finessed the ouster of Knazko as deputy prime minister and minister of foreign affairs. In addition to anger at Knazko's support of Michal Kovac in the election, which he considered to be insubordination, Meciar considered Knazko's personal friendship with President Kovac a liability for the cabinet's independence and his own personal authority. Knazko could become a conduit of presidential influence on cabinet decisionmaking.[7] In addition, Meciar disagreed with Knazko's pro-Western foreign policy. He rather saw Slovakia as a "bridge" between East and West and wanted to maintain good relations with Russia.[8] Meciar also resented the bluntness of Knazko's criticisms. Typical of what annoyed Meciar was an observation harshly critical of the prime minister's abrasive political style that Knazko reportedly made on his last day in office, that "authoritarian ways of solving problems have started to play a larger role in the government of the country."[9]

The ouster of Knazko turned out to be a political liability for Meciar. Knazko shortly formed a new liberal party, the Alliance of Democrats of the Slovak Republic (ADSR), taking some MDS parliamentary deputies with him and thereby weakening the coalition and Meciar's personal political power.[10] Moreover, Knazko's successor as foreign minister, Jozef Moravcik, also was sympathetic to a pro-West foreign policy for Slovakia and eventually he too broke with Meciar to form still another splinter party made up of ex-MDS members dissatisfied with the prime minister.

Meciar Weathers a Political Storm

By mid-1993, Meciar's strong-arm tactics not only had antagonized his MDS colleagues and drove some of them to defect to splinter groups set up by Knazko and Moravcik, but also alienated the SNP. Indeed, Meciar's relations with SNP supporters in the parliament had become difficult.

Strains in the MDS-SNP Coalition. The SNP caucus disliked Meciar's seemingly high-handed ways of dealing with its leadership, in particular his failure to consult with them and his apparent determination to keep their influence over policy-making to a minimum. Economics Minister Ludovit Cernak, an SNP leader, and others demanded a more equitable powersharing agreement with the MDS. An especially provocative gesture was Meciar's appointment of General Imrich Andrejcak, an independent, as defense minister when Cernak expected the post to go to an SNP member. On March 16, Cernak resigned his post as economics minister in protest.[11] At the same time, some radical members of the SNP parliamentary group were annoyed by Meciar's seemingly indulgent policy toward the Hungarian minority. They wanted the prime minister to be more aggressive in discouraging what they perceived to be a dangerous Hungarian separatism that could lead to an annexation of the territory the Hungarians inhabited in southeastern Slovakia by Hungary. They wanted Meciar to limit the use of the Hungarian language in public life as a first step toward assimilation of the Hungarian minority, a policy Meciar was not ready to embrace despite a sympathy for SNP concerns.[12]

Cernak's resignation emboldened the opposition, in particular the CDM, the PDL, the Hungarian parties, and the new Alliance of Democrats, to go after Meciar and try to force him out of office with the threat of a parliamentary vote of no confidence and a new round of elections. The aggrieved SNP deputies momentarily flirted with the idea of joining in such a move to censure the overbearing prime minister.[13]

Fearing that a no-confidence vote and parliamentary elections might not turn out so well for his party, though he himself remained quite popular with voters, Meciar tried to head off the attack by replacing the SNP in his coalition with a more reliable partner. He turned to the PDL.[14] This was a strange move by Meciar that can only be explained by an acute frustration over what he perceived as treasonous behavior by the SNP. But the PDL was skeptical of an alliance with the MDS, especially as long as Meciar was prime minister. PDL leader Weiss told the MDS leadership that they would have to get rid of Meciar before his party would cooperate with them. Since Meciar had not the slightest intention of accommodating the PDL and since there was some concern within the MDS parliamentary group that a coalition with ex-Communists would tarnish Slovakia's image in the West, where there already was concern about the number of former Communists still in power, an MDS-PDL coalition never materialized.[15]

The PDL, consequently, was marginalized. From Meciar's vantage point the PDL was eccentric and unreliable, more eager to criticize than to cooperate. Indeed, PDL leader Weiss had joined other opposition leaders in condemning Meciar's overbearing style of leadership. Given its background, the PDL had nowhere else to turn and remains on the periphery of the Slovak political spectrum with few ties to either the government coalition or the opposition, despite occasional agreement with its policies.[16]

The SNP Returns to the MDS Fold. Meciar decided as a measure of last resort to patch up differences with the SNP. Initially, he agreed that the SNP would have a more formal role in policy-making, though he was not very specific and did nothing to compromise his personal political dominance. The SNP was responsive. It had little to gain and much to lose from a no-confidence vote and new parliamentary elections in which its chances of winning enough seats to participate in the government were uncertain, given its narrow voter constituency in the June 1992 elections.[17] For the moment it preferred to get along with Meciar, hoping that this approach might give it the increased visibility in policy-making it had sought earlier in the year.

But both sides remained suspicious of one another. The SNP parliamentary group in fact was divided over cooperation with Meciar. Some SNP deputies were still annoyed by Meciar's aggressive political style. They dreamed of cooperation with MDS members who shared their misgivings about Meciar and who might be willing to try to undermine him with the eventual goal of ousting. But, Meciar was too strong to be edged out of power. Moreover, other SNP deputies were reluctant to push Meciar's critical colleagues too far. After all, the most important SNP objective was to retain some influence, however modest, over Slovak policy-making. If the SNP overstepped the line with Meciar, not known for his tolerance of criticism from colleagues, never mind rivals and opponents, it could be shut out of power.

In mid-October 1993, the two parties finally reached an agreement that, not surprisingly, was more favorable to the MDS and Meciar than many SNP politicians liked. The SNP leadership approved the continuation of its coalition with the MDS without receiving control of any key cabinet ministries such as finance, privatization, economy, or health.[18]

Meciar Triumphant. Meciar had weathered this political storm rather well. He was as politically strong as ever or perhaps stronger. In his remade coalition the SNP had even less influence than earlier over cabinet decisionmaking, which was dominated by Meciar. Indeed, from Meciar's vantage point, after all was said and done, the weakened SNP was an ideal coalition partner.

Conflict with President Kovac

In building his strong power base, Meciar inevitably clashed with President Kovac. In the mid-1990s their increasingly frequent confrontations over Meciar's policies became very bitter, undermining the credibility of Slovak democracy abroad as well as at home.

Sources of Disagreement. Meciar's ill-concealed strategy of concentrating decisionmaking authority in his hands and those of his close supporters was a key source of conflict with Kovac, who criticized the prime minister's blatant efforts to pack the government with loyalists, to restrain the press when it challenged his policies, and to foster a crude personality cult through a complex system of patronage and machine building throughout the Slovak bureaucracy. The president said Meciar's behavior, which violated the spirit if not the letter of the democratic order, was the equivalent of one-party government.[19]

With the struggle over cabinet appointments in the reconstituted MDS-SNP coalition in the fall of 1993, the conflict between Meciar and Kovac was out in the open. Using his power to approve the prime minister's nominees for ministerial posts, Kovac held his own consultations with MDS and SNP members of the parliament regarding composition of the new cabinet. Kovac successfully blocked Meciar's appointment to head the Ministry of Privatization of Ivan Lexa, a crony of the prime minister and a conservative who, like his mentor, was skeptical of privatization and inclined to slow up market reforms. By the end of 1993, the prime minister and the president were virtually at war with one another. In December 1993, Kovac demanded Meciar's resignation. Relations between the prime minister and the president now reached a nadir.[20]

Meciar's Political Decline

By early 1994, Meciar was in political trouble. He had begun to lose much of the popularity with Slovak voters he enjoyed at the time of independence. His strong-willed and abrasive leadership had alienated friends, colleagues, and supporters in the parliament.

Loss of Popularity. Many Slovaks—about 56 percent of the population according to a Bratislava polling agency—were beginning to regret the split away from the Czechs. Had the federation survived, they believed, money from the well-off western part of the country would have flowed eastward to the economically depressed parts of Slovakia, as it had in the past. Popular willingness to go along with independence in 1992 had given way in 1993 and 1994 to a pervasive popular sullenness and disappointment with the country's political evolution under Meciar's leadership.[21]

Between October 1992 and January 1993, Meciar's popularity rating plummeted from 74 percent to 34 percent and from January to February 1993 it dropped another 10 percent to an all-time low of 25 percent.[22] Slovak voters increasingly blamed Meciar for the country's economic problems after independence. In an opinion poll conducted by the Slovak Statistical Office at the beginning of 1993, almost 60 percent of the respondents said that their economic situation had worsened in the latter part of 1992 and that they expected their living standard to fall even further in 1993, as in fact it did.[23]

Erosion of Support in Parliament. By early 1994, Meciar's support in the parliament also had eroded. In February, there were more defections from the coalition, severely weakening it. Then, Knazko's successor as foreign minister, Jozef Moravcik, and Roman Kovac, to whom Meciar had given the deputy prime ministership, bolted the MDS, announcing their support of Knazko's new group in the parliament, which called itself the Alternative of Political Realism, which soon became the Democratic Union of Slovakia (DU).

Meciar responded in the usual way: He sought the dismissal of both Moravcik and Roman Kovac. President Kovac resisted. To circumvent the president, Meciar proposed a referendum in which voters would be asked to decide whether deputies who bolted from their party should be expelled from parliament since it could be said that they no longer stood for the constituency that had elected them. If the voters said yes, as Meciar hoped they would, he could then replace Moravcik and other renegades with loyalists. The referendum, however, was never held. President Kovac's office asserted that of the more than 420,000 signatures on the petition for the referendum submitted on March 2, only 232,000 were genuine, not enough under the constitution to hold a referendum.[24]

Meciar Loses His Parliamentary Majority. By March 1994, having alienated a large number of colleagues and supporters, Meciar's cabinet lost its political majority in the SNC and was vulnerable to a no-confidence vote. His enemies now tried to maneuver him out of office. They focused on the National Property Fund (NPF), an organization charged with implementing the sale of state enterprises authorized by the Ministry of Privatization. The NPF's job was to establish the government's legal ownership of state property and find buyers for it. Under the control of the privatization ministry, headed by Meciar himself after his failure to get Lexa appointed, the NPF had become a great source of patronage. Meciar's critics in the SNC joined forces to pass a law that gave the legislature power to appoint and dismiss members of the fund's governing board. This action was a significant setback for Meciar.[25]

President Kovac added his weight to the anti-Meciar movement in parliament in a speech on March 9 in which he accused the prime minister of incompetence and obstruction of democracy. He called attention to Meciar's packing government posts with loyalists, many of whom, he said, had little competence to fulfil the administrative responsibilities assigned to them. He accused Meciar of mismanaging the economy and of adopting "practices that create a confrontational atmosphere in political life." He called Meciar unfit to govern.[26]

Meciar was deeply offended by Kovac's attack, viewing it as treachery because of the president's past membership in the MDS leadership and his support of the MDS-led campaign for Slovak independence. On March 11, Meciar tried to answer the president's attack in a lengthy speech full of threats, slurs, and innuendos. After the speech, PDL leader Weiss called for Meciar's resignation. Meciar refused. Meanwhile, Meciar's MDS parliamentary colleagues were getting ready to cooperate with the opposition, which was mounting a campaign for a no-confidence vote against the prime minister. On March 11, a majority of the NCS voted against the government. After the vote, Meciar walked out of the parliament in a huff, pledging that "in opposition the MDS will do everything possible to remove the current head of state."[27]

Meciar's defiant attitude suggested that his opposition in suceeding weeks and months would be anything but constructive, which meant more trouble for Slovakia's fledgling democracy. Meciar and his MDS supporters in the parliament were ready to lie in wait, so to speak, for the new government, to criticize, oppose, and undermine it rather than to offer helpful alternatives to its policies and work to persuade the new leadership to accept them. Meciar was in a position to do considerable damage to his successor. Indeed, despite his defeat, he remained one of the most influential politicians in the country. There was still a substantial public sympathy for Meciar, and the MDS was still the strongest single party in Slovakia.[28] Meciar's opposition to rapid privatization still resonated with many voters. Moreover, although he lost the prime ministership, Meciar retained his seat in the SNC and still had the loyalty of a substantial number of MDS deputies.

MORAVCIK'S "INTERREGNUM"

President Kovac promptly appointed Moravcik as Meciar's successor. In the latter part of March 1994, Moravcik formed a government based on a "grand coalition" of groups including the CDM, PDL, DU, and several other small parties. This new government, despite its diverse membership, seemed eager to move forward with market reforms, in particular privatization, and the rapid integration of Slovakia into Western Europe.[29]

A Government of Weakness and Drift

Popular expectations of real political change were never fulfilled. Moravcik was a weak leader. His control of parliament rested on a highly fragile coalition of five parties, whose programs ran the entirety of the political spectrum. The raison d'être of the coalition seemed to be little more than keeping Meciar out of power, despite rhetoric about proving to the country that there could be an alternative to Meciar and moving ahead with liberal reform at home and achieving international respect for the new state.[30] Indeed, as one Slovak source reportedly put it, the new government was more political than professional, lacking not only an economic program but the consensus needed to transact policy.[31]

By the end of the summer of 1994, the new government's achievements were modest. While there was a momentary improvement in Slovak relations with Hungary, which had been strained by a perception in Budapest of a systematic Slovak discrimination against the Hungarian minority, which Moravcik had tried to dispel, his government accomplished little else. It was given more to postponement than passage of laws on urgent economic and social problems. The only exception, perhaps, was some progress in the areas of privatization and "lustration," a term that refers to the removal of former Communists from positions of political and economic power. Reflecting discontent with the government's drift, the SNC called for early elections to be held on September 30 and October 1, 1994.[32]

Having been in power only four months, the coalition really did not have time to develop credibility with voters who still had much sympathy for the charismatic Meciar and his MDS. Although the government had managed to remove many of Meciar's cronies from positions of power in the national ministries and on local levels of administration, it gained little political advantage. Meciar and his supporters condemned the government, and some called the personnel changes a "purge," a view that seemed to resonate with many Slovaks still enamored of Meciar.[33]

The September 1994 Parliamentary Elections

With parliamentary elections scheduled for the end of the summer, Meciar and the MDS began an aggressive campaign to regain power, focusing as much on Meciar himself as on issues that had provoked public discontent, such as the disastrous state of the economy with a double-digit rate of unemployment. Meciar was very skillful, telling voters what they wanted to hear. He said he was no fan of Czech-style shock therapy, especially rapid privatization. He stressed the need to safeguard valuable national property from ownership by greedy investors at home and especially abroad. He opposed "dirty property transfers," or the sale of state-owned property to government insiders at below market prices, a brazen position given his responsibility for such transactions during his last prime ministership. He also played the nationalist card, condemning Moravcik's conciliatory policy toward Hungary as a "sellout." At the same time, Meciar challenged the constitutionality of his ouster in March and criticized President Kovac for his role.[34]

The outcome of the elections favored Meciar and the MDS, which won 35 percent of the popular vote. The rural part of the country was an important source of Meciar's strength. The MDS showing was a plurality to be sure, but it was a bit smaller than the 37 percent won in June 1992. With only about a third of the electorate behind the MDS, Meciar really did not have the kind of popular backing he wanted to reinforce his power base in parliament. He would still need the help of other parties to obtain a majority of parliamentary support, which meant a coalition and diminished leadership authority. The so-called Common Choice Bloc made up of the PDL and other smaller parties on the left won the second largest share of votes. While the DU won 10 percent, not a bad showing for a very new party whose leader, Moravcik, had not done all that well in governing the country in the past several months, the SNP won only 6 percent, less than the 9 percent it had won in June 1992, a setback in popularity the party had always feared could happen at the polls.[35]

Meciar Returns to Power

To regain the prime ministership Meciar needed to forge a coalition, which took several months of dealmaking with other parties. Weaker than he had been in 1992, Meciar had a tough time getting their support. He ruled out a coalition with the PDL despite shared views on many economic issues, mainly because of a personal dislike of PDL leader Weiss for having publicly expressed a willingness to cooperate with the MDS if Meciar resigned. Although some followers of Moravcik, many of whom had been members of the MDS, were willing to cooperate with him, Meciar was not interested. He could not forgive their betrayal of him in March. He again preferred the weak and all-but-ineffectual SNP, which was willing to add its 9 seats to his 61. But an MDS-SNP agreement would still leave Meciar 5 seats short of the parliamentary majority he needed to form a government. With the help of the Association of Slovak Workers (ASW), an offshoot of the PDL and more successful than the SNP in the recent elections (it won 13 seats), he had his majority in the SNC.[36] By mid-December 1994, the coalition, consisting of the MDS, the SNP, and the ASW, was formally set up and ready to govern, though it had been unofficially administering the country throughout November. The coalition controlled 83 of the 150 seats in parliament. On December 13, 1994, Meciar began his third prime ministership. This new coalition was quite fragile since the SNP and ASW were on opposite ends of the political spectrum. Keeping the parties loyal given their divergent ideological commitments would be difficult but possible, given Meciar's readiness to "bang heads" if that were necessary to preserve unity.[37]

MECIAR'S LEADERSHIP SINCE OCTOBER 1994

In this recent period of his leadership, Meciar went to extraordinary lengths to consolidate political power, dismissive of democratic principles and practices to which he and his government professed allegiance.[38] He pursued punitive and repressive policies that, more than at any time earlier, were incompatible with and subversive of the democratic order. But, while Meciar's leadership became increasingly harsh, causing some Slovaks to compare it with the Communist dictatorship, it had a base of popular support for reasons having to do with not only the peculiarities of Slovakia's political environment but also Meciar's own personal traits, especially his enormous charisma among many Slovaks in different walks of life. He continued to enjoy the support of many Slovak voters despite criticism in the media of his political behavior, especially his growing intolerance of criticism, never mind opposition, and his penchant for harsh retribution against anyone who tried to defy his leadership.

Retribution against the DU

One example of how retributive Meciar could be toward former party colleagues who dared question or criticize his policies involved DU members who had defected from the MDS in the early months of 1994. He viewed their behavior as treason not only to the MDS but also to its leadership of the country. Initiating a legal challenge to the participation of the DU in the new parliament, Meciar called into question the DU's claim to the parliamentary seats it had won in the September 1994 elections. Despite Electoral Commission and Constitutional Court rulings that the DU had registered properly for the election, a parliamentary commission comprised only of government parties heavily dominated by Meciar's supporters continued to investigate the DU in 1995, and Meciar continued to accuse it of election fraud. In the spring of 1995, the government authorized an additional police investigation. DU leaders charged that these actions were intended to intimidate voters and ruin the party's popular base of support.[39] Although Meciar eventually failed to obtain the removal from parliament of the DU members being investigated and failed to discredit the DU, he did succeed in intimidating party colleagues by making clear the extent to which he was willing to go to punish disloyalty.

More Conflict with President Kovac

Meciar was in office for only a few weeks after the formation of his government in December 1994 when his conflict with Kovac resumed. It was now more vicious and more divisive than ever. It is not an exaggeration to say that at times Meciar and Kovac acted as if they were the bitterest of enemies determined to destroy each other politically.

The renewal of conflict was evident as early as November 1994, before Meciar's new cabinet had been formally installed in power. It centered around Meciar's effort to annul all decisions on privatization that had been made by the Moravcik leadership after September 6. It was a high-handed gesture that reflected not only his opposition to the selling off of state enterprises, but also his anger at losing an opportunity to make personal gain from privatization. Kovac refused to approve the legislation and returned it to the parliament, where Meciar's followers promptly passed it again. Opposition leaders in the SNC as well as President Kovac requested the Constitutional Court to judge its legality. In May 1995, the court declared the cancellation illegal.[40]

Meciar wanted to oust Kovac from power, and in May 1995 the parliament passed a resolution expressing "no confidence" in President Kovac. The vote was inspired by allegations that Kovac had used the Slovak Intelligence Service (SIS), an "FBI-style" criminal-investigation and intelligence-gathering organization, to obtain confidential information concerning the activities of political parties, in particular the MDS, and of certain state officials for use in mobilizing the parliamentary opposition to Meciar's government that led to the March 11 no-confidence vote. To have the effect of impeachment, however, the resolution required the support of 60 percent of parliament, which it failed to get. It therefore had no impact, except perhaps a psychological one. The president was now under no illusion about the lengths to which Meciar was ready to go to weaken and discredit him and eventually force him from power. Kovac could take some consolation from the fact that the opposition parties were sympathetic to him and ready to support and cooperate with him against the prime minister. For example, the CDM and the DU organized mass popular rallies in support of the president in Bratislava and Kosice. Public opinion polls affirmed that Kovac was still popular with many voters.[41]

Meciar then tried another tack against Kovac. Although the evidence is circumstantial, many people believe that Meciar may have had a hand in the kidnapping of President Kovac's son, Michal, Jr., at the end of August 1995, in an effort to distract and demoralize the President. Michal, Jr., claimed that he was abducted from his car in Bratislava, made to drink a bottle of whiskey, and transported in the trunk of another car to Austria, where his abductors called the Austrian police and told them that they could find a fugitive—he was wanted for questioning in a fraud case in Germany—in a car parked in a particular place. Although Kovac's son eventually returned to Slovakia, it was a bizarre and frightening incident for Kovac. The Slovak police apparently suspected that the SIS was involved; when they expressed their suspicion, top police officials were fired.[42]

By late 1997, the abduction was still unresolved. An important witness in the case died in a car explosion. An Austrian court ruled that the abduction was most likely the work of Slovak authorities, although Meciar repeatedly denied this, saying that there was no evidence to support a charge of official Slovak complicity.[43]

In 1996 and 1997, Meciar had another incentive to force Kovac from office. He believed that if the president left office prematurely, requiring parliament to elect a successor, there would be a deadlock because neither the government nor the opposition had the 60 percent support needed to elect a president and that he would benefit, at least temporarily, from such a deadlock because the Slovak constitution provides that the prime minister takes some of the president's power if the parliament cannot elect a new president. If Meciar thought he could induce Kovac's premature departure from office through a campaign of harassment, he was quickly disabused of this idea when Kovac declared in mid-1996 that he would never be broken.[44]

The ongoing confrontation between Slovakia's prime minister and president had some troublesome implications for Slovak democracy. Kovac's challenges of Meciar's policy encouraged the president's office to become the focal point of opposition to government policy. Such conflict-breeding dualism in the executive undermined the credibility, already fragile, of the democratic order. Meciar's effort to discredit and weaken the Slovak presidency also compromised the constitution's checks on the government's behavior. In trying to weaken the presidency because of his hostility to the incumbent, Meciar increased the possibility of a prime ministerial dictatorship, an especially dangerous prospect given the absence from the Slovak political environment of the deeply rooted principles of limited government and respect for individual rights found in the West.

More Pressure on the Media

In his effort to maintain a tight grip on power as well as to resist Kovac, Meciar increased government control over the Slovak media. In Meciar's view the media were too critical of the government and its policies, and he sought to curtail their freedom to broadcast and print. He tried to mobilize public sympathy for his pressure on the media by playing the nationalism card. He called media criticism of the government subversive of the country's cultural identity and of its hard-won sovereignty. Meciar pressured both the electronic and the print media.

The Electronic Media. In November 1994, shortly after resuming power, Meciar replaced the directors of the state radio and television networks with political allies.[45] He restricted coverage by state-run networks of opposition activities and discontinued broadcast of programs that satirized government policy. At the end of February 1995, when Peter Susko, the Slovak radio's Washington correspondent, reported that the Slovak trade delegation to the United States appeared unprepared, Meciar ordered him home and closed down the Washington office.[46]

During 1995 and early 1996, the diversity of views, the scope of political coverage, and the degree of objectivity of new and documentary programming on Slovak television diminished sharply. Opposition views received scant coverage in news programs, a disturbing trend because 84 percent of the Slovak population watched the state-run television.[47] Slovak television also carried little coverage of President Kovac.[48] Kovac complained that he was denied access to television. In an interview with journalists in May 1997, he reportedly said he had tried to appear on television in 1996 and again in March 1997 in connection with a planned referendum on Slovakia's membership in NATO, in which he wanted voters to support Slovak entry into the Western alliance. His efforts on both occasions, he said, were "in vain."[49]

In response to complaints from the Western democracies about antidemocratic restrictions on freedom of the press, Meciar's government allowed Slovakia's first private television station, known as *Markizia*, to start broadcasting at the end of 1996. With objective presentation of domestic problems, the station's programs became quite popular. But the government became alarmed and restricted its transmission capability to 60 percent of the country.[50] In addition, in December 1996, the government replaced state television director Jozef Darmo with Meciar supporter Igor Kubis, who had attracted attention with programs critical of President Kovac's son.[51]

The Print Media. The Meciar government was equally aggressive in dealing with the press in ways that appeared to many journalists as ill-disguised censorship. A so-called Mass Media Council was set up in February 1995 to monitor the media to assure their "adherence to the constitution."[52] Early in March 1995, MDS politicians threatened to impose sharply increased taxes on independent newspapers, which would have forced them out of business. As it was, the independent newspapers had to be careful of government retaliation. They were dependent on the government for distribution of scarce supplies of newsprint to keep the presses rolling.[53] In the spring of 1996, Meciar's culture minister, Ivan Hudec, pushed forward a sweeping law requiring the Slovak media to distinguish between information and opinion, news and commentary, forbidding the media to present anything that in a hidden or open way offends Slovak statehood, state symbols, or nationality.[54]

Fortunately for both the print and the broadcast media, President Kovac vetoed this law. International criticism, especially by the U.S. Department of State, discouraged the Slovak parliament from revising it and resubmitting it to the president. Indeed, in May 1996, the United States–based Committee for the Protection of Journalists included Meciar on its list of the ten "worst enemies of the press." When Meciar declared that no lawsuits had been brought against journalists in Slovakia, Karol Jezik, editor-in-chief of the independent *Sme*, promptly issued a statement that "the Prime Minister did not tell the truth."[55]

Government pressure on the press continued throughout 1996. When Tatiana Repkova, publisher and editor-in-chief of *Narodna Obroda*, wanted to transform it into a nonpartisan economic-oriented daily, Meciar's government intervened. Concerned that *Narodna Obroda* would become critical of his policies, Meciar saw to it that a large government-controlled steel enterprise, VSZ, bought the publishing house that produced the paper. In mid-November 1996, Repkova was dismissed.[56]

Sme was also under pressure. In November 1996, it lost a libel case and was ordered by a district court in Banksa Bystrica to apologize to all 18 members of Meciar's cabinet for a critical piece published on May

14 saying that the government was undertaking a "cold war" against Slovak citizens. The court also required *Sme*'s publisher to pay each minister about $13,000 in compensatory damages.[57]

By the end of 1996, many in the media were convinced that Meciar wanted to restore a Communist-style censorship. Certainly he has not allowed the kind of freedom of expression the Slovak constitution guaranteed. Perhaps recognizing the smaller audience for radio, the government has allowed a greater discretion in audio programming.[58] Meciar's overall policy of restraint on the media, despite the absence of formal censorship and the existence of a variety of independent broadcast media, remained a serious obstacle to post-independence Slovakia's efforts to develop a stable and secure democratic system.

Other Restraints on Freedom of Expression

Closely related to the Meciar government's efforts to limit media criticism was an attempt to curtail the individual's freedom of expression. In March 1996, the government approved a piece of legislation called the "Law on the Protection of the Republic" that defined as subversive "organized public rallies aimed at subverting the constitutional system . . . the defense capability of the country or destroying its independence." Individuals found guilty could be jailed for six months to three years; if the crime were committed by "an organized group," the punishment was up to five years in jail.[59]

This law caused an uproar among opposition parties and journalists, who likened it to a 1961 criminal law of the Communist regime that had provided for punishment for "the subversion of the socialist state system" and had contained other wording used in the new "Law on the Protection of the Republic." The 1961 law was used to jail dissident Vaclav Havel in 1979.[60] Jozef Szilvassy, chief editor of the Hungarian-language daily *Uj Szo*, which had the largest circulation among Slovakia's Hungarian minority, said of the law that "it will certainly put psychological pressure on journalists." Karol Jezik, chief editor of *Sme*, said, "The law can put pressure on journalists to practice self-censorship and create an environment of fear."[61]

When the law reached his desk, President Kovac refused to sign it and sent it back to parliament in April. In December 1996 a revised version of "the Law" was passed by parliament, and again the president rejected it. By this time opposition to "the Law" had galvanized and expanded, with the president as chief critic, along with the Roman Catholic Church, the opposition parties, and other social groups. Comparison of the law with Communist restrictions had become an embarrassment to the government. Meanwhile, the European Union warned

Meciar that final enactment of "the Law" would be a serious infringe-ment of Slovak democracy bound to complicate Slovakia's efforts to integrate with the West.[62]

The Gaulieder Affair. Another kind of assault on free speech involved parliamentarian Frantisek Gaulieder. In late November 1996, he al-legedly resigned from the MDS, reducing the number of seats held by the MDS-led coalition in the parliament to 81 out of 150, further weakening its ability to muster the 60 percent parliamentary majority needed to amend the constitution, pass constitutional laws, and elect the president. Gaulieder accused his former party of not fulfilling its campaign promises. Meciar was furious at Gaulieder and worried that his resignation might encourage other defections from the MDS ranks in the parliament, provoking a political crisis that would endanger his leadership.[63]

Meciar decided to punish Gaulieder as a warning to other would-be defectors from the MDS and to protect his government's power base in parliament. Presumably on his signal, the parliament's Mandate and Immunity Committee voted to oust Gaulieder from his seat based on a letter of resignation it allegedly had received but which Gaulieder denied writing. Gaulieder decided to fight the regime both to protect his career and establish the right of parliamentarians to bolt their parties if they wanted to do so. He denied writing the letter of resigna-tion, maintaining that it had been falsified, and said he wanted to remain a member of parliament. On his side, he had the Slovak consti-tution, which states that parliamentary mandates are held by individ-uals, not by the parties to which they belong. In July 1997, the Constitutional Court upheld his position, ruling that the decision to strip him of his seat was unconstitutional. However, in succeeding months the Mandate and Immunity Committee refused to restore his seat.[64]

Strengthening the Prime Minister and Cabinet

During 1995 and in the early months of 1996, Meciar persuaded parliament to enact laws that would considerably strengthen the prime minister's influence over the running of secondary schools and univer-sities and place limits on the ability of the Constitutional Court to declare laws unconstitutional. For example, in April 1995 the SNC passed a law transferring the authority to appoint and recall school principals from local authorities to the Ministry of Education in Bratislava. Eventually, the government approved and parliament passed a law on universities giving the Ministry of Education in

Bratislava broad powers over academic affairs, over the objection of President Kovac.[65] In September and again in December 1995, the parliament refused to include any opposition representation on the body that oversees the SIS.[66]

Part of Meciar's effort at expanding the cabinet's authority involved a concurrent reduction in the prerogatives of the presidency. In 1994 and 1995, the parliament passed laws giving the cabinet the right to appoint the heads of the statistical office and the Academy of Science, the chief of the General Staff, and the director of the SIS. Previously these positions were filled by nominees of the president.[67] Other steps to strengthen the cabinet at the expense of the presidency included cutting funds for the construction of a new presidential palace and for the operation of the president's office.[68] Meciar would have liked to combine the offices of prime minister and president of the republic to create a superexecutive and proposed an amendment of the constitution to this effect, significantly, on September 1, 1995, Constitution Day. He probably considered filling this new superexecutive post himself.[69]

The idea of combining the presidency and the prime ministership went nowhere. It was too controversial, too much of a threat to the system of checks and balances, and too favorable to Meciar politically. It is significant largely as a reflection of Meciar's power-grabbing ambitions, which the opposition and President Kovac were determined to resist.

Meciar also tried to strengthen the cabinet's influence over local government. In July 1996, a new administrative structure divided the country into eight regions and 79 administrative districts, and redrew local boundaries that among other things had the effect of reducing the political influence of the Hungarian minority. Heads of newly created regions and counties were appointed by the central government, giving Meciar a significant source of additional patronage. Opposition parties, especially those representing the Hungarian community, complained that the new arrangements provided the government with a new source of leverage, in particular over those areas inhabited by Hungarians. The new law also adjusted the special status of Bratislava, a strong center of reformist and liberal opposition to Meciar's conservative rule, to reduce its political influence on government.[70]

By 1997, Meciar had contrived an undemocratic concentration of power in the cabinet that, when taken together with MDS control of parliament, established something of a political dictatorship. He could act in arbitrary ways with near impunity. This situation, which challenged the democratic character of the Slovak government established in the 1992 Constitution, was evident in the preparations for the referendum on Slovak membership in NATO held on May 23 and 24, 1997.

The May 1997 NATO Referendum

In early 1997, the government proposed a referendum on the issue of Slovak membership in NATO that asked voters to answer three questions: "Are you in favor of Slovakia entering NATO? Are you in favor of nuclear weapons being placed in Slovakia? Are you in favor of NATO military bases being located in Slovakia?"[71] With a majority in the Slovak parliament, the government obtained a resolution calling upon President Kovac, who agreed to the referendum, to set a date for it. The constitution required the president to act within 30 days of the parliamentary motion.[72]

Purposes and Objectives. Meciar believed that a referendum on Slovak membership in NATO would demonstrate to the West that he and his government believed in democratic processes. He also knew that NATO membership was favored not only by Slovak Foreign Minister Pavol Hamzik but also by President Kovac and the opposition parties. Hamzik in fact was optimistic about Slovakia's chances of receiving an invitation to be among the first wave of central European countries to become members of NATO. Meciar also was certain that there would be a big public turnout for the referendum.[73]

But Meciar was not as supportive of Slovak membership in NATO as his rhetoric sometimes suggested.[74] He was concerned about Russian opposition to the admission of former Soviet allies to the Western alliance, and he wanted to maintain good relations with the Kremlin. Moreover, his coalition partners, the SNP and ASW, opposed Slovak entry into NATO, citing the costs of modernizing the Slovak military to meet NATO standards. They preferred Slovak neutrality vis-à-vis Russia and the West.[75] In addition some polls showed that many Slovak voters, if given a chance, would vote against membership in NATO to avoid the deployment of foreign nuclear weapons and military bases on Slovak soil, even though the NATO allies had agreed that they would not deploy nuclear weapons on the territory of new member states from central Europe.[76]

The opposition speculated that Meciar may have wanted the referendum precisely because he thought people would vote "no." If that happened, his government would have an alibi to explain away a refusal of NATO to invite Slovakia to join.[77] Meciar realized that, in light of recent Western criticisms of his domestic policies, in particular his perceived disregard of democratic freedoms, and contrary to Foreign

Minister Hamzik's optimistic assumption that Slovakia would be in the first wave of new members from central Europe, NATO in fact would not invite Slovakia at this time to join. Certainly German Chancellor Helmut Kohl and U.S. President Bill Clinton recently had signalled Bratislava that Slovakia would not be among the first countries to be admitted because of "domestic problems," an Aesopian reference to Meciar's repressive leadership. The opposition believed Meciar included questions two and three to frighten voters into voting against Slovak membership in NATO and closer ties to the West. These questions raised the specter of foreign weapons on Slovak soil, which could not have been very attractive so soon after the era of Soviet control and the achievement of Slovak independence.[78]

Plans for holding the referendum were complicated also by the intrusion of another issue quite unrelated to Slovak membership in NATO. President Kovac, the opposition parties, the trade unions, and the Catholic Church believed that Meciar's proposal of a referendum on NATO was intended to distract the public's attention from a campaign they had begun to win public support for a change in the Slovak constitution that would allow the president of the republic to be elected directly by the people instead of by the parliament. To maintain public interest in this issue, they proposed a fourth question for the NATO referendum, asking voters whether they approved a constitutional amendment providing for the direct election of the president. They had a lot of public support, and by mid-February 1997 more than 350,000 voters had signed a petition favoring a referendum on direct election of the president.[79]

Why this popular interest in changing the method of electing the president of the Slovak Republic? Given the balance of political forces in the parliament, the country was faced with the prospect that the parliament would not agree to a president in the next election and that during the stalemate Meciar as prime minister would assume some of the president's power. President Kovac and the opposition parties were determined to prevent this from happening. Furthermore, critics of Meciar reasoned that because a directly elected president would hold office with a mandate from the voters themselves, he would be much stronger in relations with the prime minister.[80]

Meciar and his MDS colleagues not surprisingly opposed asking voters about direct election of the president.[81] Of course, Meciar realized that such a change would weaken his power and benefit Kovac, who might very well be reelected. Although Kovac insisted that he would not run for reelection, he had never definitely ruled it out. There was a lot of support among the opposition parties, especially those representing the Hungarian minority, to draft him.[82] Meciar tried to argue that a directly elected president would preside over what he called a "semi-imperial system."[83]

Meciar was determined to do what he could to avoid including a question on direct election of the president in the NATO referendum. His first step was to raise a legal question: Did the constitution allow the basic law to be amended by a referendum? On April 22, the government petitioned the Constitutional Court for an opinion on the legality of using the referendum to amend the Slovak constitution.[84] It then instructed the Minister of the Interior and the chairman of the Statistical Office to halt distribution of the now-printed referendum ballots that contained the question on direct election of the president.[85]

Kovac denounced these actions, saying they contravened the President's constitutional prerogatives.[86] The opposition for its part accused the government of intentionally delaying its decision to go to court until a few weeks before the referendum was scheduled, hoping that the justices would not render a verdict until after the May 23 date on which the referendum was to be held, thereby causing either its postponement or its cancellation.[87]

If Meciar's government in fact had plotted to prevent the holding of the referendum with a question on direct election of the president on the scheduled date in the expectation that it might never be held at all, it was both surprised and disappointed. The court responded to the government's petition on May 13, declaring that it was perfectly legal to place the question of direct election of the president on a referendum. The court ruled that the referendum on direct election of the president actually would not constitute an amendment to the constitution, which could only be made by the parliament, but would allow the people to have their views on the constitutional issue heard. The court ordered the government to distribute ballots with the four questions. However, in a sop to the government, it dismissed on a technicality a motion by the President that his constitutional prerogatives as head of state had been violated when the Ministry of the Interior had suspended preparations for the referendum to await the court's rulings.[88]

Meciar was still determined to have his own way.[89] He saw to it that the Ministry of the Interior distributed ballots to polling stations throughout the country with only the three questions on NATO, omitting the question on the direct election of the president.[90]

President Kovac and the opposition leaders were outraged. They asked voters to insist when they arrived at the polling place on a ballot with four questions; they were asked to refrain from voting if denied this ballot.[91] President Kovac announced that he would not vote without a ballot containing the four questions.[92] DU leader Eduard Kukan was especially outspoken, blaming the Interior minister "for marring the referendum, forging ballot papers." Kukan accused him of "[abus-ing] . . . public office." He told journalists on May 23, the first day of voting, that "today is the 'funeral' of democracy in Slovakia." Given that the government succeeded in manipulating this referendum, there was no guarantee, Kukan added, that it would not behave in the same way again, say, during the parliamentary elections scheduled for the autumn of 1998. He considered the government's behavior on this occasion "serious and alarming" from the standpoint of the future. He even went so far as to say, quite correctly as matters turned out, that the referendum, which all of Europe was watching, would "thwart all Slovakia's chances of remaining in the first group of applicants for EU membership."[93]

Outcome of the Referendum. The outcome of the referendum was a political embarrassment for the nation. Only 9.5 percent of eligible voters participated in the referendum. Of those who voted, an over-whelming majority said no to Slovak membership in NATO, to the deployment of nuclear weapons on Slovak soil, and to the establish-ment of foreign military bases. In a way it was a victory but, given the low turnout, a Pyrrhic one for Meciar.[94]

There followed a vitriolic exchange of complaints by each side against the other for frustrating the referendum. While Meciar's government insisted it had done nothing wrong and condemned Kovac and the opposition for insisting on the inclusion of a question that should have been addressed in some other way, the opposition denounced the gov-ernment for wrecking the referendum by its distribution of illegal ballots and called for the immediate resignation of the prime minister and his minister of the interior.[95]

Voters also were up in arms. Many who went to the polling stations refused to accept a ballot with only three questions.[96] One angry voter was reported to have said, "How dare the government play such dirty tricks on us? The Communists were mere amateurs compared with these."[97]

A Setback for Democracy? The outcome of the referendum demon-strated once more the Meciar government's willingness to ignore prin-ciples of democracy for the sake of political expediency, convincing the NATO allies, especially Germany and the United States, that Slovakia was hardly ready to join NATO or for that matter the European Union, with which President Kovac and the Opposition parties wanted the country linked. President Kovac thought that the failure of the referen-dum had significantly weakened Meciar. So few voters had participated in the referendum that it suggested that most people deplored his

high-handed political behavior and were ready for a change in leadership. Meciar dismissed the low turnout for the referendum, insisting
that Kovac was responsible for the fiasco, and called his presidency a
"tragicomedy" that "will not be repeated" in the next presidential
election.[98]

MECIAR'S RESILIENCY

Despite this severe criticism of his handling of the May 1997, referendum, Meciar's power seemed minimally affected. By the end of 1997,
he was very much the leader of his country, with no hint of his stepping
aside or being made to step aside prior to parliamentary elections
scheduled for late 1998.

Sources of Popularity

Meciar's political resilience stems from his popularity with most of
the Slovak people, even those whom one would expect to be critical of
his antidemocratic style of leadership, such as the youth and the well
educated. The popular affection for him had provided Meciar a foundation from which to consolidate his power. Respect for Meciar was
strongest among rural voters, who were older and less well educated
than voters in the large urban centers like Bratislava. Rural Slovak
voters with little understanding of or sympathy for Western-style pluralistic democracy approved his conservatism and thought the country
needed it. They distrusted and feared change and had little faith in
politics. They took to Meciar also because he simplified the issues and
spoke to them in reassuring terms.

Popular support for Meciar was also the result of the fragmented and
conflict-ridden character of the opposition, which by late 1997 still was
able to unite behind a single leader or develop a common program that
offered an alternative to Meciar. Meciar shrewdly kept the opposition
on the defensive and rarely missed an opportunity to discredit and
denigrate it. The opposition has yet to produce a spokesman who can
match him.

Furthermore, Meciar did well in playing the nationalist card. Much
of what he said and did was in the name of Slovak sovereignty and
independence. He frequently said things that went to Slovakia's sense
of being special. He said that Slovakia should have its own national
culture, different from that of the West, which he criticized for having
"too much sex and not enough sense" and too much "American trash."[99]
His emotional and somewhat romantic view of the Slovak state resonated with many Slovaks. He skillfully played the role of the conscience

of his country. After hearing one of Meciar's speeches, Martin Mozer, a university student and deputy chairman of the National Movement of Slovak Youth, said that he supported Meciar because "we want Slovakia to be independent."[100]

Working to the advantage of Meciar's quasi-authoritarian style of leadership was a continuing nostalgia for the country's fascist experience during World War II, when Slovakia was an independent state despite its subservience to Nazi Germany. For example, in April 1995, *Matica Slovenska*, the nationwide Slovak Cultural Organization, sponsored an exhibit extolling wartime Slovak president Tiso. The exhibit depicted Tiso as the savior of the Slovak nation during the war and as a martyr for Slovak independence. The Bratislava government formally endorsed this exhibit, despite protests by the country's Jewish community.[101]

Indeed, an unpleasant aspect of this nostalgia for the authoritarian past was the reappearance of public anti-Semitism. For example, a blatant expression of it occured in August, 1995, with the desecration of a Jewish cemetery in Stupava, near Bratislava. Meciar, playing to this anti-Semitism, presented a journalism award to a weekly that had printed anti-Semitic cartoons and targeted international philanthropist George Soros for being a Jew.[102]

Political Prospects

Meciar unquestionably antagonized large portions of the electorate in his leadership of Slovakia during the early and mid-1990s. He alienated many former political supporters, who took up arms against him, like Knazko, Moravcik, and Kovac, to mention only the most prominent of his antagonists. By the late 1990s, a coalition of democratic groups seeking to challenge the MDS in parliamentary elections scheduled for the fall of 1998. Whether this kind of voluntary strategic discipline among party groups with little experience in democratic politics is possible remains to be seen. A straw in the wind may be the pointed public criticism of Meciar by the DU leadership in mid-April 1997, in connection with the NATO referendum. In addition, the DU also had complained about governmental mismanagement and abuse of power in the settlement of serious societal problems, a situation that it said could only be corrected "by changing the ruling style."[103]

Moreover, in the immediate aftermath of the NATO referendum, opposition parties continued to attack and criticize Meciar, accusing him of criminal behavior and of "wasting the referendum." Voters displayed their anger and disillusionment over the handling of the referendum by antigovernment demonstrations like the one held on

June 3 in front of a government building in Bratislava. Participants chanted the slogan "Don't Let Them Silence Us!" In Nitra in western Slovakia a similar demonstration was called by the CDM, DU, DM, and some Hungarian parties. There were efforts to hold similar anti-government protests elsewhere, such as in Zilina in northern Slovakia, in Trnava in western Slovakia, and in Kosice, where 250 people gathered in a parking lot outside a government office to demonstrate their frustration with the government.[104] In another display of anger, the opposition parties told journalists on June 6 that they were refusing to participate in all-party talks proposed by Meciar as a post-referendum conciliatory gesture until Interior Minister Krajci, whom they blamed for the foiled referendum, resigned.[105]

The opposition emerged from the referendum much stronger than it had been at any time earlier. Voter turnout at less than 10 percent suggested that its appeal to boycott the referendum had been heeded by most of the electorate. More important, in the summer of 1997 the CDM, the DU, and the Democratic Party (DP) plus two small center-left parties, the Slovak Social Democratic Party (SSDP) and the Slovak Green Party (SGP), joined forces with the three Hungarian parties (Coexistence, the Hungarian Christian Democratic Movement, and the Hungarian Civic Party) to form a broad coalition called the Slovak Democratic Coalition (SDC). The SDC intended to confront the MDS and its allies in the parliamentary elections to be held in September 1998 as a single electoral organization. An opinion poll conducted in June 1997 indicated that an opposition alliance of this kind would gain a clear majority.[106]

By the fall of 1997, however, the opposition parties still did not have either a platform for the electorate or a leader. They also lacked a vision of Slovakia's future that could inspire voters. The opposition still offered no viable alternative to Meciar and his MDS. Moreover, it is not at all certain that the CDM and DU have fully overcome their ethnically based prejudices toward the Hungarian parties with which they seemed to be aligned in the SDC. Concerned to avoid the appearance of being pro-Hungarian, they said little to suggest that their willingness to cooperate with the Hungarian parties within the framework of the SDC was inspired primarily by preference rather than expediency.[107]

At the same time, while Slovakia's new industrial entrepreneurs had much to complain about in Meciar's leadership, there was no certainty that they would support the SDC in 1998. The opposition parties unwisely suggested that if they defeated Meciar in the 1998 parliamentary elections, they would punish many of the beneficiaries of his discriminatory and corruption-ridden privatization policies. A fear of retribution may well outweigh in the minds of this new economic elite, which the opposition needed to cultivate rather than intimidate, any dissatisfaction with Meciar's policies and encourage renewed support of the MDS as the only viable alternative.[108] Whether the opposition parties can adjust their electoral strategy, let bygones be bygones, so to speak, and look more to the future and less to the past was not at all clear in early 1998.

A wild card has been Meciar's ambition to be president of Slovakia.[109] With the failure of the May 1997 referendum to change the traditional method of electing the president, Meciar had a chance if, as many feared, the parliament could not muster the 60 percent majority needed to elect a successor to Kovac. As prime minister, Meciar would be obliged under the constitution to assume presidential powers temporarily. He could use this situation to his advantage, say, by pushing through a reform of the present law governing the election of members of parliament, either to eliminate proportional representation, which has kept the MDS from gaining an absolute majority in recent elections, or to create a mixed system that also would enhance MDS chances of gaining the majority needed to put him in the presidency. Not surprisingly, Meciar's government opposed a call by Kovac for parliamentary elections to be held before presidential elections, fearing the prospect of a parliamentary majority that would support his reelection. The opposition as well did not want early parliamentary elections that would shorten the time needed to mobilize a popular majority against Meciar and the MDS.

EPILOGUE

As expected by all sides in the SNC, presidential elections in anticipation of the end of President Kovac's term and his departure from office on March 2, 1998, ended in a stalemate. In February and again in March, the SNC could not muster the 60 percent majority needed to elect the next president. And again as expected, and as feared by the opposition parties, Prime Minister Meciar in the absence of a duly elected chief of state, assumed presidential power. And when it was learned that he intended to seek legislative approval of changes in the electoral law favorable to the MDS and prejudicial to the smaller opposition groups, in particular a curtailment of proportional representation that had allowed small parties in recent parliamentary elections to win a few seats and thereby deny the larger parties, especially the MDS, a majority of voter support, there was an explosion of public wrath.[110] In May, however, despite public criticism, the MDS-dominated SNC gave Meciar his way and approved an amendment to the electoral law designed to assure an MDS victory in September. The amendment required each party within an "alliance" to cross a 5 percent threshold in order to seat its deputies in the parliament.[111] As the summer of 1998 got underway, the worst fears of the opposition materialized with Meciar trying to use his greatly enhanced influence over the Slovak government to consolidate his power and perpetuate it into the new century. For the moment the new SDC, which responded to the May amendment to the electoral law by transforming itself into a single party, was stymied. Former President Kovac and other opponents of Meciar now worried that they might never be able to dislodge him from power.

CONCLUSIONS

Commenting on authoritarian tendencies in Slovak political life during the past several years of Meciar's leadership, Frantisek Sebej, chairman of the foreign relations committee in the Czechoslovak federal parliament from 1990 to the end of 1992, and in 1995 a member of the Slovak opposition, said: "We are becoming an authoritarian country run by people with no ideology, just an insatiable hunger for power. The word fascism doesn't fit, but this is becoming an intolerant highly centralized nationalist state."[112] Ordinary Slovaks also were critical of the country's mixed record in developing democracy since the end of Communist rule in 1989. An opinion poll conducted in November 1995 found that 51 percent of respondents believed that the Bratislava government did not adequately respect human rights. And 67 percent of respondents disapproved of the country's preparations for democracy while only 27 percent said they were satisfied with Slovak democracy.[113]

Certainly authoritarianism is more embedded in the system than the constitution would appear to allow. But after three years of independence, Slovakia does have a political system that works reasonably in accordance with the principles of Western parliamentary democracy. Free, open, and nonviolent parliamentary elections have been held. When confronted with a vote of no confidence by the Slovak parliament in March 1994, Meciar did not try to hold on to power illegally; he resigned. And government efforts to monitor and control the media have not yet—and may never—physically prevent them from criticizing and opposing its policies. Furthermore, the United States, which has been severely critical of the Slovak government for "disturbing trends away from democratic principles," acknowledged in 1996 that "the (Slovak) Constitution provides for freedom of speech and the press and 'the Government generally respects this right in practice.'"[114] It also acknowledged in 1997 that "the (Slovak) Constitution provides for (freedom of peaceful assembly and association) . . . 'and the (Slovak) Government generally respects them in practice.'"[115]

NOTES

1. National Council of the Slovak Republic, *The Constitution of the Slovak Republic* (Privatpress Presov, Slovakia); see also Pavel Mates, "The New Slovak Constitution," *Radio Free Europe/Radio Liberty Research Reports* (hereafter cited as *RFE/RL Research Report*), vol. 1, no. 43 (October 30, 1992), pp. 39–42; Eric Stein, *Czecho/Slovakia: Ethnic Conflict, Constitutional Fissure, Negotiated Breakup* (Ann Arbor, Michigan: University of Mich. Press, 1997), pp. 273–282.

2. Jan Obrman, "The Czechoslovak Elections," *RFE/RL Research Report*, vol. 26 (June 26, 1992), pp. 12–19, passim, cited in Carol Skalnik Leff, *The Czech and Slovak Republics: Nation versus State* (Boulder, Colo.: Westview Press, 1997), p. 147.

3. See Sharon Fisher, "Is Slovakia Headed for New Elections?" *RFE/RL Rearch Report*, vol. 2, no. 32 (August 13, 1993), pp. 34–36.

4. Jan Obrman, "Internal Disputes Shake Slovak Government," RFE/RL RR, vol. 2, no. 14 (April 2, 1993), p. 13; see also United States Department of State, *Country Reports on Human Rights Practices for 1995: Report Submitted to the Committee on International Relations, U.S. House of Representatives and the Committee on Foreign Relations U.S. Senate April 1996*, "Slovakia" (hereafter cited as U.S. Department of State, *Human Rights Practices for 1995*, "Slovakia") (Washington, D.C.: U.S. Government Printing Office, 1996), p. 1023.

5. Leff, *Czech and Slovak Republics*, p. 148.

6. Ibid.

7. Fisher, "Is Slovakia Headed for New Elections?," p. 37.

8. Ibid.

9. Obrman, "Internal Disputes Shake Slovak Government," p. 15.

10. Fisher, "Is Slovakia Headed for New Elections?," p. 37.

11. Ibid.

12. Obrman, "Internal Disputes Shake Slovak Government," pp. 15–16.

13. Fisher, "Is Slovakia Headed for New Elections?," p. 37.

14. *Prague Post* (June 23–29, 1993).

15. Fisher, "Is Slovakia Headed for New Elections?," p. 38.

16. Ibid.

17. Milan Nic, Jan Obrman, and Sharon Fisher, "New Slovak Government? More Stability?" *RFE/RL Research Report*, vol. 2, no. 47 (November 26, 1993), p. 27.

18. Ibid.

19. Ibid., p. 29.

20. Sharon Fisher, "Unraveling the Enigma of SIS Director Ivan Lexa," *Transition*, vol. 2, no. 13 (June 28, 1996), p. 45.

21. Jane Perlez, "Slovaks Come Out Loser in Break with Czechs," *New York Times* (hereafter cited as *NYT*) (February 7, 1994); U.S. Department of State, *Foreign Broadcast Information Service Daily Report Eastern Europe* (hereafter cited as FBIS/EEU) 94-068 (April 8, 1994), pp. 8–9.

22. Polling information from *Mlada Fronta DNES* (October 29, 1992), *Pravda* (February 12, 1993), and *CSTK News Agency* (Prague, March 17, 1993), cited in Obrman, "Internal Disputes Shake Slovak Government," p. 17.

23. Obrman, "Internal Disputes Shake Slovak Government," p. 16.

24. Sharon Fisher and Stefan Hrib, "Political Crisis in Slovakia," *RFE/RL Research Report*, vol. 3, no. 10 (March 11, 1994), pp. 20–22; see also Sharon Fisher, "New Slovak Government Formed after Meciar's Fall," *RFE/RL Research Report*, vol. 3, no. 13 (April 1, 1994), p. 12.

25. Fisher and Hrib, "Political Crisis," pp. 23–24.

26. Fisher, "New Slovak Government Formed after Meciar's Fall," p. 8.

27. Ibid., p. 9; "Hilfe Country Report—Slovakia," Comment, Analyses, Statistics, Tables, Forecasts (July 1996), available on-line *Lexis-Nexis*, Library: Europe, File, Quest Economy Database: Janet Mathews Information Services (1996), hereafter cited as *Hilfe Country Report*, "Slovakia" (July 1996), *LN/EL*, Quest Economy Database, JMIS (1996).

28. Fisher, "New Slovak Government Formed after Meciar's Fall," p. 13.

29. Ibid., p. 10.

30. Leff, *Czech and Slovak Republics*, pp. 150–151.

31. *FBIS-EEU*, vol. 94, no. 053 (March 18, 1994), p. 6.

32. Leff, *Czech and Slovak Republics*, p. 151; Fisher, "New Slovak Government," p. 12.

33. See Sharon Fisher, "Slovak Government's Personnel Changes Cause Controversy," *RFE/RL Research Report*, vol. 3, no. 21 (May 27, 1994), pp. 10–15.

34. Leff, *Czech and Slovak Republics*, pp. 151–152.

35. *The Europa World Yearbook 1995* (hereafter cited as *EWY 1995*) (Rochester, Kent, U.K.: Europa Publications, Ltd., 1995), p. 2711; see also Leff, *Czech and Slovak Republics*, p. 152; Sharon Wolchik, "Democratization and Political Participation in Slovakia," in Karen Dawisha and Bruce Parrott (eds.), *The Consolidation of Democracy in East-Central Europe* (Cambridge, U.K.; Cambridge University Press, 1997), pp. 211–213.

36. Jane Perlez, "Unlikely Allies for Coalition in Slovakia," *NYT* (December 12, 1994).

37. Ibid.; Sabrina P. Ramet, *Whose Democracy? Nationalism, Religion, and the Doctrine of Collective Rights in Post 1989 Eastern Europe* (Lanham, Md: Rowman and Littlefield, 1997), p. 127.

38. Stephen Kinzer, "West Says Slovakia Falls Short of Democracy," *NYT* (December 26, 1995).

39. Leff, *Czech and Slovak Republics*, p. 153; see also Commision on Security and Cooperation in Europe (CSCE), *Human Rights and Democratization in Slovakia* (Washington, D.C.: CSCE, September 1997), p. 12.

40. Ibid.; *EWY 1995*, p. 2711.

41. *EWY 1995*, p. 2711.

42. Sharon Fisher, "Kidnapping Case Continues to Complicate Political Scene," *Transition*, vol. 2, no. 13 (June 28, 1996), p. 41; Ramet, *Whose Democracy?*, p. 129.

43. Jane Perlez, "Abduction Casts New Doubts on Slovak Chief," *NYT* (December 17, 1996).

44. *Facts on File*, vol. 56, no. 2904 (August 1, 1996), p. 541.

45. U.S. Department of State, *Human Rights Practices for 1995*, "Slovakia," p. 1024; see also Sharon Fisher, "Slovak Television in Disarray," *RFE/RL Research Report*, vol. 3, no. 27 (May 27, 1994), pp. 29–33.

46. "Slovakia Takes a Wrong Turn," *NYT* (March 7, 1995); see also Andrej Skolkay, "Slovak Government Tightens Its Grip on the Airwaves," *Transition*, vol. 2, no. 8 (April 19, 1996), pp. 18–19.

47. U.S. Department of State, *Human Rights Practices for 1995*, "Slovakia," p. 1026.

48. Ibid.

49. "President Denied Airtime to Address Nation on Referendum," *CSTK News Agency* (Prague, May 15, 1997), *LN/EL*, Library: Europe, File Eastern Europe TXTEE, BBC Monitoring Service (May 17, 1997).

50. Sharon Fisher, "Slovakia Heads toward International Isolation," *Transition*, vol. 3, no. 2 (February 7, 1977), p. 13.

51. Ibid.

52. Anne Nivat, "Slovak Media under Government Fire," *Transition*, vol. 2, no. 9 (May 6, 1996), p. 60.

53. Stephen Kinzer, "2 Year Old Slovakia Toddling Toward Democracy," *NYT* (March 19, 1995).

54. Nivat, "Slovak Media under Government Fire," p. 60.

55. Sharon Fisher, "Slovakia's Troubled Print Media," *Transition*, vol. 2, no. 21 (October 18, 1996), p. 47.

56. Fisher, "Slovakia Heads toward International Isolation," p. 13; U.S. Department of State, *Human Rights Practices for 1996*, "Slovakia," p. 1117.

57. U.S. Department of State, *Human Rights Practices for 1995*, "Slovakia," p. 1024.

58. U.S. Department of State, *Human Rights Practices for 1996*, "Slovakia," p. 1118.

59. Peter Javurek, "Slovakia Approves Draft Law on 'Subversion,'" *Reuters* (Bratislava, March 8, 1996), *LN/EL*, Europe, Reuters Textline, Reuters News Service—CIS and Eastern Europe (March 8, 1996); see also Ramet, *Whose Democracy?* p. 134.

60. U.S. Department of State, *Human Rights Practices for 1996*, "Slovakia," p. 1118; Peter Javurek, "Slovakia Approves Draft Law on 'Subversion,'" *LN/EL*, *Reuters* (Bratislava, March 8, 1996), Reuters Textline, Reuters News Service—CIS and Eastern Europe (March 8, 1996); "Anti-Subversion Bill Withdrawn from Parliament," *CSTK News Agency* (Prague, October 24, 1996), *LN/EL*, Reuters Textline, BBC Monitoring Service: Eastern Europe (October 26, 1996); Ramet, *Whose Democracy?*, p. 135.

61. Jan Krcmar, "Slovak Journalists Slam Draft Anti-Subversion Law," *Reuters* (Bratislava, March 11, 1996), *LN/EL*, Reuters Textline, Reuters News Service—CIS and Eastern Europe (March 11, 1996); Ramet, *Whose Democracy?*, p. 135.

62. Peter Javurek, "Slovak Parliament Changes Controversial Law," Reuters (Bratislava, October 24, 1996), *Reuters* Textline, Reuters News Service—CIS and Eastern Europe (October 24, 1996); Fisher, "Slovakia heads toward International Isolation," p. 13; U.S. Department of State, *Human Rights Practices for 1996*, "Slovakia," p. 1118; Ramet, *Whose Democracy?*, pp. 135–136.

63. Commission on Security and Cooperation in Europe (CSCE), *Human Rights and Democratization in Slovakia* (Washington, D.C.: CSCE, September, 1997), p. 13;

"Another Constitutional Issue in Slovakia," *CSCE Digest*, vol. 20, no. 8 (August 1997), p. 85.

64. "Another Constitutional Issue in Slovakia," p. 88.

65. Ramet, *Whose Democracy?* p. 133; Kinzer, "West Says Slovakia Falls Short of Democracy;" see also Peter Javurek, "Slovak Deputies Show Contempt for Democracy Fears," *Reuters* (Bratislava, October 23, 1996), *LN/EL*, Reuters Textline, Reuters News Service (October 23, 1996).

66. *Hilfe Country Report—Slovakia* (July 1996), *LN/EL*, Quest Economy Database, JMIS (1996).

67. U.S. Department of State, *Human Rights Practices for 1995*, "Slovakia," p. 1025.

68. Ibid.

69. *Hilfe Country Report*, "Slovakia" (July 1996), *LN/EL*, Quest Economy Database, JMIS (1996); CSCE, *Human Rights and Democratization in Slovakia*, pp. 19-20.

70. The Economist Intelligence Unit, *Country Report: Slovakia, 1997/1998 Prospect* (London; 1998); Leff, *Czech and Slovak Republics*, pp. 167, 250.

71. "Commission Says Referendum to Include Four Questions," *Tasr News Agency* (Bratislava, May 16, 1997), *LN/EL*, Eastern Europe TXTEE, BBC Monitoring Service: Eastern Europe (May 19, 1997).

72. Peter Javurek, "Slovak Deputies Approve Referendum on NATO Bid," *Reuters* (Bratislava, February 14, 1997), *LN/EL*, Reuters Textline, Reuter News Service—CIS and Eastern Europe (February 14, 1997); for a succinct summary of the political and constitutional issues raised by the referendum and details about the preparation for it, the balloting, and the outcome, see CSCE, *Human Rights and Democratization in Slovakia*, pp. 14-18.

73. "Slovak Foreign Minister Says Ready to Join NATO," Reuters (Bratislava, February 18, 1997), *LN/EL*, *Reuters* Textline, Reuters News Agency—CIS and Eastern Europe (February 18, 1997); "Slovakia Will Be in First Wave of NATO Expansion," *CSTK News Agency* (Prague, February 21, 1997), *LN/EL*, Eastern Europe TXTEE, BBC Monitoring Service: Eastern Europe (February 22, 1997).

74. CSCE, *Human Rights and Democratization in Slovakia*, pp. 15–16.

75. Peter Laca, "Slovak Coalition Party Warns against Entry into NATO," *Reuters* (Bratislava, March 2, 1997), *LN/EL*, Reuters Textline, Reuters News Service—CIS and Eastern Europe (March 2, 1997); "Russia, USA Discussing Slovak Neutrality, Says Coalition Party," *CSTK News Agency* (Prague, March 14, 1997), *LN/EL*, Eastern Europe TXTEE, BBC Monitoring Service: Eastern Europe (March 17, 1997); "Ruling Coalition Party against Joining European Structures," *CSTK News Agency* (Prague, March 20, 1997), *LN/EL*, Eastern Europe TXTEE, BBC Monitoring Service: Eastern Europe (March 22, 1997).

76. A public opinion poll in December 1996 showed only 35.5 percent of Slovaks supported NATO membership and 25.5 percent opposed it. See Peter Javurek, "Slovakia Sets NATO, Presidential Poll Referendums," *Reuters*, *LN/EL*, Reuters Textline, Reuters News Service—CIS and Eastern Europe (March 13, 1997).

77. Peter Javurek, "Slovak Opposition Calls for Referendum Yes on NATO," *Reuters* (Bratislava, May 7, 1997), *LN/EL*, Reuters Textline, Reuters News Service—CIS and Eastern Europe (May 7, 1997).

78. *CSTK News Agency* (Prague, February 13, 1997), *LN/EL*, Eastern Europe TXTEE, BBC Monitoring Service: Eastern Europe (February 15, 1997).

79. "Slovak President May Run Again If Asked," *Reuter* (Bratislava, May 20, 1997), LN/EL, Reuters Textline, Reuter News Service—CIS and Eastern Europe (May 20, 1997).

80. Peter Javurek, "Slovak Opposition Says Referendum Petition Success," *Reuter* (February 18, 1997), LN/EL, Reuters Textline, Reuters News Service—CIS and Eastern Europe (February 18, 1997); see also "Opposition Collects Enough Signatures for Direct Presidential Election Referendum," CSTK News Agency (Prague, February 23, 1997), LN/EL, BBC Monitoring Service: Eastern Europe (February 23, 1997).

81. "Government Halts Distribution of Referendum Ballots on Presidential Elections," *Pravda* (Bratislava, April 23, 1997), *LN/EL*, Eastern Europe TXTEE, BBC Monitoring Service: Eastern Europe (April 25, 1997).

82. "Presidential Referendum Undemocratic and Dishonest," *CSTK News Agency* (Prague, April 24, 1997), *LN/EL*, Eastern Europe TXTEE, BBC Monitoring Service: Eastern Europe (April 26, 1997).

83. "Slovak President May Run Again If Asked," *Reuters* (Bratislava, May 20, 1997), *LN/EL*, Reuters Textline, Reuter News Service—CIS and Eastern Europe (May 20, 1997).

84. "Government Halts Distribution of Referendum Ballots on Presidential Elections," *Pravda* (Bratislava, April 23, 1997), *LN/EL*, Eastern Europe TXTEE, BBC Monitoring Service: Eastern Europe (April 25, 1997).

85. Ibid.

86. Ibid.; see also Peter Javurek, "Block on Slovak Referendum Illegal, Says Opposition," *Reuters* (Bratislava, April 23, 1997), *LN/EL*, Reuters Textline, Reuters News Service—CIS and Eastern Europe (April 23, 1997).

87. "President Launches Direct Communication with People," *Sme* (Bratislava, May 9, 1997), *LN/EL*, Eastern Europe TXTEE, BBC Monitoring Service: Eastern Europe (May 15, 1997).

88. Jan Krcmar, "Slovak Court Opens Way for Presidential Referendum," *Reuters* (Bratislava, May 14, 1997), *LN/EL*, Reuters Textline, Reuters News Service—CIS and Eastern Europe (May 14, 1997); CSCE, *Human Rights and Democratization in Slovakia*, pp. 16–17.

89. "Deputy Premier Says Court Ruling 'Last Ditch Attempt' to Save President," *CSTK News Agency* (Prague, May 15, 1997), *LN/EL*, Eastern Europe TXTEE, BBC Monitoring Service: Eastern Europe (May 17, 1997).

90. Peter Javurek, "Confusion Mars Voting in Slovak Referendum," *Reuters* (Bratislava, May 23, 1997), *LN/EL*, Reuters Textline, Reuters News Service–CIS and Eastern Europe (May 23, 1997).

91. Peter Javurek, "Confusion Mars Voting in Slovak Referendum"; "Opposition Urges Boycott of Referendum with Three Questions," *CSTK News Agency* (Prague, May 22, 1997), *LN/EL*, Eastern Europe TXTEE, BBC Monitoring Service: Eastern Europe (May 24, 1997).

92. "President Calls Interior Minister's Referendum Moves 'Illegal,'" *Slovakia 1 Radio* (Bratislava, May 22, 1997), *LN/EL*, Eastern Europe TXTEE, BBC Monitoring Service: Eastern Europe (May 24, 1997); Peter Juvarek, "Slovak President Refuses to Vote in Own Referendums," *Reuters* (Bratislava, May 23, 1997), *LN/EL*, Reuters Textline, Reuters News Service—CIS and Eastern Europe (May 23, 1997)

93. "Today Is the Funeral of Democracy in Slovakia," *CSTK News Agency* (Prague, May 23, 1997), *LN/EL*, Eastern Europe TXTEE, BBC Monitoring Service: Eastern Europe (May 26, 1997).

94. "Referendum Turnout under 10%," *CSTK News Agency* (Prague, May 25, 1997), *LN/EL*, Eastern Europe TXTEE, BBC Monitoring Service: Eastern Europe (May 27, 1997).

95. "Controversial Referendum Ends," *CSTK News Agency* (Prague, May 24, 1997), *LN/EL*, Eastern Europe TXTEE, BBC Monitoring Service: Eastern Europe (May 26, 1997).

96. Ibid.

97. Peter Javurek, "Slovak President Refuses to Vote in Own Referendum," *Reuters* (Bratislava, May 23, 1997), *LN/EL*, Reuters Textline, Reuters News Agency—CIS and Eastern Europe (May 23, 1997).

98. "Premier Says President Is the Reason for the Political Struggle," (Radio 1, Bratislava, June 6, 1997), *LN/EL*, Eastern Europe TXTEE, BBC Monitoring Service: Eastern Europe (June 9, 1997).

99. Perlez, "Abduction Casts New Doubts on Slovakia Chief."

100. Ibid.

101. U.S. Department of State, *Human Rights Practices for 1995*, "Slovakia," p. 1026.

102. Ibid.

103. "Democratic Union Calls on People to Demand Change in Ruling Style," *TASR News Agency* (Bratislava, April 19, 1997), *LN/EL*, Eastern Europe TXTEE, BBC Monitoring Service: Eastern Europe (April 21, 1997).

104. "Some Opposition Parties Stage Protest Rallies against Foiled NATO Referendum," *TASR News Agency* (Bratislava, June 3, 1997), *LN/EL*, Eastern Europe TXTEE, BBC Monitoring Service: Eastern Europe (June 5, 1997).

105. "Talks Conditional on Minister's Resignation—Opposition [(Says)]," *CSTK News Agency* (Prague, June 6, 1997), *LN/EL*, Eastern Europe TXTEE, BBC Monitoring Service: Eastern Europe (June 9, 1997).

106. The Economist Intelligence Unit, *Country Report: Slovakia*, Third Quarter, 1997 (London: The Unit, 1997) on CD-ROM; see also "Slovak Poll Shows Opposition Ahead," *Radio Free Europe/Radio Liberty Newsline* (January 15, 1998) (Prague: Paul Goble Publisher, 1998), on line @ http://www.rferl.org/

107. John Gould and Sona Szomolanyi, "Bridging the Chasm in Slovakia," *Transition*, vol. 4, no. 6 (November 1997), p. 73.

108. Ibid., pp. 75–76.

109. The Economist Intelligence Unit, *Country Report: Slovakia*, Third Quarter, 1997 (London: The Unit, 1997) on CD-ROM.

110. "Mass Protest Demonstration in Bratislava," *RFE/RL Newsline* (March 26, 1998), ON-LINE.

111. "Slovak Parliament Makes Controversial Change to Electoral Law," *RFE/RL Newsline*, (May 21, 1998), ON-LINE.

112. Kinzer, "West Says Slovakia Falls Short of Democracy."

113. Ramet, *Whose Democracy?*, p. 127.

114. U.S. Department of State, *Human Rights Practices for 1995*, "Slovakia," pp. 1022-1023.

115. U.S. Department of State, *Human Rights Practices for 1996*, "Slovakia," p. 1118.

4

Movement toward the Free Market

Problems of Reform and Recovery

In the early 1990s, post-Communist Czech and Slovak leaders identified the Communist command economy as the biggest obstacle to economic growth and development. They believed introduction of a free enterprise economy based upon capitalist principles of supply and demand could bring economic health, raise living standards, and ultimately assure political stability.

OBJECTIVES AND METHODS OF REFORM

On the advice of Western economists as well as its own experts, Slovak leaders in the early 1990s subscribed to and followed a range of policies to free up economic life. Among these were (1) privatizing large and small enterprises in industry, agriculture, and service areas like banking, insurance, and retail sales; (2) ending state monopolies; (3) accepting bankruptcies and unemployment as the price of the free market; (4) terminating centralized control of both planning and pricing and allowing prices to be influenced by supply and demand; (5) dismantling the bureaucratic planning apparatus, including removal of the former Communist nomenclature; (6) abandoning subsidies to producers and consumers; (7) using fiscal policy to restrict demand; and (8) making currency convertible by reducing budget deficits, increasing exports, and reforming an inept and inadequate national banking system inherited from communist rule.[1]

After Slovakia became independent, Prime Minister Meciar continued to implement some of these principles. He was much less an economic reformer than Czech Republic prime minister Vaclav Klaus, who was staunchly devoted to free enterprise capitalism. Meciar favored an economic system somewhere between capitalism and socialism that included a substantial amount of state control and a very gradual rate of change. He wanted to cushion the harsh effects of free market reform, notably inflation, unemployment, and a decline of state-supported social services. Nevertheless, Meciar did support the free market; and in March 1995, Jozef Sucha, an official of the economics ministry, reportedly stated that, despite delays, the Slovak government in fact was committed to development of the market economy.[2]

PRIVATIZATION POLICIES

Slovakia's privatization policies began when it was part of Czechoslovakia. In the early 1990s, these policies, set in Prague, did not adequately take into account Slovakia's vulnerability to rapid change away from the state-controlled economy of the Communist era. The Slovaks went along with the changes mandated by Prague but paid a far higher price than the Czechs.

Uncertain Beginnings, 1990–1992

In the early 1990s, the Czechoslovak government had difficulty starting up privatization, partly because people had little if any spare capital to purchase shares in industries the state wanted to privatize. They also lacked entrepreneurial experience, since the Communist government had strictly forbidden private shops or businesses. When in the early 1990s the government in Prague auctioned off state-run stores to the highest bidders, they sold at bargain prices. Furthermore, those who benefitted most from this early phase of privatization—because they were the only people with money to take advantage of the auctions— were ex-Communist officials, money-changers, swindlers, and black marketeers. At least, that was what angry Czechoslovak citizens left out of the process believed. Some managers deliberately bankrupted their enterprises so that they could buy the ruined businesses at a lower value.[3]

The Voucher System. To increase the pool of prospective buyers of state property, Czechoslovak finance minister Klaus introduced the *kuponova metoda,* or voucher system. As outlined in the privatization law of February 1991, the voucher system gave every adult citizen the right to purchase a book of coupons or vouchers at a nominal fee, well within the reach of most wage earners. The purchaser could then exchange the vouchers for shares in state enterprises to be privatized. This procedure was intended to transfer a large number of state-controlled enterprises as quickly as possible to private owners, creating a constituency of small investors much as one would find in Western capitalist countries.

Furthermore, support for the voucher system was based on an argument that it was democratic in giving all citizens an opportunity to participate in the privatization process, especially those who might otherwise be shut out because they did not have enough money. On the other hand, politicians in Slovakia with links to industrial managers skeptical of privatization and eager to slow it up preferred public auctions and direct sales.[4]

The voucher system got off to a very slow start. Not at all familiar with the meaning of investment, most Czechoslovak citizens did not really understand what the vouchers were all about. They saw little value in them and hesitated to spend even the small amount of money needed to purchase them. The idea that they literally were being offered a windfall that would have sent small American investors into the streets to celebrate escaped most Czechoslovak people mainly because they had never experienced the phenomenon of investment. By the end of 1991, the Czechoslovak government had sold only 500,000 books of vouchers, a pittance considering the 16 million citizens eligible to participate in this extraordinary scheme.[5]

Then suddenly, in early 1992, sales of the vouchers skyrocketed, thanks to the appearance of Viktor Kozeny, a Harvard-educated entrepreneur, who came forward with a plan that looked very much like a mutual fund operation. Kozeny invited owners of vouchers to use them to buy shares in his so-called Harvard Capital and Consulting Fund, an outfit that had nothing to do with Harvard University. He promised to redeem the investment in a year and a day at ten times the original value of the vouchers paid to the fund. Kozeny obviously understood, as most ordinary Czechoslovaks did not, that purchasing shares in valuable state enterprises was a very good investment. Although most Czechoslovaks did not see through this clever marketing scheme, many were willing to take a chance and accepted Kozeny's solemn pledge of a good return and bought the vouchers.[6] Still, there were complaints about the voucher system. Some called it unfair because it seemed to favor people who knew something about the enterprises for sale and appreciated how the coupons allowed easy acquisition of huge amounts of valuable property. Those who benefitted most were former Communist Party big shots and well-heeled foreign speculators who saw an opportunity to make a quick profit. Indeed, many Czechoslovaks considered the voucher system as little more than a giveaway program.

Nevertheless, the voucher system did stimulate a lot of popular interest in privatization. Eventually people did take the vouchers quite seriously. Kozeny's fund was quickly followed by other investment firms that helped people to use their vouchers to make investments and to learn about risk taking. By January 1992, 8.7 million Czechs and Slovaks had used their vouchers to obtain shares with over 400 investment firms.[7]

A first wave of large-scale privatization using the voucher system was completed in both the Czech and Slovak republics in December 1992, though voucher holders had until June 30, 1993, to trade their coupons for property. In the Slovak republic 9,676 small businesses sold for 14.5 billion crowns by the end of 1992, while property with a book value of 79.9 billion crowns (91.7 percent of the total property offered) was transferred in the first round of large-scale privatization. Between 75 percent and 80 percent of Slovaks took part in voucher privatization, and more than 70 percent invested their vouchers in 165 privatization funds.[8]

Privatization in Slovakia after Independence

Following the achievement of independence on January 1, 1993, most Slovak political leaders believed that curtailment of state control over Slovak economic life was important for growth and prosperity. The commitment to privatization transcended party lines. Moreover, the Slovak government was under international pressure, especially from the European Community (EC), now called the European Union (EU), in which Slovakia sought membership, to move forward with privatization. But, privatization of state enterprises after independence in January 1993 proceeded slowly. By the beginning of 1994 only 5 percent of Slovakia's state-owned enterprises had been privatized, in contrast with the Czech Republic, which had privatized 40 percent of state enterprises by mid-1994.[9]

The rate of privatization accelerated temporarily when Jozef Moravcik succeeded Meciar as prime minister in March, 1994. Shares in 88 companies that had remained unsold after the voucher privatization had begun in 1991 were offered for sale, and by late July 47 percent had been sold. At the same time the Moravcik government announced that all the conditions needed to begin another wave of voucher privatization had been met. On August 12, 1994, the Economic and Budget Committee of the Slovak National Council (SNC) approved a list of 632 state firms worth 262.9 billion crowns for privatization, with 20 percent to be sold off by the voucher method. In September, registration for the purchase of vouchers started.[10]

When Meciar returned to power following parliamentary elections at the end of September 1994, privatization continued, but only very slowly, with most of heavy industry under state control. Moreover, Meciar criticized Moravcik's privatization efforts as "hasty" and even "a robbery of the people." In late 1994, the SNC, dominated by Meciar's Movement for a Democratic Slovakia (MDS), canceled the Moravcik government's privatization deals and postponed completion of a second wave of privatization, despite strong evidence of popular interest. When Slovak courts subsequently overturned the parliament's action, the voucher sale was rescheduled, to take place in the summer of 1995. With Meciar in charge, the plan to continue large-scale privatization was whittled down and eventually canceled.[11]

Still, there was some privatization. By the end of 1995, 60 percent of the gross domestic product (GDP) came from the private sector.[12] In 1995, a second major wave of privatization for a two-year period to end in 1997 was initiated. The Meciar government invited large and small investors to purchase bonds, which bore interest annually, could be redeemed within a five-year period, and could be used to buy not only shares, as had been the case with vouchers, but also apartments, additional health and pension insurance, and participation in an employee joint-stock company. The objective was to create a genuine entrepreneurial group, which the vouchers had not been able to do. By 1996, the proportion of economic activity generated by the private sector reached 76.8 percent, up from 62.6 percent in 1995.[13]

The Slovak government envisaged further privatization following the conclusion of the second wave. In May 1997, in a document titled "The Timetable for the Transformation of State Property in 1997," the government called for the privatization in 1997 and 1998 of public utilities administered by the economy and agriculture ministries, in particular water and sewage treatment plants, over which in the past the government had wanted to maintain control.[14]

Controversy over Bank Privatization. Perhaps no industry better illustrates the Slovak struggle to move cautiously and carefully to the free market than banking. In the mid- and late 1990s, Meciar-led governments were committed to bank privatization partly because they had promised the Organization for Economic Cooperation and Development (OECD) to move forward in this area. Without a private banking system, Slovakia had little chance of gaining membership in the OECD.

Meciar sought bank privatization for other reasons. Many publicly owned banks were on the threshold of bankruptcy because of portfolios loaded with uncollectible loans.[15] Deputy Prime Minister and Minister of Finance Sergej Kozlik believed that banks like *Vseobecna Uverova* (General Credit Bank [VUB]), if under private control, would do better than under state control at generating funds needed to keep the National Property Fund (NPF), the agency responsible for selling off state enterprises to private investors, liquid and capable of redeeming bonds given to individuals in compensation for vouchers no longer being sold.[16]

The SNC, however, was less enthusiastic than the Meciar government about relinquishing state control over the banking system. Many deputies were uncomfortable over the transfer of the state's banking system, which influenced many aspects of the country's economic life, to private interests motivated primarily by profit. They wanted the state to continue to dominate this section of the national economy. In June 1996, the parliament approved a law freezing bank privatization until March 31, 1997. Meciar suffered a setback here partly because his coalition partners, in particular the Association of Slovak Workers (ASW), did not support bank privatization. The ASW broke ranks and joined the opposition in the SNC to support the freeze.

Meciar, however, was determined to move forward with bank privatization. He was still under intense international pressure to establish a privately owned and managed banking system in Slovakia. Moreover, the benefits that would accrue to the government, especially the NPF, from the sale of the banks were substantial in terms of both foreign policy and domestic economic development. The opposition remained adamant; and on February 13, 1997, in anticipation of the March 31 expiration, the parliament voted to freeze the privatization of four major banking institutions until 2003.[17] Meciar said that the vote would make it impossible for him to honor a pledge to the OECD that the banks would be privatized by the end of March 1997. Meciar predicted that failure to complete the privatization of the Slovak banking system would compromise the economic transformation of Slovakia.[18]

The prime minister asked President Kovac to send the bank privatization freeze bill back to the parliament, which the president had to do according to the constitution despite his reservations. Meciar also lectured the ASW on its divergence, saying its behavior on February 13 was not the first time it had acted independently and in opposition to its coalition partners. He warned that to remain in the coalition it could not make a habit of supporting the opposition. At the same time, to pressure the parliament to approve privatization of the banks, Meciar said he might link passage of the bill to a vote of confidence in the government.[19]

When ASW leader Luptak learned of Meciar's linkage plan, he said publicly that the ASW would "stick to its guns" and support freezing bank privatization until 2003, even if that meant destroying the coalition. If the coalition collapsed, he declared, the ASW could not be blamed. Responsibility would lie rather with those who linked the bill to confidence.[20]

Ironically, Meciar was faced with a line of reasoning from the advocates of a freeze on bank privatization with which he himself might have agreed had not the stakes from his perspective been so high. Advocates of the freeze worried that the banking system, so much the heart of the country's well-being, would be in the hands of greedy profiteers, a version of the old Communist line; but it held some truth as well, since Meciar and his supporters stood ready to profit from the privatization, just as the opposition feared.

In mid-February 1997, PDL leader Peter Weiss strongly denounced bank privatization. He called the government a "hostage" to a very greedy lobby eager to privatize the banks to finance their operations abroad. Weiss said, "The debtors want to get hold of the assets of their creditors, taking over the Slovak economy and politics. Its a big threat to democracy." He argued that this lobby was using OECD recommendations to privatize the Slovak banking system for their own ends." Weiss said the lobby went by the slogan, "What is good for us, the new [entrepreneurial] oligarchy, is good for Slovakia."[21]

The Slovak central bank, known as the National Bank of Slovakia (NBS), recommended only a partial privatization of the four Slovak banks, expressing a fear that they would be taken over by those who owed them money. While the central bank memorandum stated unequivocally that "complete privatization ... would not be appropriate,"[22] it did approve the sale of some shares in the banks to private investors if only to demonstrate the government's good faith to the OECD in seeking to free up Slovakia's banking sector. State control over the management of the banks for the most part must continue until it was clear that private owners of the banks could not abuse the power that would accompany their control of the banks.[23]

The NBS proposed that private investors should have no more than a 50 percent interest in the banks. *Investicna Rozvojova Banka* (Investment and Development Bank) was the exception and could be fully privatized. Furthermore, the NBS suggested that the government should have a controlling interest in the bank known as *Slovenska Sporitelna* (Slovak Savings Bank [SS]), which held over 75 percent of the deposits of the Slovak population, and make this money available to other banks. Otherwise, owners of SS would be in a position, according to the NBS, to exert undue influence over interest rates and eventually over the entire banking sector. The NBS advised that the private stake in SS should be no more than 49 percent. It also recommended that the state retain a "blocking" stake of no less than 34 percent of shares in *Slovenska Poistovna* in light of its dominant position in the Slovak insurance market.[24]

Eventually, Meciar and the parliament reached a compromise based on a recommendation of the NBS. On March 12, 1997, the parliament approved a new privatization law that provided for the sale of *Investicna Rozvojova Banka and Vseobecna Uverova Banka* (General Credit Bank [VUB]). The state would retain a 35 percent share of *Rozvojova* and 51.49 percent of VUB. The privatization of *Poistovna* and *Sporitelna* would occur after the parliamentary elections scheduled in the fall of 1998. In the interim the state would control 91.3 percent of *Sporitelna* and 50.5 percent of *Poistovna*.[25]

Neither side was altogether satisfied with the compromise. The opposition believed the government had exaggerated the pressure for bank privatization coming from the OECD and pointed out that the OECD had raised other equally important concerns about Slovak membership. According to PDL parliamentary deputy Birgitta Schmognerova, the OECD was critical of the government's restrictions on foreign investment in strategic companies and its tendency to sell companies at unrealistically low prices to insiders.[26] For his part, Meciar regretted the parliament's decision to postpone privatization of *Poistovna* and *Investnica*, saying that the sale of these banks would have provided a much-needed source of capital for improving their operations.[27]

Restitution of Church Property. Still another complication with privatization had to do with restitution of property confiscated by the Communists, and no area was more sensitive in this regard than church property. In the early and mid-1990s, the Meciar governments favored returning confiscated property to the church. There also was some economic logic to restitution. The Roman Catholic Church, which claimed land and property valued at up to $1.2 billion, and other religious institutions were impoverished at the end of the Communist era and were dependent on state subsidies. Meciar wanted to provide the churches with the means for self-support to end a drain of scarce funds from the national treasury that could be used for other purposes.[28]

There also were constitutional and political incentives for restitution. Meciar wanted to strengthen the country's commitment to the constitutional principle of separation of church and state. He also hoped that by cultivating the clergy he could discourage it from imitating the Polish clergy's aggressive political role, which involved actively opposing government policies it disliked. By returning confiscated property to the church, he wanted to strengthen public support. Meciar realized there was a lot of popular sympathy for returning at least some property confiscated by the Communists to the church. In 1991, 60 percent of Slovaks claimed membership in the Catholic Church, and in 1993 that figure had risen to 72 percent.[29]

Although in September 1993 a restitution bill easily passed the Slovak parliament, with most Slovak political parties sympathetic to restitution, there were some concerns. The PDL thought the churches should not be awarded huge tracts of land, arguing they should have only the property needed to carry out their necessary functions. There was some public support for this position. While a majority of Slovak voters favored the return of Church buildings, they thought differently about farmland, meadowland, and forests. They believed that this kind of agricultural property should remain under the control of the state or of private owners who would make more productive use of it than the church.[30]

Furthermore, President Kovac objected to a provision which allowed the church to receive property without compensation to owners (the state, private people, and cooperative farms) who had bought and paid for it and had legal possession of it. As Kovac pointed out, restitution without compensation was a violation of personal property rights protected in the Slovak constitution.[31]

When the bill reached his desk in October 1993, President Kovac refused to sign it and sent it back to parliament. The government agreed to amend the bill to provide for compensation. The amended law, which was promptly passed, provided for state compensation to private owners for loss of legally owned land claimed by the church to have been seized by the Communist government.[32]

The restitution of church property strengthened Slovakia's commitment to democratic processes by strengthening the separation of church and state and punctuating the country's renunciation of its Communist past, especially in the area of religion. It signalled the government's determination to have good relations with the country's churches.

Problems with Free Market Reform

By the end of 1997, despite much progress, Slovakia remained behind its central European neighbors, notably Hungary, the Czech Republic, and Poland, in the percentage of GNP coming from the free sector. A major reason was Meciar's own skepticism about privatization. But other problems complicated and slowed privatization. Among them were a scarcity of foreign investment, concern about giving up state control of "strategic" companies, and the cost of restructuring poorly managed, rundown enterprises to make them saleable. Perhaps also important was fear of unemployment and of other risks of the free market for Slovak workers. A larger obstacle to rapid privatization was corruption at the highest levels of the Slovak government.

Skepticism about Privatization. In early 1993, Lubomir Dolgos, Slovak privatization minister and deputy chairman of the MDS, correctly attributed the slowness of privatization to a lack of interest on the part of the government, in particular the Trade, Agriculture, and Economics ministries and ultimately of Prime Minister Meciar himself, who for a time was Acting Minister of Privatization and controlled the National Property Fund.[33] While Meciar never opposed privatization in principle, he questioned the virtue of transferring massive amounts of state property to private ownership. Having once belonged to the Slovak Communist Party, he had the Marxian distrust of private enterprise. His populist approach to leadership increased his concern about the hardships that accompanied the curtailment of state control over the country's economic life. At the very least he favored not only a very gradual movement away from the highly regulated economy of the Communist era, to which most Slovaks had become accustomed, but also an expansive, and expensive, social security net to cushion the impact on Slovak workers of the inflation and unemployment that were the immediate consequences of an expansion of private enterprise.

For Meciar and his colleagues privatization was politically risky in an impoverished society that could not afford to take risks at the expense of individual citizens, especially as they had been promised an improvement in their level of material well-being once Slovakia became independent and no longer was obliged to pursue the costly reformist policies advocated by the Czech leadership in Prague. Indeed, a major reason for Slovak independence had been the freedom to move very slowly if at all toward the free market, with its unpredictability and unreliability.

Furthermore, according to Ivan Simko, a member of the Christian Democratic Movement (CDM) in the SNC, for Meciar "privatization has become a way to concentrate political power instead of a means of economic transformation."[34] Meciar saw in government ownership and management of the weapons-producing enterprises an important source of political patronage as well as a means of keeping a substantial number of potential electoral supporters employed indefinitely in firms that otherwise might be closed down because of their inability to operate at a profit.

Scarcity of Foreign Investment. Throughout the early 1990s, as the privatization process got started, Slovakia trailed its neighbors in obtaining foreign investment. In this period Slovakia attracted only about $620 million in direct foreign investment, whereas Hungary received more than $11 billion. Foreign investment in Slovakia also compared unfavorably with that in the Czech Republic, with Slovakia receiving only one dollar of foreign investment for every nine dollars received by the Czech Republic.[35]

In the mid-1990s, there were some disincentives to foreign investment in Slovakia. For example, as former privatization minister Ivan Miklos observed in mid-January 1993, the prospects of inflation and economic instability scared off private investors who distrusted the country's weak currency.[36] Reflecting a subliminal suspicion of outsiders, the Meciar government also did little to attract foreign investment, saying that foreign money would discourage domestic buyers. As Privatization Minister Peter Bisak explained in May 1996, "If we let in foreign capital from the very beginning, local entrepreneurs would have [had] no chance."[37] Given the poverty of most Slovaks, who could not be even small investors in the proposed new companies, this was a specious argument at best.

For their part, the governments of EU countries and the United States did not go out of their way to encourage private investment in Slovakia for political reasons. They disliked Meciar's authoritarian behavior and his reluctance to give up personal control over the scope and pace of economic reform.[38] Meciar's refusal to pay much attention to the criticisms by well-heeled Western governments of his overbearing style of leadership that at times struck them as blatantly anti-democratic, did little to encourage a sympathetic attitude toward Slovakia.

Other disincentives included the Meciar government's reluctance to transfer to private ownership "strategic companies," such as banks, public utilities, and weapons-producing industries. Meciar believed, as did many in the SNC, that these industries were so important for the general welfare, security, and defense of the country that they should never be in private hands. Thus, in July 1994 the government approved special conditions for privatizing power and gas companies, requiring that 51 percent of shares in power companies and 67 percent of shares in the gas industry continue to be owned by the state.[39]

At the end of 1996, in response to its restrictions on privatization of strategic companies, the World Bank warned the Meciar government that limiting foreign participation would compromise Slovak entry into the EU because it was a violation of the fair and open competition in national economies required of EU members. The Bank called upon the Slovak government to support an increase in the flow of foreign development capital into Slovakia and pointed out that as a result of Slovak discrimination against foreign investors in the sale of strategic companies, direct foreign investment in Slovakia continued to lag behind that in its neighbors.[40]

Difficulties of Enterprise Restructuring. Even with strategic companies restricted, there was much left that could be privatized, but there were additional problems. Many state-owned enterprises sold to private investors were transferred "as is," without any improvement in their plant equipment, much of which dated back to the Communist era. The Slovak government expected private owners to spend what was needed to make these companies profitable, although in the sale of clearly inefficient enterprises with outmoded or worn-out equipment, it did "forgive" half the purchase price as long as the saving was reinvested in the enterprise.[41] The reluctance of private investors to sink large amounts of capital into unprofitable enterprises the state wanted to sell off impeded privatization.

Rise in Unemployment. Unemployment was almost inevitable with the movement toward a free market, given the difficulty many enterprises had in cutting costs and earning profits. State enterprises were especially hard hit as the Slovak government gradually reduced subsidies to inefficient enterprises. In the 1990s, with governments in Prague and later in Bratislava increasingly willing to let state-run enterprises sink or swim depending upon their ability to function without large infusions of public money, deadbeat firms closed down and their employees joined the swelling ranks of unemployed. Making unemployment worse in the early 1990s was a sharp decline in foreign trade, a result of economic and political turmoil inside Slovakia's traditional trade partners, notably the former Soviet Union. In 1991, Slovak unemployment increased in some industrial centers from 13 percent to 20 percent.[42]

Slovak unemployment continued to rise in the mid-1990s. In March 1993, it had risen from an annual rate of 11.26 percent to 12.01 percent. Throughout 1993 unemployment continued to rise, reaching 14.3 percent in December 1993, and 14.9 percent in early 1994.[43] In 1993, the number of industrial workers declined by 11 percent and of construction workers by 14 percent. There was little improvement in 1994 with a stagnant economy that caused a decline in GDP by about 3.7 percent.[44] While these figures were below those for Poland and Hungary, they were cause for concern in Slovakia after the long period of near full employment under the Communists, a situation that Slovaks now missed—hence the popularity of Meciar, who had made unemployment a major campaign issue.

To save jobs, Meciar opted to continue subsidizing Slovakia's inefficient and unprofitable arms industry, which had brought a measure of well-being to Slovakia under the Communists. In the early 1990s, the arms industry fell on hard times partly because of Czechoslovak president Vaclav Havel's decision to curtail the country's arms exports abroad and partly because of the collapse of the traditional Soviet market. The Meciar government in June 1993 spent 15.5 billion crowns to reinvigorate arms industry.[45]

Psychological Stress and Resentment. Rising unemployment had a troubling impact on the psyche of Slovak workers who had become accustomed to guaranteed employment under communist rule. They may not always have had a job that made them happy, but they were assured a minimal well-being that they took for granted. Slovak workers still expected the government, despite its rejection of Communist ideology, to guarantee jobs. Indeed, they expected the government to assure a level of material well-being that went beyond a regular paycheck to include affordable housing, guaranteed vacations, and generous medicalcare. When unemployment in Slovakia soared in the early 1990s to almost 15 percent by early 1994, workers lost not only income but other benefits they always had enjoyed under Communism.[46]

At the same time, workers had limited means of influencing government policy to improve their living conditions. Unions were and remain weak and for the most part ignored by the government. In part this weakness is the result of the subservient behavior of unions under the Communists, when they were little more than stooges of the Communist Party. Workers had little respect for them. Even after the adoption of democracy, Slovak trade unions had little credibility with workers.

Seeking another means to improve living conditions, workers were attracted to a new party in the Slovak parliament following the September 1994 elections. The Association of Slovak Workers (ASW) was founded by former members of the PDL who wanted an organization committed to the interests of workers and willing to cooperate with Meciar. They disliked PDL leader Weiss's refusal to cooperate despite shared concerns about the negative consequences for labor of free market reform. ASW chairman Jan Luptak said that the high rate of unemployment and other hardships for workers in post-Communist Slovakia were unexpected and unaddressed by government leaders. In the new Slovakia, he lamented, as jobs diminished, wages decreased, and prices soared for workers, the ministers, bankers, enterprise managers, and similar big shots in the new economic order were thriving. The ASW leadership wanted to know where the money was coming from to purchase privatized property. It wanted an accounting, and it was angry over what it correctly perceived as widespread corruption among the elite while many workers were impoverished.[47]

Luptak struck a responsive note with the SNC. Along with many ordinary Slovaks, members of the parliament suspected that a small elite of wealthy investors, consisting of former Communist managers and bureaucrats who had hidden away funds, were now in a position ironically to benefit from reforms they had ideologically opposed. For many Slovaks this was not only unfair but repugnant. Why should ex-Communists have a way to continue their control over the economy and derive enormous personal benefit? In early 1994, the parliament raised questions about how investors had obtained the money needed to buy state enterprises. And in late 1997, the Slovak public was as skeptical as ever of the benefits of privatization. According to a poll conducted by the Institute for Public Opinion Research in September 1997, 85 percent of respondents were "more or less" satisfied with privatization with 40 percent of those polled holding the view that privatization had only improved the living standards of a small select group of entrepreneurs and speculators, and with only 2 percent of those polled agreeing with the view that the official objective of privatization—to add to all Slovaks' living standards—had come true.[48]

Corruption and Privatization. The SNC did not have to look far to find out who was wrongly benefitting from privatization. In the early 1990s, Prime Minister Meciar and his supporters in the government were among the chief culprits, provoking more complaints about how a special elite was making a killing out of free market reforms. Using his position as privatization minister and chairman of the NPF, Meciar had limited sales as much as he dared to political allies, close friends, and relatives. He had arranged sales of state companies earmarked for privatization at bargain-basement prices. He reportedly had allowed his personal chauffeur to purchase a state-owned meat packing plant at a price equivalent to 5 percent of its real value.[49]

In the early months 1994, incensed by this chicanery, many of Meciar's own party colleagues in the SNC withdrew their support of him, opening the way in March for the vote of no-confidence in his leadership that led to his resignation as Prime Minister. In anticipation of losing power, Meciar actually speeded up privatization, approving the sale of about 45 state firms at discount prices to chosen party colleagues and other political supporters.[50]

The new Moravcik government resented Meciar's self-serving gesture. Milan Janicina, the new privatization minister, decided to examine in detail Meciar's last-minute sales of state property to determine their propriety. He said that all sales in the preceding month would be canceled if found to be damaging to the state budget. In June 1994, the parliamentary Committee on Privatization ruled that projects approved by the Meciar government in the last weeks of its tenure in fact violated the privatization law.[51]

When he returned to power in October 1994, Meciar resumed the practice of using privatization to distribute patronage. His behavior again provoked a political crisis, this time with the SNP leadership, his coalition partner, but for the wrong reason. SNP leaders were not concerned with either the illegality or immorality of Meciar's privatization policies. Rather, they complained that Meciar was not giving them enough opportunity to purchase state enterprises on the cheap. They had their eye on *Slovenska Poistovna*, the lucrative state bank heavily involved in the insurance business and about to be privatized. SNP leaders told Meciar they wanted a share in the management of the NPF, which was handling the transfer of *Slovenska Poistovna* to private ownership. The competition between the SNP and MDS leaders for a moment threatened to pull the coalition apart. Eventually SNP leaders backed off when Meciar hinted that he might look to the PDL as an alternative coalition partner.[52]

By this time the government's self-serving management of Slovak privatization was drawing the attention of the press, which reported links between relatives of coalition leaders with key firms that had been privatized.[53] Outsiders also took notice of the Slovak government's lack of transparency in the management of privatization. The World Bank had been closely monitoring Slovak economic policies and in December 1996 called attention to continuing discrimination in favor of government officials. It reported that investors with contacts in political circles were being given preference in purchase-and-sales agreements to the detriment of investors from abroad. The Bank accused the NPF of selling companies for unrealistically low prices to these "preferred customers," many of whom were close to Prime Minister Meciar.[54]

The Persistence of Government Interference

Although by the end of 1996 Slovakia had made significant but halting progress in moving away from a command to a market-based economy, with almost 79 percent of GDP coming from the private sector, the Bratislava government's control over the country's economic life was still quite substantial. The Meciar leadership was still reluctant to sell off strategic companies, notably transportation, communication, and energy-producing enterprises; and there was still much political favoritism in the transfer of state property to private ownership.[55] Furthermore, to control inflation, which had increased slightly in early 1997 to an annual rate of 6.5 percent, and to limit unemployment, the government took several steps that increased its influence over the country's economic life. For example, it imposed import restrictions, wage controls, and tax increases. Wages were allowed to rise only in proportion to productivity and profitability, a controversial gesture strongly opposed by the trade unions and also by the main association of employers who disliked this interference in their managerial decisionmaking.[56]

In April 1997, the SNC passed a controversial "enterprise revitalization" law allocating 70 billion crowns to keep insolvent enterprises afloat. Under the law, companies selected by a government-appointed committee of economic officials were exempted from bankruptcy proceedings for three years, a clear deviation from free market principles. The engineering sector of the Slovak economy, because it had great difficulty switching its capacity to nonmilitary production since the post-1989 collapse of armaments production, was among the main beneficiaries of the "enterprise revitalization" law. By mid-1997, 14 engineering companies, headed by former Slovak finance minister Julius Toth, applied for revitalization benefits. Toth defended the application by claiming that the assisted companies would help raise Slovak exports. At a meeting of the government's Council on Economic Development in mid-1997, Meciar emphasized the law's goal of preserving current employment levels in the armaments industry. Given the limited range of armaments in which Slovak producers are competitive and the fact that production capacity already exceeded demand, the credibility of the arguments of Toth and Meciar in defense of the kind of government intervention the law provides was questionable.[57]

President Kovac, supported by free market advocates in and out of government and others who thought the law was unconstitutional because of the arbitrary character of the bankruptcy committee's decisionmaking, severely criticized "enterprise revitalization." The law nevertheless was readopted in June.[58]

These developments suggest that Slovak government decisionmaking under Meciar's leadership is still inspired by values and attitudes prevalent in the era of Communist paternalism. They suggest the Slovak government's continuing distrust of the free market as an appropriate mechanism for economic growth and development.

RECOVERY

As the Slovak economy moved toward the free market economy through an extensive though somewhat halting privatization of state-controlled enterprises in the early and mid-1990s, there was a noticeable recovery of economic strength, a kind of economic upswing in terms of annual increases in gross domestic product (GDP). A major consequence of improving economic health was the appearance of a new interest in the environment and the development of public pressure to diminish the pollution caused by decades of Communist dismissiveness and neglect, especially in the area of energy production. Indeed, one of the most serious economic controversies of the mid- and late 1990s in Slovakia centered on the development of nuclear power plants and their negative impact on the country's already troubled environment.

An Economic Upswing

By the mid-1990s, there was much evidence of a steady improvement in Slovakia's overall economic health. Gross Domestic Product (GDP) increased, and rates of unemployment and inflation declined. There was also an expansion of foreign investment. By mid-1997, advances and achievements in these areas made Slovakia look good not only in an absolute sense but also when compared with economic development in its neighbors. Moreover, Slovakia received some recognition of its success from the IMF.

Increasing GDP. In 1994, real gross domestic product increased by 4.8 percent after declining by 14.5 percent in 1991, by 2.4 percent in 1992, by 4.1 percent in 1993, and by about 4.3 percent in 1994. Although in 1993 industrial production had declined by 13.5 percent, compared with 1992, in 1994 it increased by 6.4 percent.[59] During 1995, the country's GDP grew 7.4 percent from the previous year, while industrial output grew by 8.3 percent.[60] In 1996, the GDP was an impressive 7 percent, with Slovakia recording the highest rate of annual GDP growth of any of the mainstream central and East European economies, even more than officially anticipated.[61]

Decline of Inflation and Reduction of Budget Deficits. In the early 1990s, poor management, government interference in the economy, and huge spending to keep outdated industrial enterprises functioning and pay for an extensive social net provoked inflation. But, by the mid-1990s, with better controls, in particular a valued-added tax (VAT) imposed in January 1994 and a 10 percent devaluation of the crown in June, the annual rate of inflation at 23 percent in 1993 began to decline. The VAT, in addition to raising revenue, slowed demand and relieved pressure on prices. The devaluation also gave Slovak exports a boost, which eased unemployment and provided the country with additional foreign exchange.[62]

The decline of inflation continued into 1994, with the annual rate at 15.5 percent in March and at 14.6 percent in June. By the end of the year it was down to 12 percent.[63] And in 1995, there was a further decline to 6.2 percent, partly because the Slovak central bank limited the money supply, despite a negative impact on living standards.[64] By the end of 1996, Slovakia was the region's low inflation country. Consumer prices in September 1996 increased at only a 5.2 percent annual rate, despite an increase of retail sales by 14.3 percent in the first half of the year. Several factors were responsible for the government's continuing success in controlling inflation in 1997, in particular a reduction in the VAT rate, a temporary suspension of import duties on small automobiles, and the introduction of public and private sector wage controls.[65]

Unemployment Stabilizes. After 1994, the rate of unemployment stabilized at about 15 percent.[66] By the end of October 1996, it was down to 12.23 percent, though it was still above rates in Hungary and the Czech Republic.[67] Unemployment continued to decline, given Slovakia's present growth of GDP at about 4 percent, its highly trained labor force, and good supporting infrastructure. One thing the Communists did leave Slovakia was a good transportation system. However, by early 1998, Slovakia still had a 12 to 13 percent rate characterized by severe regional disparities, with unemployment in Bratislava as low as 5 percent, compared with a 25 percent rate in many predominantly agricultural towns in the south and east of the country.[68]

Expansion of Foreign Investment. In the mid-1990s, foreign investors began to figure out that the Slovak economy in fact was doing better than at any time in the past. In early 1994, foreign investment rose by 6.7 percent, with the largest share coming from Austria and Germany.[69] By the end of 1996, Austria ranked first, with a 22 percent stake in overall foreign investment. Germany was second, with a 20 percent stake, and the Czech Republic was third with a 15.5 percent stake. Four other large investing countries were the United States, Britain, France, and the Netherlands, each having invested at least 1 billion Slovak crowns. The most important foreign companies investing in Slovakia by the end of 1996 were America's K-Mart and Germany's Volkswagen.[70]

Western capital mostly benefitted Bratislava, where unemployment consequently has been mild, running at about 6 percent a year; in rural sections of the country, the rate is over 20 percent. Slovakia still lags way behind the Czech Republic, Poland, and Hungary in receiving foreign investment largely because of fear about the country's political stability and uncertainty about Meciar's commitment to free market reform.[71]

Improved Comparative Standing. In the mid to late 1990s, Slovak economic development, when compared with that of its neighbors, was good. Its unemployment rate, though higher than that in the Czech Republic, was lower than levels in Poland and Hungary and even lower than levels in some West European countries like Portugal and Greece. Moreover, Slovak economic growth rates in 1994 and 1995 were actually higher than those in the Czech Republic.[72]

External Recognition of Economic Progress. The IMF acknowledged Slovakia's efforts at economic reform. When Moravcik was prime minister in mid-1994, it approved a loan of $263 million for Slovakia's economic renewal and general stabilization.[73] However, when Meciar returned to power after the October 1994 parliamentary elections and privatization slowed down, the IMF proceeded cautiously. Since 1995 the IMF has linked further credit to a curtailment of government expenditures and a sustained reduction of the budget deficit. In 1995, concerned that these constraints would have a negative impact on the safety net he promised voters to maintain to ease the hardships accompanying free market reforms, Meciar refused to accommodate IMF requests to raise the retirement age from the present 60 for men and 53–57 for women and to reduce family benefit payments. He bragged to the Slovak public that Slovakia's neighbors seemed to have raised the retirement age and that Slovakia in 1997 was ahead of them in terms of increased pensions and other benefits.[74]

The Social Net Continues. Meciar was determined for political and ideological reasons to preserve a good portion of the social net inherited from the Communists. In this, Meciar had broad support. Even the centrist reformer Moravcik, during his brief tenure as prime minister from March to September 1994, was sympathetic to the preservation of a social net. In June 1994 his government increased pension payments.[75] Meciar knew most Slovak voters counted on the government to assure them at least a minimum level of material well-being. He also knew that sensitivity to the hardships accompanying free market reforms, such as the retreat from the full-employment policies of the Communists, was essential to his popularity and that of his MDS.[76] At the same time, his concern for the well-being of Slovak workers derived also from his Marxist background and his conviction that the state did have a moral responsibility to cushion the effects of change whatever the costs.[77]

Energy and the Environment

Throughout the 1990s an important part of Slovak economic recovery involved the generation of sufficient energy to sustain industrial growth, and its impact on the environment. Although Meciar and the Slovak leadership threaded their way through many of the economic dislocations raised by the former Communist regime, they have yet to come to grips with the economic and environmental costs of energy. Slovakia is not unlike other ex-Communist countries in central and Eastern Europe in its search for an affordable power supply. Like the rest of Europe, it does not have enough energy resources. Beyond an inadequacy of fuel sources, the country suffers from the Communist legacies of wastefulness and ineptitude in the management of energy and other resources. Apart from contributing to pollution because of their obsession with pollution-causing heavy industries, such as coal mines and steel mills, the Communists used twice as much in resources as the West to produce a unit of industrial output and made no effort to conserve fuel by improving technology. Moreover, as a general rule the Communists paid little attention to pollution and considered information about its growth a state secret. When they left office at the end of 1989, many parts of Slovakia were heavily polluted as the result of acid rain, the use of brown coal, and the unfettered emission of pollutants by iron, steel, aluminum, and chemicals industries whose pollution was worsened by their location in mountain valleys where pollutants were trapped.[78]

In any event, Communist leaders of Slovakia and other central and Eastern European countries looked to nuclear energy as a panacea. The Soviet Union provided them with the material and technology to build nuclear power plants. But Soviet nuclear technology was primitive, especially when concerned with safety, and poorly applied to the construction and management of nuclear power plants the USSR helped build. There was and continues to be a lot of opposition abroad as well as within Slovakia to the completion of the Soviet-designed nuclear power plant at Mochovce in the center of the country. Construction of the plant in Mochovce was first approved by the Czechoslovak government in 1978; and construction began in the early 1980s and stopped in 1991 for lack of funds. Reactor units one and two were 90 percent and 75 percent completed while reactor units three and four were only 50 percent completed.[79]

In addition to this almost-completed plant, there are others in western Slovakia in operation but already obsolete and dangerous, and the Slovak government would like to close them down. They were built with outdated Soviet technology and managed by inept Communist bureaucrats. These plants in western Slovakia continue to operate even though in 1994 French and German utilities joined with the state-owned Slovak Electricity Enterprise to resume, update and improve with western technology, and complete construction of the Mochovce project, with financial help from the European Bank for Reconstruction and Development.[80]

There was much anxiety about completing the new project at Mochovce. The plant was to use an untested system to contain radiation leaks that raised fears about its safety.[81] Opposition from Austria to the completion of the project increased in 1995. Mochovce is only 190 kilometers away from Vienna, and the Austrian government was terrified by the possibility of another Chernobyl-like tragedy on its doorstep. Antinuclear sentiment is very strong in Austria. Partly because of Austrian opposition, Germany withdrew from the consortium financing the completion of the project, and other Western help evaporated.[82]

Opposition to the project was fueled also by a report from the World Bank on the environmental impact and financial costs of the project. The report pointed out that while some concerns about safety were addressed by the construction of reactors with up-to-date technology, especially with regard to the working of an emergency cooling system, the reactors were still not in the same class in the matter of safety with reactors in Western nuclear energy plants. The Bank also concluded that hazards to safety remained. They involved the cooling systems. There was a risk of fires, flooding, and earthquake damage. There were also significant environmental concerns such as the safe disposal of the plant's nuclear waste. The biggest concern was the adequacy of containment procedures in the event of a Chernobyl-like meltdown. All this suggested that the project could not meet the Bank's own conditions.[83]

In the meantime Russia saw an opportunity to show how Soviet-designed nuclear stations could be upgraded to Western standards. In 1995, the Kremlin invested the equivalent of $150 million in the Mochovce project. In addition the Czech engineering firm Skoda Praha expressed interest in helping to complete the project. This offer did not materialize, because of the uncertainty of getting the project completed according to Western standards and in the face of the unrelenting opposition of Austria, which gained support from Denmark, Norway, Holland, Portugal, and Greece. The management of Skoda Praha also was sensitive to European and more recently American opposition to the completion of Mochovce.[84]

Meciar nevertheless wanted to complete the project, partly for reasons of national pride and partly because Slovakia needed an abundant source of cheap energy, especially since one of the old plants at Bohunice was being phased out of operation. Meciar also imagined the day when Slovakia would export energy. Moreover, he thought he could capitalize on the West's concern about allowing Slovakia to increase its dependence on Russian sources of energy.

Limits and Obstacles to Recovery

During 1997, Slovak economic recovery had certain weak spots. Whereas GDP growth was driven in 1995 by strong industrial production and export growth, in 1996 and early 1997 it was the result of consumer spending encouraged by generous wage settlements and by public spending that the Meciar government had decided to curtail in order to discourage a growth in inflation. In 1997—and presumably this will be the case in the remainder of the 1990s—Meciar faced the task of balancing increases in private consumption, to allow an improvement in living conditions, with concerns about inflation and efforts to limit it. In 1997, he opted to control consumer spending by wage controls and reduced government spending on social services.[85]

Meanwhile, in 1996 and early 1997, another obstacle to the country's economic recovery was stagnation in industrial production a result of weak foreign demand and the high interest rates, charged as a means of controlling inflation, that discouraged investment. The production of the country's leading industries—petroleum, steel, chemicals, and transportation equipment—and construction were falling by the spring of 1997. Indeed, in 1997 and for the foreseeable future, a major drag on the Slovak economy would continue to be the difficulty of expanding exports to traditional markets in the east, mainly Russia, where there has been economic turmoil, and in the West, where the inferior quality of Slovak goods weakens their competitiveness in comparison with Western manufactures.[86]

Slovak entrepreneurs continue to have problems setting up joint ventures with foreign producers, partly because of politics, notably Meciar's continuing suspicion of foreign investors in Slovakia's economy. For example, in the beginning of the summer of 1997, Meciar's government discouraged Toyota from setting up its first central European manufacturing facilities in cooperation with VSZ, Slovakia's leading producer of flat-rolled steel products. The Toyota deal would have allowed Slovakia to diversify and expand its exports with a product that would not have to be finished abroad and would have benefitted Toyota by providing it with a talented low-cost labor pool.[87]

Finally, although the flooding of rivers in central Europe during the summer of 1997, which wreaked havoc in Poland and the Czech Republic, did less damage to Slovakia, the western part of the country suffered and required a diversion of funds from the Ministry of Public Works and Construction. The Zilina district and areas along the Moravia River on the border with the Czech Republic were hardest hit. According to preliminary estimates available in the fall of 1997, property damage amounted to 4.2 billion crowns, with damage to agriculture accounting for roughly half this amount. Damage to homes and personal property was estimated at 135 million crowns. The Bratislava government agreed to assist property owners, whose losses exceeded 100,000 crowns, by giving each one-time payments of 30,000 crowns. At the same time the government had to appropriate money for the repair of damaged infrastructure, in particular reservoirs, roads, and levies.[88]

CONCLUSIONS

Post-independence Slovakia has made great strides in the areas of economic reform and recovery. Seventy-nine percent of the country's GDP now comes from the private sector, and there is abundant evidence of steady and substantial economic growth and development.

There is still a large gap between what Slovak voters expect and what they now have. Improvement of living conditions has been the number-one issue in elections. It also is true that an overwhelming majority of Slovaks, like everybody else in central and Eastern Europe, want change without pain, or at least with pain that is minimal and bearable. However, the more the Slovak governments of both Meciar and Moravcik tried to minimize the pain of economic change, the slower they were obliged to proceed.

Complicating the processes of reform and recovery are a variety of circumstances not unlike those that have slowed change in Slovakia's neighbors, notably Poland, Hungary, and the Czech Republic. The most serious is an apparent obsession of the Meciar leadership with obtaining personal gain from privatization. Since both government and voters already had reservations about abandoning government control and introducing free enterprise throughout the country's economic life, the corruption has further undermined public faith in reform and increased skepticism about the real extent of recovery. With unemployment still persistent, the negative psychological as well as material consequences of reform continue to affect Slovak workers and cause them to be fearful of further change.

Meciar, as the leader of Slovakia with only a brief interruption since it became independent on December 31, 1992, must bear much of the responsibility for the tardiness of economic reform and recovery and for the failure of the economy to deliver the kind of improvement in living conditions Slovak voters expected after independence. Other reasons why Slovakia has lagged behind Poland, Hungary, and the Czech Republic in achieving economic health, however, have to do with the inevitably harsh consequences of freeing up a highly controlled, paternalistic economy. For the moment it seems that many Slovaks are willing to trade a speedy achievement of the level of material well-being it is said free market reforms will bring them for a gradual rate of change that will assure at least some of the stability, certainty, and predictability they had in the Communist era.

NOTES

1. Jan S. Prybyla, "The Road from Socialism: Why, Where, What, and How," *Problems of Communism* (January–February 1991), pp. 2, 7–8.

2. Stephen Kinzer, "2-Year-Old Slovakia Toddling toward Democracy," *New York Times* (hereafter cited as *NYT*) (March 10, 1995); see also Sharon Fisher, "Economic Developments in the Newly Independent Slovakia." *Radio Free Europe/Radio Liberty Research Report* (hereafter cited as *RFE/RL Research Report*), vol. 2, no. 30 (July 30, 1993), pp. 42–48.

3. Sharon Fisher, "The Slovak Economy: Signs of Recovery," *RFE/RL Research Report*, vol. 3, no. 33 (August 26, 1994), p. 64.

4. Otto Ulc, "The Bumpy Road of Czechoslovakia's Velvet Revolution," *Problems of Communism*, vol. 41, no. 3 (May–June 1992), pp. 24–25; Bernard Wheaton and Zdenek Kavan, *The Velvet Revolution 1989–1991* (Boulder, Colo.: Westview Press, 1992), pp. 156–157.

5. Carol Skalnik Leff, *The Czech and Slovak Republics: Nation versus State* (Boulder, Colo.: Westview Press, 1997), p. 192; see also Eve Marikova Leeds, "Voucher Privatization in Czechoslovakia," *Comparative Economic Studies*, vol. 35 (Fall 1993), pp. 19–23.

6. Ibid.

7. Gale Stokes, *The Walls Came Tumbling Down: The Collapse of Communism in Eastern Europe* (New York: Oxford University Press, 1993), pp. 198–199.

8. Sharon Fisher, "Economic Developments in the Newly Independent Slovakia," p. 46.

9. *The Europa World Yearbook 1995* (Rochester, Kent, U.K.: Europa Publications, Ltd., 1995) (hereafter cited as *EWY 1995* p. 2712; see also "Pace of Privatization Called 'Outright Tragic,'" U.S. Department of State, *Foreign Broadcast Information Service Daily Report Eastern Europe* (hereafter cited as *FBIS-EEU*), 93-010 (January 15, 1993), p.15; 93-216 (November 10, 1993), p. 18.

10. Leff, *Czech and Slovak Republics*, p. 194; Fisher, "Slovak Economy," p. 64.

11. Leff, *Czech and Slovak Republics*, p. 194; see also "Slovakia, Rough Rider," *LN/EL*, Eastern Europe TXTEE, Euromoney Central European (May 29, 1996).

12. U.S. Department of State, *Country Reports on Human Rights Practices for 1995: Report Submitted to the Committee on International Relations, U.S. House of Representatives and the Committee on Foreign Relations U.S. Senate April 1996,* "Slovakia" (Washington, D.C.: U.S. Government Printing Office, 1996), p. 1021.

13. "Slovakia, Rough Rider," *LN/EL*, Eastern Europe TXTEE, Euromoney Central European (May 29, 1996); The Economist Intelligence Unit, *Country Report: Slovakia 1997/1998 Prospect* (London: The Unit, 1998).

14. "Cabinet Approves Privatization Schedule for 1997," *Narodna Obrada* (Bratislava, May 7, 1997), *LN/EL*, Eastern Europe TXTEE, BBC Monitoring Service: Eastern Europe (May 15, 1997); see also The Economist Intelligence Unit, *Country Report: Slovakia*, Third Quarter 1997 (London: The Unit, 1997), on CD-ROM.

15. "Premier Urges Completion of Privatization of Banks," Radio 1 (Bratislava, February 28, 1997), *LN/EL*, Eastern Europe TXTEE, BBC Monitoring Service: Eastern Europe (March 3, 1997).

16. "Slovak Parliament Approves Compromise over Bank Privatization," *CTK* (Bratislava, March 12, 1997), *LN/EL*, Eastern Europe TXTEE, CSTK Ecoservice (March 12, 1997).

17. "Parliament Freezes Privatization of Four Major Banks until 2003," *CTK News Agency* (Prague, February 13, 1997), *LN/EL*, Eastern Europe TXTEE, BBC Monitoring Service: Eastern Europe (February 20, 1997).

18. "Premier Interviewed on Bank Privatization, NATO Referendum," *1 Radio* (Bratislava, February 14, 1997), *LN/EL*, Eastern Europe TXTEE, BBC Monitoring Service: Eastern Europe (February 17, 1997).

19. Ibid.

20. Peter Javurek, "Slovak Party Says Banking Row May Bring Early Poll," Reuters News Service (Bratislava, February 21, 1997), *LN/EL*, Reuters Textline, Reuters News Service—CIS and Eastern Europe (February 21, 1997).

21. "Cabinet Hostage to Privatization Lobby - Opposition Leader (Says)," *CTK News Agency* (Prague, February 27, 1997), *LN/EL*, Eastern Europe TXTEE, BBC Monitoring Service: Eastern Europe (March 1, 1997).

22. "Central Bank against Complete Sell-off of Four Biggest Banks," *TASR News Agency* (Bratislava, February 27, 1997), *LN/EL*, Eastern Europe TXTEE, BBC Monitoring Service: Eastern Europe (March 6, 1997).

23. "NBS Wants Bank to Recover before Privatization," *CTK News Agency* (February 26, 1997), *LN/EL*, Eastern Europe TXTEE, CSTK Ecoservice (February 26, 1997).

24. Ibid.

25. "Slovak Parliament Approves New Bank Privatization," Reuters (Bratislava, March 12, 1997), *LN/EL*, Reuters Textline, Reuters News Service (March 12, 1997).

26. "Slovak Parliament Approves Compromise over Bank Privatization," *CTK* (Bratislava, March 12, 1997), *LN/EL*, Eastern Europe TXTEE, CSTK Ecoservice (March 12, 1997).

27. "Premier Reaffirms Need for Bank Privatization," *TASR News Agency* (Bratislava, March 6, 1997), *LN/EL*, Eastern Europe TXTEE, BBC Monitoring Service (March 13, 1997).

28. Sharon Fisher, "Church Restitution Law Passed in Slovakia," *RFE/RL Research Report*, vol. 2, no. 46 (November 19, 1993), pp. 51, 53.

29. Ibid.

30. Ibid.

31. Ibid.

32. Ibid.

33. Fisher, "Economic Developments," p. 46.

34. "Slovak Is Balking at Privatization," *NYT* (February 13, 1994).

35. "Eastern Europe Sings Currency Blues: Slovakia—To Devalue or Not," *International Herald Tribune* (November 12, 1996); see also Leff, *Czech and Slovak Republics*, p. 262.

36. "Pace of Privatization Called 'Outright Tragic,'" *FBIS-EEU* 93-010 (January 15, 1993), p. 15.

37. "Slovakia, Rough Rider," *LN/EL*, Eastern Europe TXTEE, Euromoney Central European (May 29, 1996).

38. Leff, *Czech and Slovak Republics*, p. 262.

39. Fisher, "Slovak Economy," p. 64.

40. Peter Javurek, "World Bank Report Says Slovak Policy EU Barrier," Reuters News Service (Bratislava, December 18, 1996), *LN/EL*, Reuters Textline, Reuters News Service CIS—Eastern Europe (December 18, 1996).

41. "Slovakia, Rough Rider," *LN/EL*, Eastern Europe TXTEE, Euromoney Central European (May 29, 1996).

42. Fisher, "Economic Developments," p. 43; see also "Study Assesses State of Economy," *FBIS-EEU* 94-068 (April 8, 1994), pp. 8–9.

43. Fisher, "Slovak Economy," p. 60.

44. "Study Assesses State of Economy," pp. 8–9; see also Jane Perlez, "After the Uncoupling Slovakia Seems Unnerved," *NYT* (July 30, 1993).

45. See Sharon Fisher, "The Slovak Arms Industry," *RFE/RL Research Report*, vol. 2, no. 38 (September 24, 1993), pp. 34–39.

46. Leff, *Czech and Slovak Republics*, p. 197; Sharon Wolchik, "Democratization and Political Participation in Slovakia," in Karen Dawisha and Bruce Parrott (eds.), *The Consolidation of Democracy in East-Central Europe* (Cambridge, U.K.: Cambridge University Press, 1997), p. 225.

47. Leff, *Czech and Slovak Republics*, p. 201

48. Ibid., p. 194; Fisher, "The Slovak Economy," p. 64; "Privatization Rejected by Most Slovaks—Poll," Czech News Agency (CTK) (Bratislava, October 23, 1997), *LN/EL* General News, CTK National News Wire (October 23, 1997).

49. Leff, *Czech and Slovak Republics*, p. 194; see also "Slovak Is Balking at Privatization."

50. Fisher, "Slovak Economy," p. 63.

51. Ibid.

52. Sharon Fisher, "Meciar Retains Control of the Political Scene," *Transition*, vol. 2, no. 16 (August 9, 1996), pp. 32–36.

53. Ibid.

54. "IBRD Warns Slovakia on Discrimination against Foreign Investors," *CTK News Agency* (Bratislava, December 18, 1996), *LN/EL*, Eastern Europe TXTEE, CSTK Ecoservice (December 18, 1996).

55. U.S. Department of State, *Country Reports on Human Rights Practices for 1996: Report Submitted to the Committee on International Relations, U.S. House of Representatives and the Committee on Foreign Relations U.S. Senate February 1997*, "Slovakia" (Washington, D.C.: U.S. Government Printing Office, 1997), p. 1115.

56. The Economist Intelligence Unit, *Country Report: Slovakia*, Third quarter, 1997 (London: The Unit, 1997) on CD-ROM.

57. Ibid.; while revitalization is taking place, according to the law, the enterprise in question may not pay dividends; must accept limitations on asset management;

provide an audited balance sheet annually to the ministry responsible for supervising it; and pay a committee-appointed commissioner who will oversee implementation of the revitalization plan. The law also stipulated that there is no judicial or administrative recourse for appeals against committee decisions. See The Economist Intelligence Unit, *Country Report: Slovakia 1997/1998 Prospect* (London: The Unit, 1997) on CD-ROM.

58. The Economist Intelligence Unit, *Country Report: Slovakia*, Third quarter, 1997 (London: The Unit, 1997) on CD-ROM.

59. *EWY 1995*, p. 2712; for a discussion of Slovak economic improvement see Fisher, "Slovak Economy," pp. 58-65.

60. "Slovakia: To Devalue or Not?"

61. Dean Calbreath, "While Slovakia Grows, Its Companies Don't," *Central and Eastern Europe Report*, vol. 5, no. 6 (July–August, 1997), p. 18; Michael Wyzan and Ben Slay, "Central, Eastern and Southeastern Europe's Year of Recovery," *Transition*, vol. 3, no. 2 (February 7, 1997), p. 59.

62. Fisher, "Slovak Economy," p. 59.

63. Ibid.

64. *Hilfe Country Report — Slovakia*: Comment, Analyses, Statistics, Tables, Forecasts (July 1996), available on-line, *Lexis-Nexis*, Library: Europe, File, Quest Economy Database: Janet Mathews Information Services (1996); hereafter cited as *Hilfe Country Report*, "Slovakia" (July 1996), *LN/EL*, Quest Economy Database, JMIS (1996).

65. Wyzan and Slay, "Central, Eastern, and Southeastern Europe's Year of Recovery," p. 60; The Economist Intelligence Unit, *Country Report: Slovakia 1997/1998 Prospect* (London: The Unit, 1998).

66. Fisher, "Slovak Economy," p. 60.

67. "Unemployment Rate Reaches 13.73%," *CTK News Agency* (Bratislava, February 16, 1996), "Slovak Unemployment at 12.23% in September," *CTK News Agency* (Bratislava, October 30, 1996), Eastern Europe TXTEE, CSTK Ecoservice (February 19, 1996; October 30, 1996, respectively); see Wyzan and Slay, "Central, Eastern, and Southeastern Europe's Year of Recovery," p. 60.

68. Wyzan and Slay, "Central, Eastern, and Southeastern Europe's Year of Recovery," p. 60; The Economist Intelligence Unit, *Country Report: Slovakia 1997/1998 Prospect* (London: The Unit, 1998) on CD-ROM.

69. Fisher, "Slovak Economy," pp. 62–63.

70. "Foreign Investment…in Slovakia at End of September (1996)," *CTK News Agency* (Bratislava, November 22, 1996), *LN/EL*, Eastern Europe TXTEE, CSTK Ecoservice (November 22, 1996).

71. Fisher, "Slovak Economy," pp. 62–63.

72. Leff, *Czech and Slovak Republics*, p. 188.

73. Fisher, "Slovak Economy," pp. 62–63.

74. "Premier Says Life Is Good in Slovakia," *Radio 1* (Bratislava, March 7, 1997), *LN/EL*, Eastern Europe TXTEE, BBC Monitoring Service: Eastern Europe (March 11, 1997).

75. Fisher, "Slovak Economy," p. 61.

76. See "Poll on Views after Fall of Communism," *FBIS-EEU* 94-015 (January 24, 1994), p. 22.

77. *Hilfe Country Report*, "Slovakia" (July 1996), *LN/EL*, Quest Economy Database, JMIS (1996).

78. Leff, *Czech and Slovak Republics*, pp. 205–207; The Economist Intelligence Unit, *Country Report: Slovakia 1997/1998 Prospect* (London: The Unit, 1998) on CD-ROM.

79. Leah D. Wedmore, "The Political Costs of Mochovce," *Transition*, vol. 1, no. 10 (June 23, 1995), pp. 46–47.

80. Ibid.

81. Ibid.

82. Ibid., pp. 49–50.

83. Ibid.

84. Ibid.

85. The Economist Intelligence Unit, *Country Report: Slovakia*, Third quarter, 1997 (London: The Unit, 1997), on CD-ROM.

86. Ibid.

87. John Gould and Sona Szomolanyi, "Bridging the Chasm in Slovakia," *Transitions*, vol. 4, no. 6 (November 1997), pp. 74–75.

88. The Economist Intelligence Unit, *Country Report: Slovakia*, Third quarter, 1997 (London: The Unit, 1997), on CD-ROM.

5

Societal Democratization

Setbacks and Advances

Setbacks to societal democratization in post-independence Slovakia concern mainly the country's ethnic minorities, which have complained about discrimination. In addition, Slovak women endure prejudice in public life that compromises their well-being. In addition, there has been a disturbing resurgence of anti-Semitism, apparently part of a continuing nostalgia for Slovakia's fascist past that seems incongruous with and subversive of the new democratic environment that most Slovaks seem to enjoy and want to preserve. Finally, the Slovak public has become worried about a decline of personal security as a result of increasingly frequent outbreaks of crime and violence, especially in neighborhoods where economic hardship has had the greatest impact. While these problems have roots in the Communist past, they became more dangerous to the stability and harmony of Slovak society in the post-independence era of the mid-and late 1990s.

Balanced against these negative aspects of post-independence Slovak society are some advances that augur well for democratization. The Slovak Catholic Church has been willing to speak out against the government's authoritarian style. Another development is a new civic activism in which increasing numbers of Slovak citizens are getting involved in politics to articulate issues of special interest to them, especially government policies that seem to badger and coerce them in ways reminiscent of the Communist dictatorship. Also, a conspicuously nonpolitical military has been an advantage for Slovak democratic development.

ETHNIC MINORITIES

The most serious threat to Slovak social peace comes from the Slovak government's discriminatory treatment of its ethnic minorities, especially the Hungarian community, which is the largest non-Slovak ethnic group at about 10.7 percent of the country's total population. Smaller minorities, like the Roma people, with about 1.5 percent of the total national population, and Ruthenians, many of whom are of Ukrainian extraction, also complain about official discrimination.

Discrimination occurs despite the fact that the Slovak constitution provides minority groups with the right to develop their own culture, receive information and education in their mother tongue, and participate in decisionmaking in matters affecting them. Discrimination threatens the stability of post-independence Slovakia and certainly has raised questions about the country's overall commitment to Western-style democracy.

The Hungarian Minority

Following the collapse of Communist rule and the introduction of a pluralistic parliamentary democracy in the Czech Republic and Slovakia, the Hungarian minority asked the Slovak government in Bratislava for recognition of "collective rights." These included increased control over local administration and respect for the Hungarian cultural identity, which meant the freedom of Hungarians as a community to use their language in local administration and in local schools in towns and villages where they were in the majority. Contending that they were not migrants, the Hungarians pointed out that the land they inhabited has been theirs for centuries. It was only by accident that they found themselves no longer under Hungarian but Czechoslovak rule after World War I. Their view is that border shifts, such as those delineated in the 1920 Treaty of Trianon ending World War I that assigned territory with Hungarian populations to some of Hungary's neighbors, in particular to Czechoslovakia, Romania, and Yugoslavia, should not deprive them of their cultural identity simply because foreign diplomats arbitrarily changed the administrative jurisdiction under which they lived.[1]

In the early 1990s, Hungarian anxiety about the future increased with discussions surrounding the Slovak government's proposed minorities program put forward in June 1992, just before the Czech-Slovak split. Although the program promised full respect for minority rights in accordance with international norms, members of the Slovak republic parliament, called the Slovak National Council (SNC), representing the Hungarian community, said that the sections of the program dealing with minority rights were much too general, hard to monitor, and lacking in obligations to observe international agreements. These Hungarian deputies asked Slovak Prime Minister Vladimir Meciar for autonomy in cultural affairs, which meant rights to use their language in public places and to control the schools in communities where Hungarian citizens were in the majority. If the Hungarian community received cultural autonomy, they said, they would support Meciar's coalition.[2] At the same time, the Hungarian parties in the SNC opposed the split of the country and Slovakia's independence when the Declaration of Sovereignty came up for a vote on July 17, 1992. Fearing that the Hungarian community would suffer if there were no longer any pressure on Slovak leaders from the federal government in Prague to respect its rights and those of other minority groups in Slovakia, some Hungarian deputies in the SNC favored a referendum on the issue of separation of the two large ethnic communities that made up the Czechoslovak state, arguing that the Slovak people directly should pass on sovereignty, not their representatives. Other Hungarian deputies said that the sovereignty declaration was incompatible with the Czechoslovak constitution. What clearly was of most concern to the Hungarian politicians, however, was what would happen to Hungarian-speaking people as a distinct cultural community once Slovakia was independent.[3]

Hungarian deputies in the SNC, therefore, were critical of the proposed new Slovak constitution. They focused on Article 6, which stipulated that the Slovak language was the state language on the territory of Slovakia and that the use of other languages in official dealings is to be regulated by a special law. This stipulation, they believed, discouraged bilingualism.[4] They also balked over a clause in Article 6, which seemed to preclude the possibility of future local self-rule. The clause in question said that the exercise of the rights guaranteed by the constitution to "citizens belonging to national minorities and ethnic groups cannot lead to the breakup of the Slovak republic and to discrimination against the rest of the population."[5]

When the new Slovak Constitution was approved on September 1, 1992, Hungarian deputies walked out of the SNC in protest. Their behavior and especially their demand for the nationwide use of more than one language made Meciar think, wrongly so, that they were disloyal and gave him an excuse for denying them any opportunity to loosen Bratislava's strong administrative grip over them.[6] For their part, the Hungarian community not only became determined to obtain a clear, unequivocal endorsement by Bratislava of their cultural rights, but they also renewed demands for increased control over their local administration, especially in education.

During 1993, policies of Meciar's government only added to the Hungarian community's anxiety about their future in an independent Slovak state. The SNC passed laws forbidding bilingual signs on local roads and forbidding the signature of names in birth registers to be in Hungarian. Meciar also refused to create regions based on ethnic principles and obtained legislation establishing new territorial districts stretching from north to south, rather than east to west, that divided the Hungarian community into five administrative units in which they would be outnumbered by Slovaks. The Hungarian community saw a substantial loss of political influence in this gerrymandering of administrative districts.[7]

Hungarian goals were inspired by more than cultural differences. Many of the Hungarian political leaders believed that the Hungarian community would do better economically, especially in regard to attracting foreign investment, if it enjoyed control over its local affairs. Under the Slovak government in Bratislava in 1992 and 1993, the unemployment rate in southeastern Slovakia, where most of the Hungarian minority resided, was much higher than almost everywhere else in the country. In places like Dunakska, Streda, and Komarno, unemployment in 1993 was running at about 19.5 percent versus the much lower rate of a little over 11 percent elsewhere in the country.[8]

Meciar's Opposition to "Collective Rights." Meciar and other Slovak leaders had no intention of changing their policies to grant the Hungarian community demands for "collective rights." Slovak officials, including Meciar, always contended that the Hungarian community already enjoyed rights "on a higher level" than was the case for minorities elsewhere in Europe. Rather, the Slovak government contended that the demands of minorities for rights guaranteeing them cultural, educational, and territorial autonomy threatened the integrity of Slovakia. Slovak officials also said that giving the Hungarian community the cultural autonomy it wanted might lead to the "Magyarization" of Slovaks living in the regions inhabited predominantly by Hungarian-speaking people and could lead eventually to pressure on Slovaks to move out.[9]

Meciar publicly accused the Hungarian deputies in the SNC of making "unrealistic and extremist demands." Any of the forms of self-government the Hungarian community proposed were unacceptable because, he believed, their establishment would lead eventually to separate state administrative systems for the minority and the majority. He also suggested that the Hungarian deputies in the SNC were heavily influenced by the Hungarian government in Budapest, saying that they did not represent the sentiments of the Hungarian community in

Slovakia and that they would not have been elected had it not been for television propaganda from Hungary. He called Hungarian deputies in the Slovak parliament "stooges of Budapest" and blamed them for tension between Slovaks and Hungarians in Slovakia. In 1992 and early 1993, Meciar refused to meet with Hungarian parliamentary deputies belonging to Coexistence and the Hungarian Christian Democratic Movement (HCDM). He said at the time that he would speak only with Hungarians in his own MDS party and in the Democratic Left, people who in his oppinion were not making extreme demands and who wanted a real coexistence between Slovaks and Hungarians.[10]

Bratislava Makes Concessions. Meciar was under intense international pressure, mainly from the Council of Europe and the Republic of Hungary to be conciliatory toward Slovakia's Hungarian-speaking citizens. He wanted to avoid compromising Slovakia's chances of joining Western organizations like the EU and NATO. Moreover, he could not afford to antagonize Hungary, which already was a member of the Council of Europe and could bloc Slovakia's admission to this organization. Accordingly, Meciar made some concessions to the country's minorities to appease his Western critics and to mollify the government in Budapest. On his initiative, on July 7, 1993, the SNC approved a new law allowing minorities to register their names in their mother tongues and stipulating that women of nonethnic Slovak groups were no longer required to use the Slovak feminine suffix "ova" in their surnames. The SNC also amended an earlier discriminatory law limiting land restitution for ethnic Hungarians to 50 hectares by setting a 150-hectare limit for arable land.[11]

To the dismay of the Hungarian politicians in Bratislava, these gestures did not lead to real change in the Bratislava government's behavior, which remained discriminatory and in violation of pledges Slovakia had made to the Conference on Security and Cooperation in Europe (CSCE) to improve its treatment of minorities. For example, Slovak nationalists in July 1993 objected to the new law on names, arguing that it violated the Slovak constitution, which held Slovak as the official language of the Slovak Republic. Meciar then requested President Kovac to return the law to parliament, which he did. Meanwhile Slovak transportation authorities ordered the removal by force if necessary of local road signs in Hungarian, provoking widespread Hungarian complaints. The Slovak Constitutional Court upheld this action, implying that conformity with demands of the CSCE for the accommodation of the Hungarian minority in this and other areas of Slovak life was constitutionally not possible.[12]

The Crisis in Komarno. A crisis in Bratislava's relations with the Hungarian community flared up in the late summer of 1993. It seemed to grow out of the fact that six months after Slovakia's admission to the CSCE, which had been predicated on its protecting the cultural rights of Slovak minorities, the SNC had not passed any protective legislation. Indeed, in mid-December 1993, Pal   Csaky, head of the parliamentary group of the HCDM, complained that the SNC had yet to begin the serious consideration of nationality problems in Slovakia for which he had been asking for over a year and a half.[13]

Frustrated by the delays, an association of Hungarian towns and villages in the area of Zitny Ostrov, and known as ZMOZO, met in December 1993 at Komarno, in southeastern Slovakia and called for the establishment of a province inhabited primarily by Hungarian-speaking people with an independent government, public administration, and a special legal status. The Komarno meeting set January 8, 1994, as the date for another ZMOZO meeting to discuss further how this proposal could be implemented.[14]

Although the Slovak government opposed this second meeting of ZMOZO, it was held as planned on January 8. Three thousand ethnic Hungarians gathered in the Komarno sports stadium. It called on the Bratislava government to be more responsive than it had been to the interests of the Hungarian community, in particular to respect its political influence and the cultural unity of the Hungarian minority.[15] Repeating their demand for a special legal status for areas where Hungarians predominated, the participants criticized the Slovak government's proposed changes in local administration that they believed would marginalize Hungarians. They offered as an alternative the creation in the southern region of the country of either one large or three small administrative units comprised primarily of Hungarian people. They also asked that the Hungarian language become an official language, along with Slovak; that ethnic Hungarians be represented in state bodies in proportion to their population; and that the Hungarian region receive a share of the state budget and of local budgets equivalent to their proportion of the general population. The January 8 meeting, however, was restrained. There was no violence and no inflammatory rhetoric. There was no mention of the words "independence" and "autonomy." Participants affirmed the loyalty of the Hungarian community to Slovakia.[16]

Moreover, shortly afterward local Hungarian politicians in Bratislava backed away from pressuring the government on the autonomy issue. They turned out to be divided over how to proceed further in lobbying the Meciar government for more equitable treatment of the Hungarian community. On the one hand, HCDM parliamentary deputy Bela Bugar argued that there was little chance the Slovak government would ever agree to ethnically based administrative units, simply because no part of the country where Hungarians predominated was in fact ethnically pure; southern Slovakia was "ethnically mixed." In response, Coexistence chairman Miklos Duray argued in favor of ethnically based autonomous administrative units for areas inhabited predominantly by Hungarians. He favored keeping up the pressure on the Slovak leadership for administrative autonomy. Eventually, however, even Duray had softened his rhetoric, saying that his party favored what he termed "self-ruling administration."[17]

Behind this apparent weakening of Hungarian resolve was the reality of determined opposition of the Slovak leadership to any concession to the Hungarian minority that might in some way compromise the country's territorial integrity and internal stability. Moreover, this opposition was in no way mitigated by the conciliatory character of the January 8 ZMOZO assembly. Rather, the Slovak leadership still viewed any demands of the Hungarian community for autonomy as a first step toward the rejoining of southeastern Slovakia to Hungary, a prospect strengthened in the Slovak mind by the nationalistic rhetoric of conservative Hungarian politicians in Budapest like Istvan Csurka, who suggested the possibility of Hungary's reclaiming southern Slovakia, as it had done in 1939.[18]

Furthermore, Hungarian deputies in the SNC had little clout in dealing with the Slovak leadership, nor could they expect the Hungarian government in Budapest to openly support their campaign for minority rights. Indeed, Budapest sent a mixed message to the Hungarian community in Slovakia. Hungarian political leaders showed concern about the well-being of kinsmen living in Slovakia. Hungarian President Arpad Goncz asked Slovak president Kovac to do his best to mediate between the majority and the minority to assure protection of the latter's rights, and Hungarian foreign minister Geza Jeszenszky said publicly in early 1994 that Slovakia should be reorganized administratively into ethnic cantons. Goncz, however, assured Kovac that no high-ranking officials in Hungary questioned the territorial integrity of Slovakia.[19]

Renewal of Interethnic Tensions, 1995-1997. With Meciar back in power following the September 1994 parliamentary elections, no concessions of any significance were made to the Hungarian community to reassure it of its rights as a minority. For his part, Meciar was responding to other public opinion polls that showed a widespread popular prejudice toward Hungarians whom many Slovaks considered "a permanent threat to the language and ethnic sovereignty of Slovaks in their own state." Indeed, Meciar reversed plans of the Moravcik government during its brief tenure in the summer of 1994 to soften central government policies toward the Hungarian community by allowing bilingual identification of many municipalities inhabited predominantly by Hungarian-speaking people partly because of a focus poll conducted in May 1994 had found that 63 percent of Slovaks felt that Hungarians were entitled to bilingual signs in areas where they constituted 50 percent or more of the population. Meciar resumed efforts to weaken the Hungarian national identity in Slovakia, making large cuts in government subsidies to Hungarian cultural organizations. The Slovak ministry of education proposed an "alternative education" plan that sought to introduce use of the Slovak language for the instruction of certain subjects in schools where Hungarian otherwise was the primary language of instruction. When the Hungarians claimed that the plan was inspired by the government's goal of assimilating all Hungarians, the education ministry vigorously objected. Ministry officials pointed out that the initiative was entirely voluntary, that it was only being implemented in a few schools where parents had requested it, and that its real intention was to benefit Hungarian students by giving them the opportunity to strengthen their ability to use the Slovak language, the primary language of business and administration.[20]

The November 1995 Language Law. In November 1995, over the strenuous objections of Hungarian deputies, the Slovak parliament passed a law that required all public employees to speak Slovak and all public ceremonies except weddings to be held in Slovak. The law, enthusiastically supported by *Matica Slovenska*, the ultranationalist Slovak cultural society, mandated that all signs, advertisements, and announcements be made in the state language. The law had support from a broad range of political groups in the parliament, including the PDL and the liberal CDM. Slovak politicians of all ideological positions apparently accepted the position of SNP deputy Melania Kollarikova, who declared, "We must eradicate the use of foreign words from the state media and...cleanse our language of them."[21] Kollarikova and most other Slovak politicians saw the law as a key instrument to promote Slovak national identity, which is apparent in the wording of the law:

> The Slovak Language is the most important characteristic of the Slovak nation, the most valuable part of its cultural heritage, an expression of Slovak sovereignty, and the general means of communication of its citizens, guaranteeing them freedom and equality in dignity and rights on Slovak territory.[22]

Once passed, however, there was some discomfort over the law among those who had helped put it through. The law was of questionable legality, inasmuch as it seemed to contradict article 34 of the Slovak constitution, which gives minorities the right to use their own language in official contacts. Furthermore, it was by no means clear that all or most Slovak voters sympathized with this draconian measure to foster the Slovak language among the country's minorities.[23]

Furthermore, by 1995 there seemed to be a decline in the willingness of Slovak voters to champion extreme nationalist positions, such as the language law, that called for heavy-handed intrusive government policies which struck many as illiberal and even antidemocratic. Finally, it was clear that there would be problems enforcing it. For example, did the law preclude the public use of the Czech language, which would mean dubbing Czech-language movies and television programs presented in Slovakia? Would Slovak opera singers be prosecuted for violating the new law if they sang arias in Italian, French, or German?

In 1996, the Slovak government's response to these questions was a moratorium on prosecution by postponing enforcement until 1997. As a result, by the end of 1996, according to government statistical data, in southern Slovakia both ethnic Hungarians and Slovaks continued to speak Hungarian as much as they did before the November 1995 law, suggesting that seeking linguistic assimilation by legislation in all probability would be futile.[24]

Be that as it may, the law still antagonized and intimidated the Hungarian community not only because of its obvious attack on their language but also because its broadly worded provisions invited an expansion of official Slovak discrimination on all administrative levels. For example, it was, theoretically at least, no longer possible for Hungarians in Slovakia to send a telegram in Hungarian.[25] Hungarians complained that the law in fact did violate minority rights spelled out in Slovakia's own constitution as well as in the Convention on Minority Rights of the Council of Europe.[26]

The law also alarmed the EU and infuriated Budapest. Western leaders made it clear to Meciar that because of his government's failure to respect minority rights and other "problems with democracy" Slovakia would not be among the first group of countries, which included Poland, Hungary, and the Czech Republic, to be invited to join NATO at its summit meeting in Madrid in July 1997. Budapest also protested the language law, with Hungarian president Goncz calling it "an unacceptable step backwards." He also accused Slovakia of violating the European Convention on Human Rights. He said Slovakia had lost its credibility with the West.[27]

In 1996, Hungarian deputies in the Slovak parliament, weary of waiting for the Meciar government to honor a promise to the OSCE to put through a law to protect minority languages, drafted one of their own; but the SNC, dominated by the MDS, refused to act on it.[28] In mid-February 1997, the Slovak government said that "as the right to using minority languages is guaranteed by 32 valid laws, there is no need of passing a special law."[29] Culture Ministry spokeswoman Marta Podhradska declared, "We do not expect to pass a special law in the near future."[30]

Pressure on the Meciar government to enact a law on minority languages increased when the SNC in May 1996 finally ratified a new state treaty with Hungary concluded in 1995 guaranteeing borders, human rights, and the protection of minorities. President Kovac urged the Meciar government to follow through on the provisions of this treaty. During a visit to Budapest in June 1996 he assured Hungarian leaders that a law protecting minority languages would be passed and that Slovakia would respect the rights of its Hungarian-speaking minority in accordance with its treaty obligations.[31]

Throughout the rest of 1996, pressure from Western Europe on Bratislava to guarantee the language rights of minorities continued with veiled and not-so-veiled warnings about Slovakia's isolation if its policies toward minorities did not conform with Western democratic norms. The OSCE in particular kept after the Meciar government to get a minorities language law through the parliament. For example, in early November, Max van de Steel, OSCE High Commissioner for minorities, was in Bratislava telling President Kovac that his office was constantly monitoring developments in Slovakia, especially with regard to the government's treatment of the Hungarian minority. He was critical of the allocation of skimpy state subsidies for cultural, educational, and broadcasting activities for the Hungarian minority, observing that non-Hungarian minorities in Slovakia were receiving more than their fair share when compared with their Hungarian compatriots.[32]

More pressure from Western Europe on Meciar's government to address the minorities language issue continued into 1997. On February 13, European Commissioner Hags van den Broke told a member of the Slovak parliament during a visit to Brussels that he was surprised that the Slovak government had not yet submitted a bill on the use of ethnic minority languages.[33] Several days later, on the 18th, SNP official Jozef Prokes, who was deputy chairman of the parliamentary foreign affairs committee, said on Slovak television that the government in fact was preparing a law on minority languages. But in July 1997 an ethnic Hungarian teacher, Alexander Toth, reportedly was fired for using a report card in both Slovak and Hungarian.[34] But by mid-1997 the Slovak government still had not put through a minorities language law.

In early 1997 the three major Hungarian parties, Coexistence, the Hungarian Civic Party, and the HCDM, became more aggressive in promoting bilingualism in Slovakia. For example, at the end of February the three parties formed a coordinating committee in Bratislava to help deal with some practical consequences for the Hungarian community of the ban on bilingualism. This committee was to provide legal aid to every Hungarian teacher and parent in Slovakia who had grievances against the authorities arising out of the ban or was threatened for refusal to issue or accept school reports in the Slovak language.[35]

The Meciar government responded harshly to these developments, strengthening its enforcement of the language law. In May 1997 the Ministry of Education announced that it would henceforth enforce strongly an earlier decision to abolish the 76-year-old practice of issuing bilingual grade reports in Hungarian language schools. Seventy thousand parents immediately protested, but headmasters who refused to implement this order were promptly fired. In addition, the government moved quickly to make sure that their replacements would obey the new requirement by stipulating that students without an official "Slovak only" grade report would not be allowed to pursue higher education. At the same time, in a similar vein, the ministry indicated that the number of first-year classes at Hungarian-language secondary schools would be cut in half in the coming academic year. The ministry also ruled that the only university that trained ethnic Hungarian teachers would no longer provide such training.[36]

The Flap over Loyalty. Meanwhile another event escalated tensions between the Hungarian community and the Slovak government. The Meciar government demanded in May 1996 that the Hungarian political parties, that is, Coexistence, the HCDM, and the Hungarian Civic Party (HCP), make a new and explicit pledge of loyalty to Slovakia.[37] The loyalty pledge was inspired by Meciar's conviction that political representatives of the Hungarian community still favored separatism and annexation by the Republic of Hungary. Statements by Miklos Duray of Coexistence that the Hungarian minority was getting ready to declare unilateral autonomy heightened Meciar's anxieties.[38]

Hungarian politicians in Bratislava reacted angrily to the idea of a loyalty pledge. HCP leader Laszlo Nagy publicly reminded the Slovak government of how the Hungarian parties in Slovakia so often had reiterated their loyalty to the Slovak Republic, its government, and its territorial configuration. But, if a formal declaration were needed, he continued, it would be forthcoming, provided that the Slovak government reciprocated with a formal guarantee of minority rights and with adoption of a law on the use of minority languages.[39]

Jozef Kvarda, deputy chairman of the Coexistence Movement, was less conciliatory, saying loyalty could not be "enforced" but was rather the result of a process in which "the state pursues policies acceptable to the citizens." In such situations, he argued, the issue of loyalty does not arise; popular support of the state is "natural." Kvarda suggested that the Slovak government's demand for a declaration of loyalty by the Hungarian parties was not a "standard" pattern of behavior in international life, nor was it justified on the basis of the past behavior of Hungarian political parties in Slovakia.[40]

The July 1996 Budapest Conference. Relations between the Slovak government and the Hungarian community deteriorated further when in July 1996 a conference of foreign Hungarian parties including those from Slovakia convened in Budapest to discuss issues of common concern, such as minority rights. The Hungarian parties from Slovakia and from other countries with a Hungarian minority were receptive to the idea of a conference in Budapest to discuss with Hungarian Republic leaders their concern that once Hungary was integrated in NATO it would no longer be willing to address the problems of Hungarian minority communities in neighboring countries. The conference was held by the Hungarian Ministry of Foreign Affairs; the Slovak leadership assumed that the Hungarian government originated the idea. This was a reasonable enough assumption, given the Hungarian government's frequently expressed concern with the well-being of minority Hungarian communities in neighboring countries, such as Slovakia, Romania, and Serbia.

Slovak leaders were especially incensed by the conference endorsement of autonomy for Hungarian minorities in foreign countries. For the Meciar government this was more official Hungarian intrusiveness in Slovakia's internal affairs. Slovak nationalists, pointing to the presence of Slovak Hungarian parties at the conference, said that they could not be trusted and that they had a hidden "separatist" agenda. Their protestations of loyalty had little credibility. For Dusan Slobodnik, MDS chairman of the parliamentary foreign affairs committee, the Budapest Conference was an attempt at breaking up Slovakia and creating a greater Hungary.[41] Marian Andel, deputy chairman of the SNP parliamentary group, called the leaders of Slovakia's ethnic Hungarian minority "political adventurers" who wanted to break up the nation.[42]

Pal Farkas, deputy chairman of the HCDM, rejected these views. Farkas insisted that the Hungarian minority living in Slovakia saw itself as an "integral part of Slovakia which it considers its homeland." Farkas also complained that the hypersensitive Meciar leadership misunderstood the meaning of the term "autonomy" for Hungarians living outside of Hungary that was used in the communique issued by the conference at its adjournment on July 5. It meant only "self-government."[43]

The Budapest Conference emboldened those in the Slovak government who were inclined to ride herd on the Hungarian community. For example, SNP deputies in the Slovak parliament proposed stripping the Hungarian party deputies who attended the Budapest conference of their parliamentary immunity, while other SNP deputies proposed repealing the Slovak-Hungarian treaty ratified in May 1996. They accused Hungary of having violated it by convening the Budapest conference and permitting it to endorse autonomy for Hungarians living abroad. They also criticized Meciar, despite their support of him, for pushing the treaty into law.[44]

Restrictions on Foreign Flags and Emblems. It wasn't long after the conference that another effort at tightening Slovak control over the Hungarian community occurred. At the end of September 1996, the Meciar government came forward with an amendment to a law on state emblems that outlawed flying foreign flags and playing foreign national anthems unless an official delegation from the country concerned was present. This rule hurt Hungarians by denying them the opportunity to fly the Hungarian flag and sing the Hungarian national anthem at ethnocultural ceremonies.[45]

In this policy Meciar had a large measure of popular support. It seems plausible that Meciar was again playing the nationalist card for the sake of personal political aggrandizement and in particular as a means of distracting Slovak voters from continuing economic distress. Another motive may have involved foreign policy. With this law Meciar could taunt the government in Budapest to display anger and possibly provoke an aggressive response to complicate Hungary's relations with the West and jeopardize its efforts to join NATO, which had made plain on many occasions that a prerequisite for East European membership was the resolution of any unresolved and potentially explosive crisis situations in a country's relations with neighbors.[46]

The restrictions imposed on the display of flags and emblems certainly provoked tensions between Slovaks and Hungarians. The law disrupted personal relations between the two groups in southern Slovakia, which in the past had been peaceful, despite the litany of complaints by Hungarian politicians against the Meciar government.[47]

Administrative Centralization. Also fueling tensions between Slovaks and Hungarians was a law passed by the SNC in March 1996 revising the division of the country into regions and districts. From July 1, 1996, Slovakia was to be divided into eight regions and 80 districts in order, so the government said, "to bring public administration closer to citizens." Hungarian political leaders in the SNC, however, saw the law in a different light. They argued that since the law really did not provide for any new autonomy for local government, its effect was to strengthen the influence of the parties in power at the center, notably Meciar's MDS, over lower administrative authorities. They said "the law strongly disadvantages the Hungarian community in Slovakia."[48]

The Future of Slovak-Hungarian Relations. The future of relations between the two ethnic communities does not look bright. Meciar's tough policies, which amount to cultural homogenization, continue to enjoy much support among ethnic Slovaks parties despite all the trouble at home and abroad that such policies provoke. While the opposition parties are occasionally sympathetic to the Hungarian community when it is unduly badgered by Meciar and are willing to seek the cooperation of the Hungarian parties in confrontation with the MDS leadership, no Slovak-based political organization has ever been ready to embrace the cause of administrative autonomy for the country's Hungarian minority. These parties consistently support restrictions on Hungarian cultural life in Slovakia. The SNP has even proposed outlawing the Hungarian parties, viewing them as little more than instruments of Budapest's perceived influence-building among Hungarian minorities abroad.[49]

The uneasy Slovak-Hungarian relationship imposes a heavy burden on Slovak politics and a strain on Slovak democracy. It is a continuing source of confrontation in the day-to-day politics of the country. For example, there is almost an unwritten rule among Slovak opposition parties to exclude the Hungarian parties from any coalition making, despite shared policy views and despite the fact that the Hungarian parties together constitute about 25 percent of opposition strength in the parliament. As one Hungarian political activist put it, how can there be a democracy in a country where 15 percent of the population are considered second-class citizens?[50]

This exclusivity, however, may be changing. In the summer of 1997, following the failed NATO referendum held on May 24 and 25, the Slovak opposition parties, in anticipation of parliamentary elections scheduled in the fall of 1998, began to seek the cooperation of the Hungarian parties to form a united alternative to Meciar's leadership. Whether this effort will lead to a broad interethnic electoral coalition that conceivably could defeat the MDS remains to be seen. It would require a level of conciliation and compromise among the opposition groups that so far has eluded them.

Furthermore, in the short term, Meciar's discriminatory policies could well backfire on him by causing problems for the Slovak minority living with Hungarians. Traditionally, Slovaks and Hungarians in southeastern Slovak towns and villages have been good neighbors. This social peace could collapse if the Hungarian community continues to be denied what it considers its legitimate cultural and political rights. It would not be difficult for radical nationalists in the Republic of Hungary, like Istvan Csurka, to encourage anti-Slovak hostility among the Hungarian minority with a view to providing Hungary with a pretext for intervening in Slovak affairs to help those they call "beleaguered kinsmen."

Still, there is little evidence of repentance on the part of the Slovak leadership, never mind a softening of policy toward the Hungarian community. For the moment Meciar seems willing to court the popularity that comes from playing to the nationalist-inspired ethnic-based prejudices of many Slovak voters. He also seems willing to compromise ties with the West for whatever advantages he stands to gain domestically from nationalist-inspired policies of discrimination. Indeed, the Meciar leadership still considers its treatment of the Hungarian minority fair, equitable, and generous when compared with the policies of other governments in the region toward their minority communities. The position of the government was put clearly by Foreign Minister Pavol Hamzik at a meeting of Hungarian party leaders with members of the Foreign Affairs ministry in mid-October 1996. Hamzik told the Hungarian politicians "that the Hungarian minority in Slovakia enjoys a higher standard of rights compared with minorities in Europe—and significantly better than the Slovak minority's position in Hungary."[51]

The Roma

While Meciar's treatment of the large Hungarian community in Slovakia attracted the most attention, the Romani people or Roma (Gypsies) also have suffered discrimination. The Roma are about 1.5 percent of the total population, or a little over 100,000 people, who live primarily in the southeastern part of the country. The Roma are widely disliked in Slovakia because they are impoverished and seem unwilling to do much to improve their living conditions. To Slovaks the Roma seem reluctant to take full-time jobs, to make their children attend schools regularly, and to obey the law. It does not help their image in the Slovak mind that many of them speak Hungarian rather than Slovak and have Hungarian cultural roots.

Under Meciar's leadership the Slovak government tolerated discrimination against the Roma, thereby encouraging willful acts of violence against individual Roma. "Skinheads" viciously attacked Roma people while police stood by. When Roma press charges of police brutality, Slovak police often threaten what they call "counter-charges" to pressure Roma victims to drop their complaints. Medical doctors and investigators are complicitous in this police behavior by refusing to describe accurately the injuries suffered by Roma victims. Lawyers often are reluctant to represent Roma, fearing a negative impact on their practice.[52]

The Roma are worse off for their poverty and unemployment, which exceed that of ethnic Slovaks and have remained constant throughout the mid-1990s. Also, the Slovak government must bear some responsibility for the deplorable living conditions of the Roma because of official discrimination in housing, employment, and the administration of state services.[53]

Indeed, official discrimination persisted throughout the 1990s. Some members of the Slovak government were notorious for making blatantly racist remarks about the Roma, fostering a climate where anti-Roma violence could flourish. For example, Health Minister Lubomir Javorsky, a high-ranking member of the MDS, was reported in October 1995 to have said at a party rally in Kosice that "the government will do everything to assure that more white children than Romani children are born."[54] When in August 1995 Mario Goral, a young Rom, died an agonizing death after being set on fire by skinheads, Jan Slota, the head of the SNP, allegedly dismissed the crime as a reaction to "high Gypsy crime rates."[55] Slota also was quoted as saying that Roma people need "a small yard and a long whip."[56] Slota's views are shared by many Slovaks, according to a report by the nongovernmental European Roma Rights Center issued in the spring of 1997, which indicated how many Slovak localities continued to use a system of tightly controlled residency permits to restrict the freedom of movement of Roma, a practice reminiscent of the controls in place during Communist rule and in violation of the freedom of movement provisions of the Helsinki Accords. Even the Slovak government has acknowledged that despite the existence of 10 political organizations and 39 civic organizations for the Roma, "their unique way of life has caused great difficulties in coping with a new situation of diminished welfare and social support.[57]

Under these circumstances the outlook of the Roma people in Slovakia is not bright and reflects ill on the post-independence Slovak leadership. Moreover, while the government established a new administrative position called a plenipotentiary to deal with disadvantaged Slovak citizens, it refused to accommodate a request by Roma leaders to have this position focus primarily on their plight.[58] Nor is there much interest in Bratislava in doing more to protect the civil liberties of the Roma. And there is little popular support for the expenditure of scarce resources on the Roma, who remain an object of national scorn and who themselves are blamed for their unhappy lot. The nationalistic Meciar leadership feels obliged to follow the sentiments of voters, who have strong prejudices against the Roma, despite criticisms by the international community. In particular, the EU and NATO have repeatedly told Slovak leaders that integration with the West requires a greater respect for minority rights than they seem willing to offer.

Ruthenians and Ukrainians

Post-independence Slovakia has a small minority of people of Ruthenian and Ukrainian origins who make up less than 1 percent of the total population. These groups have lived in eastern Slovakia for most of this century in a region known as sub-Carpathian Ruthenia, which came under the control of the Czechoslovak state in 1918. Before World War II, Prague tried to acculturate this region by sending Czech administrators and teachers to administer it. Such policies created resentment among the local population, which considered the Czechs arrogant and condescending.[59]

While the Soviet Union annexed a portion of sub-Carpathian Ruthenia following World War II, insisting as it had since the 1920s that the people living in that region really were Ukrainians and belonged in Ukraine, small Ruthenian and Ukrainian minorities remained in Czechoslovakia and under Communist rule received legal rights to their own schools, newspapers, and cultural associations. However, Communist leaders Antonin Novotny in the 1950s and 1960s and Gustav Husak in the 1970s and 1980s did little to implement those rights. Although the 1968 Prague Spring resulted in some liberalization in the Czechoslovak government's minorities policy and although Czech and Slovak political leaders discussed the possibility of autonomy for these small minorities, nothing really changed for them following the 1968 Warsaw Pact intervention and the imposition of Soviet "normalization" policies.[60]

After the collapse of Communist rule in Czechoslovakia, as Slovak politicians became increasingly nationalistic, relations between Bratislava and the Ruthenian and Ukrainian minorities deteriorated. The two groups supported an organization known as the Union of Ukrainians and Ruthenians (UUR) to lobby their interests in Prague. The UUR compromised its credibility with Slovak leaders by supporting the preservation of a united Czechoslovakia, which it believed would be more willing to protect the rights and interests of its constituents than an independent Slovak government. Eventually, many Ukrainians joined forces with Ruthenians to create a new, more unified organization called Ruthenian Revival (RR), which looked for contacts with and support from Ukraine, where there was some popular sympathy for kinsmen stranded in eastern Slovakia. Needless to say, their opposition to Slovak independence did not endear the Ruthenians to Slovakia's post-independence leadership.[61]

After independence, the Ruthenian minority became a problem for Meciar. Apart from his reluctance to grant the Ruthenians the kind of local rights they had been accorded at least in theory by the former Communist regime, Meciar had to be careful not to antagonize Kiev, with which he wanted good relations. He could not aggressively consolidate Slovak administrative control over the small amount of sub-Carpathian territory over which Bratislava had jurisdiction for fear of fueling the demands of nationalists in Ukraine proposing annexation of this territory.

THE PREDICAMENT OF WOMEN

While women in Slovakia do not constitute a "minority," they do have some of the same problems that ethnic minorities have had in Slovak society. Despite the absence of overt discrimination and despite many benefits women enjoy in post-independence Slovakia—women are equal under the law, possess the same property-owning rights as men, and hold posts in the judicial and administrative sectors of the government in Bratislava—women face constraints in public life. They are underrepresented in many public service areas and generally receive considerably less pay than men for the same work. Between 1989 and 1993, women earned just over half what men earned. Furthermore, there is more discrimination against middle-aged and older women in employment than against men in those age groups.[62]

The Slovak government acknowledged wage discrimination against women in a 1995 report prepared by the Ministry of Foreign Affairs that was rather candid and in some respects shocking. According to the report, for the period 1988 to 1993, "gross earnings of men are 71% higher than those of women." The report concluded that "since there is little difference in the level of education achieved by men and women, and since a significantly greater number of women are graduates of technical universities as well as other institutions of higher learning, the discrepancy in wages is caused by factors other than educational achievement."[63]

Slovak women also suffer from sexual harassment and violence. According to police estimates, two-thirds of female rape victims fail to report the cases for personal reasons. The police deal with the cases that are reported as just another criminal offense; they have developed little expertise in this specialized area of law enforcement.[64]

It is difficult for Slovak women to address these problems. The male-dominated political system shows little interest in women's issues and in particular in discrimination against women in the workplace. In 1996, women were conspicuously absent from positions of leadership in government. For example, women held only 2 of 15 cabinet offices—the ministries of Labor/Social Affairs and Education—and had only 22 seats in the 150 member national parliament. In addition, Anna Okruhlicova, a psychologist and professor of women's studies at Bratislava's Comenius University, suggested that to a degree Slovak women are to blame for their economic and psychological hardships in post-Communist Slovakia. She reportedly observed that "we've got so many other social problems that a man beating his wife really takes a back seat. And, to tell the truth, most [Slovak] girls and women are stuck in their submissive traditional roles."[65]

At the same, while a feminist organization committed to the protection and furtherance of women's interests, the Democratic Union of Women of Slovakia (DUZS), exists and lobbies on behalf of women with the Slovak government, it has little influence or authority and has failed to bring about real improvement for women in Slovak society. When it seeks public money for an increase in the number of day-care centers and preschool programs, it runs into the prevailing attitude that women should focus on homemaking, a view that is reinforced by the Catholic Church. In addition, the government cannot afford large expenditures on social welfare including child-care programs. Furthermore, although the Slovak government formed the Coordinating Committee for Women's Affairs immediately following the 1995 United Nations conference in Beijing, China, to consider gender issues, a committee that included government officials, there was little subsequent public policy to improve living and working conditions of Slovak women.[66]

Although the economic and political predicament of women is also a source of instability in post-independence Slovakia, it is not likely to produce the kind of social turmoil Slovaks worry about when they think of the problems of the Hungarian and Roma minorities. Moreover, gender-based prejudice in Slovak society today and the discrimination against women it inspires are likely to diminish as democratic

values and processes take root, especially notions of equality, tolerance, and compromise. Moreover, activist Slovak women in DUZS
can look for inspiration in their campaign to improve their overall
situation in society to feminist movements and gender-based reforms
in Western Europe and the United States.

RESURGENT ANTI-SEMITISM AND NEOFASCISM

During the mid- and late 1990s, anti-Semitic sentiments continued to
pervade Slovak public life partly because of support coming from an
influential political party, the SNP, which was a member of Meciar's
government. The SNP represented a right-wing extremism in Slovak
society and has increased its ties with extremist or fascist parties
abroad, such as the Czech Republican Party, the National Front in
France, and Serbia's Radical Party led by Vojislav Seselj.

In 1996 and 1997, influential SNP members made inflammatory comments about Jews. For example, in May 1996, SNP parliamentary deputy Bartolomej Kunc said that Jews were deported to death camps by
the Slovak government during World War II under President Jozef Tiso
because they were just too wealthy and had "beggared" the Slovak
people and their deportation was therefore a necessary economic "cor-
rection."[67] The context of these disparaging remarks was another renewal of popular interest in the Tiso regime, which seemed to provide
both a moral and political justification for hostility toward Jews in
Slovakia, despite the fact that they constituted an infinitesimal minority
of less than 1 percent of the total Slovak population. In April 1997, on
the anniversary of the execution of Tiso, the SNP issued an appeal to
"all Slovaks to honor the memory of a great son of the Church and of
the nation." The party called him a "martyr to the defense of the nation
and Christianity in the face of bolshevism and liberalism."[68] At the same
time *Matica Slovenska*, the Slovak Cultural Association, which received
funding from the Slovak Ministry of Culture and was closely associated
with the SNP, publicly asserted that Tiso's trial had been manipulated
and in effect announced its efforts to rehabilitate him.

The SNP is not alone in harboring neofascist thinking; it is shared
by members of the MDS. For example, in August 1995 Meciar gave
a journalism award to a paper that had published anti-Semitic
cartoons. In April 1997 the Ministry of Education, presumably with
the approval of the MDS leadership, began distribution of a controversial, anti-Semitic textbook called *The History of Slovakia and the
Slovak Nation*, written by Milan Durica, an expatriate Slovak priest.
The Slovak Academy of Science promptly condemned the book for
putting in a positive light the universally condemned policies of the

Tiso regime of deporting Slovak Jews to certain death. The academy was especially critical of the book's description of life in Jewish labor camps as a paradise on earth. According to the academy, Durica was in effect saying that Jews were lucky to be living in Slovakia at a time when they were being exterminated.[69]

A DECLINE IN PERSONAL SECURITY

As Slovaks struggled in the post-independence period to build a sense of nationhood based on shared cultural characteristics, they must deal with what might be called in the United States a decline in family values. Slovak leaders, in particular former President Kovac, complained about a perceived increase of criminal behavior in contemporary Slovak society. In mid-December 1996, Kovac in a "state of the nation" address spoke of the way in which crime seemingly had become an integral part of Slovak society, confirmed, he said, "by the fact that there had been threatening letters and telephone calls to public officials, cars blowing up and bombs in front of family homes." He said, "We should not be surprised at the ever more frequent statements that nobody feels safe in Slovakia." He likened the situation to "the moral disintegration of public life which we criticized so sharply in November, 1989."[70]

Although Interior Minister Gustav Krajci at the end of March 1997 reported that the "security situation" had improved with a decrease in criminality and an increase in the number of crimes solved when compared with 1995 statistics, he said that organized crime remained the largest problem in Slovakia. He proposed adopting a tougher approach to criminal behavior through legislation, strengthening police organization in the new regions into which the country had been divided, and acquiring additional technical equipment and personnel.[71]

In early May 1997, Meciar added his own view that drug use was at the heart of the crime problem. He also said that too much democracy may be to blame, in particular what he called "the loosening up of certain civic inhibitors and supervision systems" that resulted in an expansion of not only civic democratic activities but also underworld activities.[72] His response seemed to be proposing increased restrictions on the personal and, presumably, political behavior of individuals.

THE CATHOLIC CHURCH
SUPPORTS DEMOCRACY

The Catholic Church, to which 60 percent of the Slovak population belongs, has played a positive role in fostering democratic values, so much so that at times it has come into conflict with the Meciar government. Mindful of the way in which the Communists attacked the church behind a slogan of fighting fascism, members of the Slovak Catholic Clergy frequently complained about undemocratic behavior of the Meciar leadership. An important consideration underlying clerical criticism of the Meciar government, undoubtedly, was the church's self-interest as an autonomous institution, but it would be unfair not to credit the church with an ethically based concern about illiberal and corrupt government behavior incompatible with the values of a democratic society and subversive of the new democratic political system.

The Catholic Church was especially disapproving of the increase in repression-like policies of the Bratislava government in the aftermath of the September-October 1994 parliamentary elections that brought Meciar back to power with a renewed determination to minimize opposition to his policies. For example, in May 1995, Catholic bishops criticized Meciar's feud with President Kovac. They characterized Meciar's efforts to oust Kovac from power as "destabilizing." The government, stung by this criticism, retaliated with an unannounced police search of the office of Bishop Rudolph Balaz, president of the Catholic Bishops Conference. Although Slovak officials said the search was triggered by alleged illegal antiquities trading, many people believed it was punishment for church criticism of the government. In response to the government's pressure on the church to keep quiet in political affairs, 3,000 Catholics demonstrated in support of Bishop Balaz in August 1995 in Banska Bystrica.[73]

In early 1996, the Bishops Conference again criticized government policies. In February, it publicly opposed the November 1995 Slovak language law. The bishops were especially upset over the way a strict enforcement of the law might require all religious services to be conducted solely in the Slovak language. In April 1996 eight bishops protested the Law on the Protection of the Republic, which would have limited free speech. Church opposition to the Law, backed by the opposition of the Evangelical Church most of the opposition parties, led to a veto by President Kovac and a decision by the parliament to leave it in limbo. SNP leader Slota reportedly denounced the bishops, calling them "anti-Slovak."[74]

A major confrontation between the church and the government occurred at the end of 1996, when the Meciar leadership announced plans to establish a Catholic university. The Meciar leadership wanted a Catholic university to help counteract the clerical hierarchy's inclination to side with the liberal opposition acting sometimes as if it were a political party. In October 1996 he reportedly complained that Slovak Catholic leaders were hostile to the government. Church leaders opposed the idea of a government-established university, arguing that only the Church could set up a Catholic university. The Church wanted such a university but without government interference. And at the end of March 1998, in another gesture reflecting its strong liberal instincts, the Slovak Catholic Church asked forgiveness from the country's Jewish community for its role in the massacre of Jews during the German occupation. In a statement released on March 26, the bishops declared "we cannot deny that the deportation of Slovak Jews took place in our midst, that certain members of the nation took part, and that Slovaks looked on in silence." On the other hand, there was no mention of Monsigneur Tiso, the Slovak chief of state during World War II for his alleged role in the murder of Slovak Jews in Nazi concentration camps.[75]

The Catholic Church may have been a conservative force in Slovak society in the pre-Communist era, but, as a result of Communist repression and atheism, it seems today to be an ally of democracy with a willingness to confront the post-independence Slovak government when it diverges from the democratic path as in its effort to enact the restrictive Law on the Protection of the Republic. Moreover, as a critic of the Meciar government's ultranationalistic cultural policies toward minorities, in particular the November 1995 language law, the church was trying to promote social peace that would strengthen and perpetuate Slovak democratic government.

A NEW CIVIC ACTIVISM

Another positive aspect of Slovak society in the post-independence era that bodes well for the successful evolution of democracy is the blossoming of a civic activism in the form of nongovernmental interest groups such as trade unions and community-based groups concerned with the environment, health-care issues, education and job training, and human rights. In January 1997, a new human rights organization appeared, calling itself "Charter 97" after Czechoslovakia's dissident human rights organization Charter 77. It is committed to monitoring the Slovak government's compliance with constitutional and international human rights norms.[76]

These new organizations, which signal a readiness of some Slovak citizens to become directly involved in politics and shed the apolitical behavior encouraged by the Communists, are also important for the specific work they do in pushing the regime to respond to their concerns, as interest groups do in Western democratic systems. For example, 8,000 people demonstrated in Bratislava in March 1995 to protest the removal of three political-satire shows from state television. That move was undoubtedly provoked by a blatant effort of the Meciar leadership to strengthen its grip on the electronic media following the September-October 1994 parliamentary elections by firing in November people critical of the government from posts on the state radio and television control board. Some 115,000 people signed a petition calling for the return of the shows. In September 1995 a new group called the Committee for the Freedom of Speech organized a public demonstration involving over 10,000 people to protest Meciar's perceived authoritarian style of government. Also in September, 20,000 trade unionists protested in Bratislava against the government's reduction of social spending, in particular the cancellation of public transportation subsidies for the needy. In May 1996, over 8,000 people demonstrated in Bratislava to demand the resignation of then Interior Minister Hudek, who was allegedly implicated in the kidnapping of President Kovac's son in August 1995. The number of public demonstrations involving thousands of people increased steadily in 1997, with angry citizens condemning antidemocratic policies of the Meciar government such as the prohibition of bilingual school report cards and protesting the Slovak government's manipulation of the May 24 referendum.[77]

This new civic activism intimidated the Meciar leadership, which immediately began trying to restrict it. For example, in 1995, on the exhortation of SNP leader Slota, a public prosecutor launched an investigation into the activities of human rights organizations sponsored by the international philanthropist George Soros, who had provoked the anger of the leadership in Bratislava by publicly criticizing it. The investigators were looking for evidence of fraud to provide an excuse to close these organizations down and punish their leadership. When they could find nothing, the investigators gave up.[78]

Then, in June 1996, the government struck a severe blow against this new civil activity with the passage of a law that required organizations, called "foundations," to have substantial resources, about $3,000, an enormous sum for many of them, in order to operate. The law also required foundations to register with the Ministry of the Interior, to document the sources and origins of property or resources donated to a foundation, and to disclose extensive information about foundation leadership. A number of groups complained that the law on foundations was extremely prejudicial to those organizations committed to human rights advocacy. Some Hungarian representatives saw the new law as aimed against the Hungarian community and other minorities, which would now find it difficult to carry on cultural activities.[79]

Although the law on foundations unquestionably put some organizations out of business, it did not completely suppress the new civic activism. Indeed, Meciar was reluctant to bear down too heavily on these interest groups lest he call attention to his already controversial rule of the country and antagonize Western Europe. Meciar tolerates these organizations, content at having forced at least some of them to go out of business. Their persistence, however, as well as that of many Slovak citizens, in publicizing criticisms of the Slovak government, especially in the area of human rights, exerts a positive influence on the development of Slovak democracy and equality. They have been capable of annoying and embarrassing the government when it tried to limit freedom of speech and in other ways stray from democratic rule.

A NONPOLITICAL MILITARY

Like the liberal instincts of the Catholic Church and the new civic activism, the nonpolitical role of the Slovak army has helped foster societal democratization. The Slovak army does not participate in politics. It has little if any influence over the selection of the political leadership or the persuit of policies. This apolitical role, which poses no threat or challenge to Slovakia's democratic development, and in fact facilitates it, is attributable to a variety of circumstances, not least the popular dislike and distrust of the army dating back to the Communist era when its leadership was blatantly subservient to Moscow. In addition, the army was severely weakened and demoralized by the purges that removed officers sympathetic to liberalization in the aftermath of the Soviet invasion of Prague and the installation of the servile Husak leadership. Its public image was tarnished further by rumors in 1989 that certain high ranking officers were willing to prop up the conservative Communist leadership when it faced an explosion of popular wrath and calls for its resignation and for the introduction of democracy.

After the collapse of Communist rule, and after the country's achievement of independence of the Czechs, the Slovak army faced other circumstances weakening it and depriving it of any influence over public policy making. The army was hurt by the decline of government spending on defense to allow an increase of investment in the country's economic and social infrastructure. In addition, during the 1990s the army was disadvantaged by the absence of any serious international crises that threatened Slovak security and by the Slovak leadership's reliance on political diplomacy rather than military power to protect the country's interests abroad. Nor did the Meciar government's ambivalence toward Slovakia's membership in NATO help the army. To the dismay of Army leaders, who wanted Slovak membership in NATO, Meciar was concerned that the costs of upgrading the country's military establishment to NATO standards could turn out to be prohibitive.

Under these circumstances, the Slovak army has been obliged to keep a low profile, make as few demands on the country's scarce resources as possible, and refrain from lobbying with leaders and the public for more attention and influence. In the late 1990s, there is nothing to suggest a threat to Slovak democracy from the army. Rather, it appears that well into the new century the Slovak army will be under the control of a loyal and professional leadership that will refrain from behavior subversive of the country's movement toward democracy.[80]

CONCLUSIONS

To some extent there are shared causes of discrimination against ethnic minorities and women and the decline of personal security in post-independence Slovakia. The most important arguably is the impact on Slovak society of the transformation from the Communist paternalistic and regimented economy to free enterprise and the focus on individual initiative, notably hardships such as inflation, unemployment, and psychological insecurity coming from the steady withdrawal of state control over the country's economic life and the end of its responsibility for the kind of "cradle to grave" social security developed by the Communists. In addition, the new open, pluralistic, democratic environment in which many restraints on personal behavior have been lifted also has been a liability for vulnerable groups in Slovak society, such as women and the ethnic minorities. Society at large is now freer than it was during the repressive and somewhat puritanical Communist dictatorship to act out its prejudices and phobias.

Underpinning official and unofficial discrimination against ethnic minorities in particular is the pervasive and strongly felt nationalism that helped inspire Slovakia's move to independence in 1992. This nationalism is highly emotional and defensive, born of a fear that Slovakia could easily jeopardize its newly achieved sovereignty, which leaders like Meciar and the voters who support him consider fragile and vulnerable, by indulging groups they perceive as threats to the country's unity and stability.

The most serious threat to post-independence Slovakia's internal stability, at least in the view of the Meciar government, comes from the discontent of the large Hungarian minority because of a pervasive, persistent, and popularly based anti-Hungarian prejudice born of the long history of Slovak subjugation to Hungary prior to World War II. This prejudice is not likely to end soon. It continues to be fed by worry in Bratislava about an eventual loss of territory inhabited by the Hungarian minority to the Republic of Hungary. Finally, this prejudice encourages intolerance of diversity and, worse, assimilationist policies that contradict the spirit, if not the letter, of the democracy Slovak leaders of all political persuasions insist they are determined to develop in their country. It also strains Slovakia's relations with the West, with which it wants to integrate, undermining the credibility of Slovak protestations of loyalty to Western values and processes, especially in the area of minority rights.

Slovak policies toward the Roma people are no less subversive of stability and democracy. These policies, which all but condone both official and personal acts of discrimination against Roma people that at times are physically brutal, seem inspired by a popular contempt for the Roma that the Slovak government is willing to tolerate. The failure of the Slovak government to protect the legal rights of the Roma minority undermines the credibility of Slovak claims of loyalty to Western-style democracy. In suggesting that life will get better for the Roma if more of them express willingness to "do an honest day's work," Meciar probably reflected the popular Slovak view that most Roma people do not have the Western work ethic and that they alone are the cause of their misery.

Balanced against the prejudice in Slovak society against minorities and the reluctance of government to take major steps to counteract it are the Slovak Catholic Church's determination to follow its strong democratic instincts and the growing willingness of Slovak citizens to abandon the apolitical behavior they were taught by the Communists and to participate in efforts to strengthen democratic values. Indeed, a popular civic activism so important for the well-being of the Western democracies seems finally to be occurring in Slovakia, signifying a real break with the Communist past and the promise of a vibrant democratic polity in Slovakia in the not-too-distant future.

NOTES

1. Carol Skalnik Leff, *The Czech and Slovak Republics: Nation versus State* (Boulder, Colo.: Westview Press, 1997), p. 166; see also William Kieran, "The Magyar Minority in Slovakia," *Regional and Federal Studies*, vol. 6 (Spring 1996), pp. 1–20.

2. Alfred A. Reisch, "Meciar and Slovakia's Hungarian Minority," *Radio Free Europe/Radio Liberty Research Report* (hereafter cited as *RFE/RL Research Report*), vol. 1, no. 43 (October 30, 1992), p. 15.

3. Ibid., p. 16.

4. Pavel Mates, "The New Slovak Constitution," *RFE/RL Research Report*, vol. 1, no. 43 (October 30, 1992), p. 39.

5. Ibid.; Reisch, "Meciar and Slovakia's Hungarian Minority," p. 17.

6. Reisch, "Meciar and Slovakia's Hungarian Minority," p. 17.

7. Sharon Fisher, "Meeting of Slovakia's Hungarians Causes Stir," *RFE/RL Research Report*, vol. 3, no. 4 (January 28, 1994), pp. 42–43; Leff, *Czech and Slovak Republics*, pp. 166–167; Ramet, *Whose Democracy?* p. 131.

8. Fisher, "Meeting of Slovakia's Hungarians Causes Stir," pp. 42–43.

9. Reisch, "Meciar and Slovakia's Hungarian Minority," p. 15.

10. Alfred A. Reisch, "The Difficult Search for a Hungarian-Slovak Accord," *RFE/RL Research Report*, vol. 1, no. 42 (October 23, 1992), p. 30.

11. Alfred Reisch, "Slovakia's Minority Policy under International Scrutiny," *RFE/RL Research Report*, vol. 2, no. 49 (December 10, 1993), p. 41.

12. Ibid.

13. Fisher, "Meeting of Slovakia's Hungarians," p. 43.

14. Ibid., p. 42.

15. Ibid.

16. Ibid., p. 46.

17. Ibid.

18. Ibid., p. 42.

19. Ibid., p. 45.

20. U.S. Department of State, *Country Reports on Human Rights Practices for 1995, Report Submitted to the Committee on International Relations, U. S. House of Representatives and the Committee on Foreign Relations, U. S. Senate, April 1996,* "Slovakia," (hereafter cited as *Country Reports on Human Rights Practices for 1995*, "Slovakia") (Washington, D.C.: U.S. Government Printing Office, 1996), p. 1027; Ramet, *Whose Democracy?*, pp. 131-132

21. U.S. Department of State, *Country Reports on Human Rights Practices for 1995*, "Slovak," p. 1027; "Slovaks Further Curb Use of Hungarian Language," *NYT* (November 16, 1995); Ramet, p. 134.

22. Sharon Fisher, "Making Slovakia More Slovak," *Transition*, vol. 2, no. 24 (November 29, 1996), p. 14.

23. Ibid., pp. 14–15; Ramet, *Whose Democracy?* p.134.

24. Ibid.

25. "Slovaks Further Curb Use of Hungarian Language."

26. Fisher, "Making Slovakia More 'Slovak,'" p. 15.

27. "Slovaks Further Curb Use of Hungarian Language."

28. U.S. Department of State, *Country Reports on Human Rights Practices for 1996 Report Submitted to the Committee on International Relations, U.S. House of Representatives and the Committee on Foreign Relations, U.S. Senate February, 1997* "Slovakia" (hereafter cited as *Country Reports on Human Rights Practices for 1996*, "Slovakia" (Washington, D.C.: U.S. Government Printing office, 1997), p. 1121.

29. Duncan Shiels, "Slovaks Must Pass Minority Language Law—Kovac," Reuters (Budapest, June 12, 1996), *LN/EL*, Reuters Textline, Reuters News Service—CIS and Eastern Europe (June 12, 1996).

30. "Slovakia Said to Be Preparing Minority Language Law After All," *CTK News Agency* (Prague, February 16, 1997), LN/EL, Eastern Europe TXTEE BBC Monitoring Service: Eastern Europe (February 18, 1997).

31. Ibid.

32. "President Suggests Foreign Politicians Tougher on Slovakia over Minorities," *TASR News Agency* (Bratislava, November 11, 1996), *LN/EL*, Eastern Europe TXTEE,

BBC Monitoring Service: Eastern Europe (November 13, 1996); Pal Farkas, deputy chairman of the Hungarian Christian Democratic Movement, had pointed out in July 1996 that state subsidies for minority culture had declined by two-thirds since 1993, see "Ethnic Hungarians Consider Themselves as 'Integral Part of Slovakia,'" *CTK News Agency* (Prague, July 17, 1996), *LN/EL*, Eastern Europe TXTEE, BBC Monitoring Service: Eastern Europe (July 19, 1996).

33. "Slovakia Said to be Preparing Minority Language Law After All," CTK News Agency (Prague, February 16, 1997), *LN/EL*, Eastern Europe TXTEE BBC Monitoring Service: Eastern Europe (February 18, 1997)

34. Ibid.

35. "Hungarian Parties in Slovakia Offer Legal Aid in Fight for Minority Rights," *Duna TV Satellite Service* (Budapest, February 25, 1997), *LN/EL*, Eastern Europe TXTEE, BBC Monitoring Service: Eastern Europe (February 27, 1997).

36. The Economist Intelligence Unit, *Country Report: Slovakia*, 3rd Quarter, 1997 (London: The Unit, 1997); In April, 1997 Vojtech Gugh, a principal who initiated a public protest against the ban on bilingual report cards was dismissed from his post. In July 1997 an ethnic Hungarian teacher, Alexander Toth, was reportedly fired from his teaching position for using a report card in both Slovak and Hungarian. And school children who accepted bilingual report cards were told that they would not be advanced to the next grade. Commission on Security and Cooperation in Europe (CSCE), *Human Rights and Democratization in Slovakia* (Washington, D.C.: CSCE, September, 1997), p. 22.

37. "Weekend Talks between Government and Ethnic Hungarians Unsuccessful," *Hungarian Radio* (Budapest, May 12, 1996), *LN/EL*, Eastern Europe, TXTEE BBC Monitoring Service: Eastern Europe (May 12, 1996).

38. "Ethnic Hungarians See No Need for Loyalty Pledge," *Radio 1* (Bratislava, May 13, 1996), *LN/EL*, Eastern Europe TXTEE, BBC Monitoring Service: Eastern Europe (May 15, 1996).

39. Ibid.

40. Ibid.

41. "Ethnic Hungarian MPs Say: We Do Not Demand Territorial Autonomy in Slovakia," *CTK News Agency* (Prague, July 21, 1996), *LN/EL*, Eastern Europe TXTEE, BBC Monitoring Service: Eastern Europe (July 21, 1996).

42. Ibid.

43. "Ethnic Hungarians Consider Themselves as 'Integral Part of Slovakia.'"

44. "Ethnic Hungarian MPs Say: We Do Not Demand Territorial Autonomy in Slovakia."

45. "Meciar Seeks to Thwart Hungary's NATO Ambitions," *Die Welt* (October 2, 1996), cited by CTK National News Wire (October 2, 1996).

46. Ibid.

47. Leff, *Czech and Slovak Republics*, p. 168.

48. "Hungarian Minority Will Seek Referendum on New Territorial Division," *CTK News Agency* (Prague, March 22, 1996), *LN/EL*, Eastern Europe TXTEE, BBC Monitoring Service: Eastern Europe (March 25, 1996).

49. Leff, Czech and Slovak Republics, p. 165.

50. Ibid., p. 166.

51. "Ethnic Hungarian Chief Pleased at New Foreign Minister's Willingness to Meet," *TASR News Agency* (Bratislava, October 14, 1996), *LN/EL* Eastern Europe TXTEE, BBC Monitoring Service: Eastern Europe (October 16, 1996).

52. *Country Reports on Human Rights Practices for 1995*, "Slovakia," p. 1027; see also Commission on Security and Cooperation in Europe, *Human Rights and Democractization in Slovakia* (Washington, D.C.: CSCE, September, 1997), p. 23.

53. Ibid.; see also Sharon Fisher, "Romanies in Slovakia," *RFE/RL Research Report*, vol. 2, no. 42 (October 22, 1993), pp. 54–59.

54. CSCE, *Human Rights and Democratization in Slovakia*, p. 23.

55. Ibid.

56. Ibid.

57. Ibid., p. 25; CSCE, *Report on Human Rights and the Process of NATO Enlargement* (Washington, D.C.: CSCE, June 1997), p. 123.

58. *Country Reports on Human Rights Practices for 1995*, "Slovakia," p. 1027.

59. Janusz Bugajski, *Nations in Turmoil: Conflict and Cooperation in Eastern Europe* (Boulder, Colo.: Westview Press, 1993), p. 46.

60. Ibid., pp. 46–47.

61. Ibid., p. 48.

62. U.S. Department of State, *Country Reports on Human Rights Practices for 1996, Report Submitted to the Committee on International Relations, U.S. House of Representatives and the Committee on Foreign Relations, U.S. Senate February, 1997*, "Slovakia" (hereafter cited as *Country Reports on Human Rights Practices for 1996*, "Slovakia") (Washington, D.C.: U.S. Government Printing Office, 1996), p. 1120; see also Paulina Brett, "The Status of Women in Post-1989 Czechoslovakia," *RFE/RL Research Report*, vol. 1, no. 42 (October 16, 1992), pp. 58–63; Swanee Hunt, "Women's Vital Voices: The Costs of Exclusion in Eastern Europe," *Foreign Affairs* (July-August 1997), p. 2.

63. *Country Reports on Human Rights Practices for 1996*, "Slovakia," p. 1120.

64. *Country Reports on Human Rights Practices for 1995*, "Slovakia," p. 1025.

65. *Country Reports on Human Rights Practices for 1996*, "Slovakia," p. 1119; Chris Sulavik, "Feminist Starts a Magazine in an Unfriendly Atmosphere," Chicago Tribune (October 31, 1993).

66. *Country Reports on Human Rights Practices for 1996*, "Slovakia," pp. 1119-1120.

67. Commission on Security and Cooperation in Europe (CSCE), *Human Rights and Democratization in Slovakia* (Washington, D.C.: CSCE, September 1997), p. 18.

68. Ibid.

69. Ibid., p. 19.

70. "President Slams Government in State of Nation Address," *Radio 1* (Bratislava, December 11, 1996), *LN/EL*, Eastern Europe TXTEE, BBC Monitoring Service: Eastern Europe (December 13, 1996).

71. "Crime Rate Down in 1996," *TASR News Agency* (Bratislava, March 21, 1996), *LN/EL*, Eastern Europe TXTEE, BBC Monitoring Service: Eastern Europe (March 25, 1997).

72. "Slovakia Not 'The Problem Child of Europe' — Premier," *Radio 1* (Bratislava, May 2, 1997), *LN/EL*, Eastern Europe TXTEE, BBC Monitoring Service: Eastern Europe (May 5, 1997).

73. CSCE, *Human Rights and Democratization in Slovakia*, pp. 25–26.

74. Ibid., p. 26.

75. Ibid., p. 27; "Slovak Catholic Church Apologizes to Jews," *RFE/RL Newsline* (March 27, 1998) (Prague: Paul Goble Publishers, 1998), on-line @ http://www.rferl.org/.

76. CSCE, *Human Rights and Democratization in Slovakia*, p. 28; for a detailed commentary on the new Slovak volunteerism see Sharon Wolchik, "Democratization and Political Participation in Slovakia," in Karen Dawisha and Bruce Parrott (eds.), *The Consolidation of Democracy in East-Central Europe* (Cambridge, U.K.: Cambridge University Press, 1997), pp. 218–220.

77. CSCE, *Human Rights and Democratization in Slovakia*, pp. 29–30; Wolchik, "Democratization and Political Participation in Slovakia," pp. 220–221.

78. *CSCE, Human Rights and Democratization in Slovakia*, p. 30.

79. Ibid.

80. Wolchik, "Democratization and Political Participation in Slovakia," pp. 221–222.

6

Slovakia between the West and Russia

Post-independence Slovakia seeks legitimacy, security, and trade in relations with the Western democracies and Russia. Above all else it fears international isolation now that administrative links with the Czechs have been severed.

The political leaders of post-independence Slovakia have not agreed on how best to reach out to the major powers on both sides. Prime Minister Meciar favored a balanced approach to both the West and Russia, enabling Slovakia to act as a kind of bridge between them. He wanted Slovakia to maintain political, economic, cultural, and strategic ties with the West after years of alliance with the former Soviet Union, even if it risked antagonizing the West. Other leaders, such as former foreign ministers Milan Knazko, Jozef Moravcik, and Pavol Hamzik and President Michal Kovac, favor giving priority to the integration of Slovakia with the West. Opposed to them were Meciar's highly nationalistic and somewhat anti-Western coalition partners, the Slovak National Party (SNP) and the Association of Slovak Workers (ASW), which favored Slovak friendship and cooperation with the Kremlin to the extent of jeopardizing Slovakia's chances of joining the North Atlantic Treaty Organization (NATO) and the European Union (EU).

Under these circumstances, in the mid- and late 1990s, Slovak foreign policy often was contradictory and unpredictable. While Meciar lobbied the West for Slovak membership in NATO and the EU, he also sought cooperation and friendship with Russia in political, economic, and military areas. Moreover, when he tried to cultivate one side, he displeased the other, with each trying to get him to assign it the priority he had been trying not to create.

RELATIONS WITH THE WEST

Since independence the Slovak government has worked hard to strengthen political, economic, and military ties to Western Europe and the United States. Slovakia needs the respect and friendship of the West to move successfully from authoritarian government to democracy and to facilitate economic transformation and growth. Good relations with the West could provide the security needed to maintain its newly won independence and sovereignty. Finally, there was much popular support for closer Slovak links to the West, especially in the Hungarian community. Polls at the end of January 1997 showed that a majority of Slovaks were sympathetic to membership in both NATO and the EU.[1]

Slovak policy toward the West involved both a campaign for membership in the EU and NATO and efforts to strengthen ties with Germany, Austria, and the United States, the three Western countries with the most interest in Slovak well-being. Slovak efforts, however, have had mixed results. Slovakia gained Western sympathy but not much material support, largely because the United States and Germany as well as most countries of Western Europe have been disappointed and dissatisfied with the Meciar government's behavior in Slovakia and abroad.

Membership in the European Union (EU)

Following independence, Bratislava campaigned aggressively for membership in the EU. In June 1993 the EU, known at that time as the European Community (EC), finalized an association agreement signed in Luxembourg in October that opened the way at least theoretically for Slovakia's full membership. Obstacles to immediate entry are substantial, not least the waiting list of other countries like those in Scandinavia that are eager to join and seem to have a priority given their solid democratic credentials, their high level of economic well-being, and their pro-West sentiment in the Cold War. Moreover, they are closer than the ex-Communist countries of central and Eastern Europe to the fulfillment of conditions for membership laid down by the EC at its summit in Copenhagen in June 1993. The conditions called on candidate countries to assure

> the stability of institutions guaranteeing democracy, the rule of law, human rights and respect for the protection of minorities; the existence of a functioning market economy, as well as the capacity to cope with competitive pressure and market forces within the Community; and the ability to take on the obligations of membership, including adherence to the aims of political, economic, and monetary union.[2]

Believing it could meet those conditions, the Slovak government submitted an application for full membership in June 1995, with the year 2000 as a target date for admission. In April 1996, Meciar acknowledged that this date might be optimistic and that it might take longer for Slovakia to meet the conditions for membership laid down by the EU.[3] Then, in October 1996, Georgios Zavvos, the EU Ambassador to Slovakia, told a town meeting in Stupava, near Bratislava, that Slovakia still had "much work to be done and in this task there can be no delay." He said that "it is only through its own efforts in the field of democracy, as in the economy, that Slovakia can hope to join the EU."[4]

In July 1997 Slovakia was not among the group of East European countries recommended by the European Commission to start talks on EU entry in early 1998. This group comprised Poland, Hungary, the Czech Republic, Slovenia, and Estonia. While the commission recognized the existence of democratic institutions in Slovakia, it maintained that these institutions were inadequately embedded in the political life of the country. It drew attention to the failure of the Meciar government to respect the powers conferred on various office holders by the constitution, pointing in particular to the constant tensions between Meciar and President Kovac and his unwillingness to recognize the rights of the opposition. It also voiced concerns about the Meciar government's disregard for the rule of law, the lack of safeguards assuring the independence of the judiciary, and the inadequate protection of minority rights. In this regard the commission took note of the Slovak government's refusal to enact a law on minority languages and its overtly discriminatory policies toward the Hungarians, especially the elimination of subsidies to their main cultural organization. In December 1997, the European Parliament affirmed the commission's decision to exclude Slovakia from the 1998 negotiations with other central and Eastern European countries over conditions for entry.[5]

Expansion of Trade

Slovakia had to move quickly to add to its trading partners with or without European Union membership. With the collapse of Communist rule, sales to Russia and other members of the former Soviet bloc, where most of its exports had gone, collapsed. In particular in the early 1990s, the lucrative sales of weapons that had brought a measure of prosperity to portions of Slovakia abruptly declined when Czechoslovakia curtailed sales of weapons carried on in the Communist era to Third World countries. Slovakia also had to cope with the loss of arms sales to its neighbors which, like Slovakia, could no longer afford to devote a substantial portion of gross domestic product to the purchase of weapons, as in the Communist era and, in fact, no longer wanted to spend as much as in the past on defense because of more urgent priorities.

Moreover, the conversion of Slovak industries from arms production to the manufacture of nonmilitary goods proved costly and complicated. The the West Europeans themselves made matters worse for Slovakia. For example, just when the East Slovak Ironworks in the southeastern Slovak city of Kosice had achieved a measure of success in transforming itself with the help of Western technology and equipment and with the benefit of cheap labor into a successful export firm — by 1992, it was selling 25 percent of its production to EC countries — its sales dropped precipitately. Strict import quotas for East European steel were imposed in response to a widespread recession in the West. The message received in Kosice was that playing by Western rules did not guarantee any special benefits and privileges. In 1997, moreover, afraid of Slovak dumping, the EU blocked the import of Slovak iron pipes for half a year, causing distress in the Slovak iron production sector, in particular in the ironworks enterprise in Podbrezova. ASW parliamentary deputy Miroslav Pacola also complained about "more such bans" that the Slovak government was tolerating in silence to avoid provoking EU governments and prejudicing them against Slovakia. The EU in this regard, according to Pacola, was no better than Russia, which was pressuring Slovakia not to draw closer to the EU.[6] In fact, EU behavior threatened the well-being of a very poor and ethnically mixed region already politically volatile.

Still, Slovakia had some success in strengthening its commercial links to the West. By 1995, the bulk of Slovak exports no longer went eastward but to the West, in particular to the Czech Republic, Hungary, Austria, and Germany.[7] Slowly but steadily Slovakia seemed to be preparing itself for close, eventually intimate trade links with Western Europe.

Membership in NATO

Slovakia sought membership in NATO, having joined the Partnership for Peace (PFP) Program in February 1994. The Slovak government was enthusiastic about the PFP program, not simply because it was seen as a stepping-stone to NATO. The PFP Program required members to pledge to respect the inviolability of borders, something Bratislava had been trying to get Hungary, also a PFP participant, to do for some time. For his part Meciar was willing to bite the bullet and improve relations with Hungary to strengthen his country's chances of gaining membership in the EU and NATO. In March 1995, he finally signed a state treaty with Hungary, which West European countries wanted as a means of resolving the long-standing and potentially explosive differences between the two countries over treatment of minorities. The treaty included the Council of Europe's recommendation on the creation under certain conditions of autonomy for minorities.

Getting parliamentary ratification of the state treaty with Hungary turned out to be quite difficult for Meciar. He was criticized by the opposition and by some of his own supporters in the MDS for accepting a treaty that was perceived as potentially detrimental to Slovak domestic interests simply for the sake of pleasing the West and hastening Slovak membership in the EU and NATO. Meciar was determined to conciliate the West, and in March 1996 Slovak Foreign Minister Juraj Schenk reiterated the importance of membership in NATO. He declared that Slovakia was not able to guarantee its security without NATO and renewed the government's interest in joining the organization.[8]

Pressure on Meciar to gain membership in NATO came from his military commanders. Slovak Army general Jozef Tuchnya, chief of the General Staff, said that the Slovak army would suffer if the country failed to win membership in NATO along with the first wave of new members from Eastern Europe that included Poland, Hungary, and the Czech Republic. Slovakia would continue to cooperate with NATO even if it were not among the first new members, General Tuchnya said, but a delay in membership would mean a delay in Slovakia's integration into the West. Tuchnya also said that a delay in Slovakia's admission to NATO would require continued Slovak cooperation with Russia because of dependence on Russian military spare parts.[9] For Tuchnya, membership in NATO meant a much-wanted declaration of real independence from Russia and an end to the closeness with the Russian army that Slovakia had over the long period of Communist rule.

Meciar's coalition partners, the SNP and the ASW, saw the case differently. They pointed out liabilities of Slovakia's membership in NATO, in particular an increase of Western military influence at the expense of its newly won independence. Russia would be unhappy. The SNP and ASW leaders wanted Slovakia on good terms with Russia at least to counterbalance Western influence and also because of some sympathy for the Kremlin's problems with reform, which were not unlike Slovakia's.

SNP leader Slota warned it would cost billions of crowns to make the Slovak army compatible with NATO forces, even suggesting that NATO might have this very goal of Slovakia's economic ruin in mind. He raised the specter of an eventual NATO troop deployment in Slovakia and compared it to the Soviet-led Warsaw Pact invasion of Czechoslovakia in August 1968: "We do not know whether we can believe their promises that no foreign military forces will be deployed in Slovakia," Slota said. "Once we are in NATO," he continued, "there will be no more chances to make our own decisions. . . . We will only be allowed to shut up and obey orders."[10]

Along the same lines, ASW chief Jan Luptak declared on March 20, 1997, in the most categorical terms, his party's opposition to "joining European structures" and stated that the omission of this position from the party's 1994 electoral manifesto was "a mistake of the party press organ." He said that NATO should open its doors to all countries without dividing them into "waves." Expressing doubt about the justification for NATO's existence now that the Warsaw Pact had ceased to exist, he also questioned the usefulness of American involvement in European affairs.[11]

Even Meciar himself, despite his frequent protestations of support for Slovak membership in NATO and EU, had misgivings. Meciar shared some of the concerns of his coalition partners. He was especially sensitive to the potentially negative impact of Slovak membership in NATO on relations with Russia, despite the Kremlin's assurance that relations between the two countries would not be compromised by Slovakia's entry into the Western alliance. Given the Kremlin's well-known hostility to NATO's eastward expansion, Meciar was inclined to discount those assurances. Moreover, he probably was more annoyed than he cared to show about the incessant criticism from EU members and the United States of his domestic political behavior.

Nevertheless, many Slovak politicians and to some extent Meciar as well were stung by the failure of Slovakia to receive an invitation to join NATO, and some were baffled. If the most compelling reason for NATO expansion was stability, Slovak leaders thought, it was difficult to understand why Slovakia was excluded from the first wave of new members from central Europe and denied any promise of membership in the near future, given the destabilizing influence this ill-concealed Western issolation of the Slovaks would likely have on the international situation in central Europe. Nor could Slovak leaders understand why Slovakia, for what they considered relatively minor offenses, was being denied membership in an organization in which Turkey was allowed to play an important role despite frequent Western complaints about the undemocratic behavior of its government, for example in the area of human rights.[12]

Western Caution and Restraint

Western governments have tended to keep Slovakia at "arms length," deferring Slovakia's membership in the EU and NATO, not least because of their critical view of Slovak domestic development. By the end of 1995, after three years of independence, Western governments concluded that Slovakia was still far from being a bona fide democratic state. They complained about Meciar's heavy-handed efforts to limit political pluralism and dissent. In 1995 and 1996, the West correctly pointed out that Slovakia still lacked a capable, nonpartisan civil service. In the Western view the Slovak bureaucracy was politically motivated, subject to periodic personnel purges, depressed by low salaries, and handicapped by the departure of many qualified Slovaks to work abroad, particularly in the Czech Republic, making it difficult for the country to make its administrative system compatible with Western norms. In October 1995, British foreign secretary Malcolm Rifkind warned the Slovak government that Britain and other EU members were worried about what he termed "the trend of recent political development in Slovakia," a reference to what the West perceived as Meciar's confrontational style in dealing with the political opposition, his ill-concealed impediments to a free press, and his unrelenting and unseemly conflict with President Kovac. In November and December 1995 the EU delivered a formal diplomatic complaint about human rights abuses with the United States, in particular urging the Meciar leadership to place "greater emphasis on the toleration of diverse opinions."[13]

Defensive Slovak Reactions. Slovakia responded to Western complaints and advice with a defensiveness that did little to persuade outsiders that they were wrong in their assessments. It almost seemed as if, in criticizing the Meciar government, the West was tapping into a deep-seated inferiority complex of Slovak leaders, who for the most part, especially Meciar, were hypersensitive to the way their newly independent country was seen by outsiders. To the Slovaks Western behavior reminded them of Czech behavior, which on many occasions they considered arrogant, patronizing, and condescending. Many Slovaks believed that their country and its leadership had been unfairly singled out by the West to be lectured and criticized for behavior that from their point of view had a logical explanation.

When warned by the EU at the end of 1995 to respect democratic principles in dealing with the opposition and with President Kovac, an MDS spokesman reportedly said the West was acting like Hitler when he sent ultimatums to states and then occupied them with tanks.[14] Meanwhile, MDS leader Dusan Slobodnik, chairman of the parliamentary committee on foreign affairs, defended Meciar by telling Western critics that he was a democratically chosen leader of the country and that he had as much right as any national leader to protect himself against subversive slander by opponents. He acknowledged that the

Slovak leadership had made mistakes, saying, "I don't deny it, but we have elections and a free press as in any democratic country."[15]

Meciar and his colleagues went on the offensive, imputing sinister intentions to Western gestures of concern with their leadership style. Parliamentary Chairman Ivan Gasparovic, a close ally of Meciar, warned that Western condemnations were creating tensions and nervousness in Slovak society, raising doubt among many Slovaks about the sincerity of Western interest in having Slovakia integrate eventually with the EU and NATO. Moreover, Slovak leaders frequently complained that outsiders "did not understand them." In mid-December 1995, German chancellor Helmut Kohl during a visit to Bratislava conspicuously omitted mention of Slovakia among candidates for immediate membership in the EU because of Bratislava's questionable treatment of minorities and slowness in moving toward the free market.[16] Foreign Affairs Committee Chairman Slobodnik reportedly said that Chancellor Kohl "is not an expert on Slovakia."[17]

SNP Deputy Chair Anna Malikova took exception to the sharp American criticisms of Slovak political behavior contained in a U.S. State Department report on human rights in 1995. According to Malikova, the State Department lacked hard information to support its conclusions about alleged human rights violations. She said that information for this report came from a Slovak think tank connected to several members of the opposition Democratic Party.[18]

Meciar also accused the West of discrimination against Slovakia in favor of Hungary. As far as the West was concerned, it was all right for Budapest to pursue nationalistic policies of interference in the internal affairs of its neighbors through its frequently stated concern about the treatment of Hungarian minorities abroad; but when it came to Slovakia, the situation was quite different. The West took a hard line. Meciar said the West was using a double standard in backing Hungary for NATO membership but not Slovakia.[19]

Bilateral Slovak Diplomacy

To help counteract this perceived discrimination, Slovakia tried hard to cultivate individual Western countries, notably Germany, Austria, and the United States, considered pivotal to the success of its efforts to become part of the Western community. While these countries have been sympathetic to Slovakia's ambition to be part of the West and have commended Slovak politicians including Meciar for having achieved Slovakia's independence peacefully, Germany and the United States have been outspoken in their concern over Slovakia's perceived divergence from democratic principles. They also worried about Meciar's perceived sympathy for Russia that could encourage further Russian resistance to NATO's recruitment of new members in the former Soviet bloc.

The United States and Germany in dealing with Meciar in the mid-1990s were in a "bind," so to speak. Critical of Meciar and skeptical of Slovakia's readiness for membership in the EU and NATO, they recognized Slovakia's importance to Western security given the strategic significance of its geographic location in the heart of central Europe, adjacent to Ukraine, Austria, and Hungary. Given Meciar's interest in maintaining good relations with Russia, which to a limited degree had responded favorably to Bratislava's interest in keeping its fences with Moscow in good repair, Bonn and Washington worried about the possibility of Slovak movement into an orbit of influence that Russia is developing that includes countries once part of the former Soviet Union.

Germany. Slovakia wants strong ties with Germany for strategic and economic reasons. Slovak foreign minister Pavol Hamzik, appointed in August 1996, considered Germany the driving force in post–Cold War Europe because of its size, its population, and its economic power. Balanced against the remarks of Chancellor Kohl that Slovakia is not yet ready for membership in the EU or NATO is Germany's long-standing sympathy in principle for the enlargement of the EU and NATO to which someday, with German help, Slovak leaders believe Slovakia will belong.[20] But in 1996 Hamzik also acknowledged that the level of relations between Slovakia and Germany "did not meet Slovakia's needs," a reflection of Slovak concern about the close and extensive links Germany had developed and sustained with the Czech Republic, which included a substantial investment in the Czech economy.[21] In the Slovak view, if Germany made equivalent investment in their economy, Slovakia could move forward and match economic conditions in the Czech Republic and elsewhere in central Europe.

For a time, Kohl tried to avoid face-to-face meetings with Meciar, a fact noted in the Slovak press. Kohl did meet with Meciar in December 1995, in Bratislava; but this was not a happy event for the Slovak leadership, because it was on this occasion that Kohl obliquely indicated that Slovakia would not be among the central European countries the West had decided to admit to NATO as full members in 1997.[22] Indeed, according to an explicit statement by CDU *Bundestag* deputy Andreas Krautscheid, Germany would not support an invitation to Slovakia to be among the first nations in central Europe to join NATO.[23] In September 1996 the Slovak press observed critically that Kohl had missed an opportunity for a summit with the Slovak leadership on his way to Kiev. Kohl has not ruled out German support of Slovakia's integration in Western Europe, saying that eventually Slovakia could meet conditions for membership but, he said, "unfortunately not at the moment."[24]

There is a real question of whether Meciar understood how Kohl and other German leaders do not want to be seen as approving Meciar's authoritarian behavior by endorsing Slovakia's bid for membership in the EU and NATO. Kohl said publicly that Meciar's illiberal policies were seriously damaging Slovakia's image abroad.

Austria. Slovakia views Austria as an ally in the post-independence era. Austria has some reasons to deal sympathetically with Slovakia. It is a neighbor of Slovakia with a history of close connections to the Slovak people. When the government in Vienna helps Slovakia integrate with Western Europe, it also enhances Austria's image as a bridge builder between the former Communist countries to its east and the developed democracies to its West. Moreover, such a policy helps Austria resist the German economic steamroller, which can and does invest more than any other Western country in the former Communist countries in central Europe. Vienna's willingness to cooperate with Slovakia sends a message that Austria has its own role to play in East European development.[25]

The United States. Meciar wanted increased American foreign economic assistance and American investment, which have always been considerably less for Slovakia than for the Czech Republic, and he wants American support of Slovakia's bid for membership in the EU and NATO. But, Meciar had problems with Washington, where he was not held in high regard. The Clinton Administration was critical of Meciar because they did not beleive he had gone far enough fast enough in breaking with the communist past. The Administration believed that post-independence Slovakia was still ruled by too many ex-Communists, starting with Meciar himself. A law of the former Republic of Czechoslovakia barring from high office people who collaborated during the Communist era with the secret police, though technically in effect in Slovakia, the State Department observed, was not really enforced. When the Slovak government replied that it could not remove many so-called former Communists from their positions because the accusations against them were based on unverifiable secret police records, Washington was skeptical.[26]

The Bratislava government's failure to determine responsibility for the kidnapping of President Michael Kovac's son caused a further erosion of Slovak-American relations. At the end of 1996, newly appointed U.S. Ambassador Ralph R. Johnson warned the Slovak government that if it wanted to join Western democratic organizations, it would have to pursue with vigor and determination the kidnapping case and the alleged killing of a witness. In the U.S. view, the Slovak government's failure to clear up the mystery of the kidnapping is part of a "cover-up" to prevent the discovery of official culpability.[27]

In a lengthy report titled "Human Rights Practices in Slovakia" for 1995, which was picked up and commented on by the Slovak press, the State Department spoke of "credible allegations of politically motivated dismissals of public officials, intimidation of opponents of government policy, police misuse of authority, and interference with the electronic media." The report went on to say that "discrimination and violence against women are serious problems" and noted that the "Roma face societal discrimination and the police fail to provide adequate protection against continued attacks on them by skinheads." The report concluded "that many actions served to consolidate the (Bratislava) Government's power in a way that led to fear for the future course of pluralism, a balanced constitution, and overall democratic development."[28]

During 1996, U.S. policy focused heavily on Bratislava's delay in ratifying the 1995 state treaty with Hungary that included provisions assuring respect for minority rights. Along with its European allies, Washington had been pressing Meciar for some time to persuade the SNC to ratify the Slovak-Hungarian treaty. In mid-March 1996, U.S. Secretary of State Warren Christopher suggested that Washington was losing patience with the Slovak government over its failure to get parliamentary ratification of the treaty. During a meeting of East European foreign ministers in Prague, Christopher reportedly implied that Slovak ratification of the treaty was a prerequisite for membership in NATO, which he called "a force for conflict prevention in this region." Christopher also observed that "the United States and every NATO ally looks forward to Slovakia's ratification of its treaty with Hungary."[29]

For their part Slovak ultranationalists considered the 1995 treaty with Hungary a big mistake, one that would encourage the Hungarian minority to seek more autonomy or even break away from the Slovak state, despite protestations of loyalty to Slovakia from leading representatives of the Hungarian community. They were prepared to stand firm despite U.S. pressure. Meciar prevailed, however, and the treaty finally was ratified in the spring of 1996. Whatever benefits may have accrued to Slovak relations with the United States as a result of ratification of the state treaty with Hungary, however, were almost immediately compromised when the SNC passed the "Law on the Protection of the Republic." This law infringed on freedom of speech and assembly. It was a concession by Meciar to the ultranationalists who were fearful that the provisions of the state treaty pertaining to treatment of minorities would provoke a new surge of Hungarian self-assertiveness. This concession not only undermined most of Meciar's diplomatic effort to smooth out Slovak-Hungarian relations, but also provoked the United States. The State Department in February 1997, in its report *Human Rights Practices for 1996*, called attention to it as a potential violation of human rights.[30]

More Defensive Slovak Reactions. Slovak reactions to American criticisms were as defensive as they had been to the EU. Typical was Deputy Prime Minister Katarina Tothova's reply on March 13, 1996, to the U.S. State Department's criticisms of Slovakia. She insisted that American views were "not based on the real situation in the Slovak Republic" and that the Americans must be put straight. She called the American complaint about lack of press freedom "absolute nonsense" and said management of the broadcast media was "not subordinated to the Government but is elected by the Slovak" parliament. Bartolomej Kunc, an SNP deputy in the parliament, was equally defensive when he called the March 1996 State Department report on human rights violations in Slovakia "a statement by observers from far away who do not view developments in our country closely." And the Slovak foreign ministry responded in early May 1997 in a tone of injured pride to critical comments about Slovakia's human rights practices by U.S. Senator Alphonse D'Amato, Republican of New York. The ministry issued a statement titled "Peculiar Interest in Slovakia," published in *Slovenska Republica* saying Senator D'Amato "discusses the human rights problem in Slovakia in a very indiscriminate manner" and his comments "do not reflect the actual situation in Slovakia." In a defensive spirit, the ministry declared "the Slovak Republic is a democratic republic with functioning democratic institutions and a democratic constitution that protects the human rights and liberties of its citizens."[31]

Dismissing Slovak reactions, the United States again accused the Meciar government of pursuing antidemocratic behavior that compromised its efforts for membership in Western institutions. At the end of October 1996, Ambassador Ralph Johnson told the Slovak government that a number of Slovak laws and proposals "do not conform to generally accepted notions of a democratic society." He listed as examples the restrictive media laws, a law governing the universities, and the November 1995 language law that the U.S. and other Western Countries as well as many Slovaks themselves beleived discriminated against the Hungarian minority.[32]

Washington and Slovak Membership in NATO. Despite criticisms of the Meciar government, Washington favored Slovakia's eventual membership in NATO and the European Union. In March, 1996, Deputy Secretary of State Strobe Talbott told Foreign Affairs Ministry State Secretary Jozef Sestak in Washington that the United States was committed to the inclusion of central and East European countries in NATO and acknowledged Slovakia's continuing interest in NATO membership.[33] U.S. policy in this regard, according to Secretary Christopher, was to enlarge NATO to discourage a permanent division of Europe into three subsystems—one formed by the prosperous countries of Western Europe, another formed by those central and Eastern European countries undergoing transformation, and a third formed by countries in East Europe threatened by isolation.[34] Furthermore, the United States was willing to discuss European security issues with Slovak representatives and invited them to Washington for joint talks at the end of November 1997.[35]

The Clinton Administration, however, was far from ready to endorse immediate NATO membership for Slovakia. In talks with Slovak Foreign Minister Hamzik in Washington in April 1997, Secretary of State Madeline Albright suggested that while no country in the former Soviet bloc had been ruled out for membership in NATO, Slovakia's chances of receiving an invitation to join the alliance were not bright because of continuing "problems with democracy."[36] Indeed, the absence of any encouragement from U.S. diplomats about an imminent membership of Slovakia in NATO led Slovak leaders, in particular Meciar, to surmise that Slovakia would not be in the first wave of former Soviet bloc countries to join NATO.

Throughout 1997, the Clinton Administration essentially opposed Slovakia's immediate entry into NATO in light of the strong criticism of Slovakia contained in the State Department's annual review of human rights practices throughout the world for 1996, which was released at the end of January 1997. The report again criticized in explicit and rather severe terms the Meciar government's disregard of democratic rules and practices.[37] The report compared Slovakia with Albania as two countries with human rights issues. The comparison with Albania struck a sensitive nerve in Bratislava. The Slovak government replied that Slovakia was well ahead of Albania and well prepared for NATO membership as much as the Czech Republic, Poland, and Hungary.[38]

Not convinced, U.S. Assistant Secretary of State John Kornblum told an audience in Bratislava in mid-March, "It appears that Slovakia has fallen out of the mainstream." He continued, "Diversity, openness and tolerance are the way to a prosperous society. But we are concerned that this message is not being heard loud enough (in Slovakia)." And in late

May in a long and detailed statement to the CSCE in Washington, D.C., Slovak Ambassador to the United States Branislav Lichardus defended his country's bid to join NATO by calling American criticisms of Slovak politics "misperceptions", giving the "impression that Slovakia is an oppressive state with no free speech and a non-existent civil society. I am here to tell you that one must really stretch reality to arrive at those conclusions."[39]

At the end of May, President Bill Clinton, dismissive of Slovak protestations, again expressed concern about aspects of Slovakia's political system in a personal letter to President Kovac, pointing out that "more work needs to be done to promote an atmosphere of openness to opposing views and concerns of minorities." Clinton all but said that Slovakia was no longer considered as being among the post-Communist countries expected to join NATO in the first phase of the alliance's eastward enlargement.[40] Clinton did not rule out eventual NATO membership for Slovakia, assuring Kovac that enlargement was an ongoing process, not a onetime event. Clinton's reassurances, however, were of little consolation to Meciar, who was now convinced that Slovakia's chances of receiving an invitation to join NATO along with Poland, Hungary, and the Czech Republic at the NATO summit in Madrid in July 1997 were almost nil. He blamed the United States for this turn of events, calling the U.S. attitude toward Slovakia "negative." Certainly any doubts Meciar may have had that his policies at home had provoked the Clinton Administration's decisive opposition to immediate Slovak membership in NATO weer removed in October 1997, when Deputy Secretary of State Strobe Talbott met with a delegation of Slovak opposition leaders in Washington, D.C. According to Frantisek Sebej, Vice Chairman of the Slovak Democratic Party and leader of the newly formed Slovak Democratic Coalition, "Talbott said something we all wanted to hear. He told us that the NATO door is still open to Slovakia with the right democratic changes."[41]

Slovakia Considers Neutrality

Meciar shared his ill feelings toward the United States with Russian Prime Minister Viktor Chernomyrdin during a three-day visit to Bratislava at the end of April 1997. Chernomyrdin undoubtedly was delighted by the American rebuff to Slovakia, reiterating Russia's strong opposition to NATO's eastward expansion and hinting that the Kremlin would be very happy to see Slovakia pursue a policy of neutrality vis-à-vis NATO.[42]

Indeed, the idea of neutrality for Slovakia in its relations with Russia and the West had a certain appeal to Meciar. The Kremlin offered

Slovakia a guarantee of its security in the event of a formal declaration of neutrality. On May 21, 1997, SNP leader Jan Slota asked whether the United States would be willing to do the same. The American response was exactly the opposite: Ambassador Johnson told Slota that while the United States was willing to recognize and respect other countries' declarations of neutrality, it would not provide a security guarantee. The United States preferred Slovakia to continue its campaign to join NATO by pursuing the changes in its political behavior necessary for membership.[43]

Slovak neutrality had some liabilities for U.S. policy, not least the opportunity it would afford Russia "to fish in troubled waters," so to speak. The Clinton Administration, while solicitous of Russian concern for its security if former allies joined NATO, wanted NATO membership for Slovakia. At the very least, the Americans believed the Slovak campaign for membership in NATO would encourage democratization in Slovakia and elsewhere in the region and could strengthen security and enhance the chances of peace and stability in a traditionally volatile area.

The May 1997 Referendum and the West. The West reacted critically to the referendum on Slovak membership in NATO held on May 24 and 25, 1997, in which only about 10 percent of the population voted.[44] Meciar included questions on the referendum concerning the deployment of nuclear weapons on Slovak soil, knowing that many Slovaks worried about such an outcome of NATO membership and probably would oppose Slovak entry into NATO for that reason even though in December 1996 the NATO Council had decided not to deploy nuclear weapons on the territory of new member states.[45] Thus, in allowing questions about deployment of Western military forces to be on the ballot at all, Meciar revealed his own ambivalence about NATO membership.

Having manipulated the questions and the polling process, Meciar and his government had to cope with the consequences. If he had intended the referendum to demonstrate to the West and in particular to the United States Slovakia's commitment to Western-style democracy, its capacity to manage democratic processes effectively, and the interest of a majority of Slovaks in their country's joining NATO, he was disappointed. The failure of the referendum to attract more than a small fraction of the population, even though polling information released in mid-February showed that 61 percent of Slovak voters would take part in a referendum on their country's membership in NATO and 65 percent would vote in favor of membership,[46] was both a political embarrassment and a significant setback for Meciar. His credibility and that of the country's commitment to democratic processes plummeted in the West.

To make matters worse for Meciar's standing abroad, the opposition, which favored Slovak membership in NATO, openly accused the government of mishandling the referendum by misprinting referendum ballots to exclude a question on the direct election of the president. In particular, the opposition charged also that the government had biased the issue of NATO membership by asking whether Slovakia should allow deployment of NATO nuclear weapons on its territory.[47] After years of military subordination to the Soviet Union, so the opposition's argument ran, Meciar certainly knew that Slovaks were sensitive to even a hint of military subordination to outsiders, including the West. According to the opposition, the government had deliberately set about to make the referendum fail, in order to have "political cover" should the country not be asked to join NATO after the Madrid summit.[48]

Meciar's effort to set the record straight for critical outsiders was not persuasive. Blaming the opposition and President Kovac in particular for spoiling the referendum by including the question on direct election of the president carried little weight in the West, given its sympathy for President Kovak in his longrunning feud with Meciar. Nor was the west impressed by the Slovak government's argument that Kovac had no legal right to ask voters to amend the nation's constitution since the amendment process was reserved to the parliament. The government's public response to the opposition's complaints about its mishandling of the referendum also was not well served by a revelation that it (the government) had chosen to ignore an advisory opinion of the Constitutional Court—that, incidentally, the government itself had sought— that it was perfectly legal to include a question on direct election of the president in a referendum.[49]

EU Reactions. EU diplomats were reported to have been disappointed by the outcome of the referendum, which appeared to have destroyed any chances of Slovakia's joining Western structures in the foreseeable future. Indeed, one EU diplomat remarked that "it is all so very sad because it will also take years for any other government to clear the damage."[50] EU external relations minister Hans van denBroek was sent to Bratislava at the end of May with a tough message for the Meciar government about the failed referendum and other aspects of recent Slovak political development that raised questions about the credibility of Slovakia's commitment to democracy and its now-diminished chances of joining NATO and the EU.[51]

At the same time, the EU issued an official statement on the results of the referendum that also was implicitly very critical. The statement expressed "regret" that the Slovak authorities administering the referendum did not act in accordance with the Constitutional Court's ruling on the compatability of the referendum on direct election of the president with the Constitution. It also called attention to the failure of the government to act in accordance with the conclusions of the Central Referendum Commission. To that extent it had violated Slovak law. The statement called upon the Slovak government "to respect the rule of law and the principles necessary for strengthening a democratic society," promising that the EU would continue to watch events in Slovakia very carefully in light of its Association Agreement and its stated interest in joining European structures.[52]

Dismayed by the political squabble surrounding the May 1997 referendum, Western leaders decided once and for all that Slovakia was not ready for admission to NATO or the EU. The decision at the NATO summit in Madrid in July was not to invite Slovakia to join NATO, along with Poland, Hungary, and the Czech Republic. The summit did not even mention Slovakia as a possible future member.

The Future of Slovak Relations with the West

In the latter half of 1997 and throughout early and mid-1998, the prognosis for Slovak relations with the West was not good. It is clear that while professing strong interest in bringing Slovakia into the EU and NATO, Meciar was equally determined to continue policies that disturbed the West and discouraged Slovak admission to Western institutions. His repressive behavior, especially toward the Hungarian minority, seemed so necessary to him that they outweighed in his mind its disadvantages for his effort to obtain Slovak membership in NATO and the EU.

SLOVAKIA AND RUSSIA

Given differences with the West, Slovakia has strong incentives to maintain good working relations with the Russian Federation. The strongest is strategic. Friendship with Russia can increase Slovak confidence in dealing with an overcritical West. Trade is another incentive and derives from the long and close relationship between the Slovak and Russian economies forged in the post–World War II era. Slovakia needs to expand trade with Russia, especially in the energy area. Its economy benefits from cheap Russian natural gas. Other incentives for good Slovak relations are the shared problems both countries have in dismantling their paternalistic economies inherited from the Communist era. Both have shown a tendency to go slowly with market reform. Also, as President Kovac told Russian Army Chief of Staff and Deputy

Defense Minister Mikhail Kolesnikov at the end of September 1996, Slovakia recognizes its historical links to Russia.[53] Finally, Slovakia and Russia are both multinational states with minorities seeking autonomy. While quiescent, these minorities have ties to Kiev, which could some-day interfere on their behalf if it felt there was nothing to fear from Moscow. Meciar's policy, therefore, has been to keep good relations with both Moscow and Kiev.[54]

For its part, the Yeltsin government, which was sympathetic to Slovakia's independence, wants good relations with Bratislava. At the end of 1992, Russian Ambassador Aleksandr Lebedev not only stressed the "great significance" of Slovakia as a political and economic partner for Moscow but also offered to "support Slovakia in the military field." Lebedev also said that Russia was willing to sign a new friendship treaty with Slovakia during Meciar's planned visit to Moscow in early 1993.[55] Behind this thinking are strategic considerations. Russia is ready to profit from Slovakia's difficulties with the West by, so to speak, "catching Bratislava on the rebound." Indeed, the Kremlin would like to encourage Slovak independence from the West and eventually in-duce an orientation eastward to Moscow. Eventually, if so inclined, Slovakia could join a new orbit of Russian influence that the Kremlin is developing in neighboring republics such as Ukraine, Georgia, and Moldova—once part of the former Soviet Union and now called the "Near Abroad." At the very least a pro-Russian Slovakia could be an impediment to further NATO expansion eastward. The former Russian Ambassador to Slovakia, Sergei Yastrzhembsky, confirmed the Kremlin's interest in cultivating Slovakia. In early September 1996 he observed in a farewell statement in Bratislava that it "was not every European state (that) can boast of visits by the Russian President, the Russian Prime Minister, and the Russian Patriarch in the past three years."[56]

Problems in Slovak-Russian Relations

Slovakia has had and continues to have problems with Russia. The most important are security and trade.

Security. The security problem involves Slovak balancing efforts that the Kremlin does not especially welcome, especially if they lead even-tually to Slovakia's entry into NATO. While Slovakia in 1993 signed a state treaty with Russia recognizing its newly won independence, pro-fessing friendship between the two countries, and renouncing claims by either side against territory belonging to the other, the security issue was not resolved. From the Kremlin's point of view the treaty seemed to give more to Slovakia than to Russia because it did not preclude Slovakia from joining Western institutions like the EU and NATO. Moscow would have prefered Slovakia, along with Romania and Bulgaria, in a Russia-oriented relationship. As none of the former Soviet Union's allies in central and Eastern Europe have been willing formally to enter a relationship with Russia similar to the defunct Warsaw Pact and CMEA, Slovakia has room to maneuver with Moscow.

Moscow Cultivates Bratislava. To lure Slovakia into a close relationship and to discourage the Meciar government from orienting Slovakia westward and in particular from seeking membership in NATO, Moscow has made concessions to Bratislava. For example, in 1993, the Yeltsin government repaid part of its $1.6 billion debt to Slovakia in the form of five MiG 29 combat aircraft with spare parts and ammunition, enabling to upgrade its air force.[57] Moscow also has carefully refrained from castigating the Meciar leadership for its hard-line approach to the Hungarian minority. Indeed, Russia is not unsympathetic to Meciar's repressive policies toward Slovakia's minorities, in particular his opposition to giving the Hungarians administrative autonomy. The Russian leadership well knows from its own experiences with minority unrest how it can unravel a multinational society. It has tried to reassure Slovakia, as well as other countries in central and Eastern Europe formerly part of the Soviet-dominated "East Bloc," that, as Army Chief of Staff Kolesnikov put it, the "times of collectively saying yes [to Moscow, as most often happened in the era of the Warsaw Pact] are over."[58]

Moscow has proceeded very cautiously in opposing NATO's eastward expansion with central and East European countries, making sure not to appear overbearing and bossy and saving its sharpest rhetoric, in particular its threats of dire consequences, for Western governments. While warning those governments that NATO expansion "would fan the flame of war across Europe," Moscow took a soft approach to NATO aspirants, such as Slovakia, assuring them that NATO membership would not negatively impact on their relations with Russia.[59] Nevertheless, with regard to the membership of central Eurropean countries in NATO, Moscow has tried to dissuade when there was a sense of wavering. For example, aware of Meciar's apparent ambivalence about Slovakia joining the Western alliance, Moscow took the opportunity to strengthen military ties between the two countries. At the end of November 1996, Russia and Slovakia concluded an agreement on defense cooperation providing for an exchange of expert groups, collaboration in military training, and the sale of Russian military equipment to the Slovak army.[60] Furthermore, Moscow worked to convince Slovak military leaders that it would not retaliate against Slovakia if it joined NATO, say, by curtailing sales of strategic raw materials and energy on which the Slovak economy was dependent. During a visit to Moscow at the end of November 1996, SNC chairman Ivan Gasparovic said he did not think "the Russian side would cut us off from their oil pipelines and gas pipelines, or not supply us with oil."[61]

Moscow's agile diplomacy had some success in encouraging the doubts the Meciar government already had about bringing Slovakia into NATO. Although President Kovac and other Slovak politicians are strongly pro-West and pro-NATO, Meciar and members of his government have spoken about "neutrality." Meciar also has told large public audiences that he does not want nuclear weapons on Slovak territory, that he does not want to rebuild the Slovak army so that it can be deployed abroad, and that Slovakia has no enemies threatening its security. All of this suggests a negative view of NATO. While the Kremlin could not determine whether he is as ambiguous as he seems to be about Slovak membership in NATO, they are pleased by what he says even though they know that whenever he meets Western diplomats, he reassures them of Slovakia's interest in becoming a member of NATO.[62]

Obstacles to a Slovak-Russian "Entente Cordiale." The Russians are unlikely to lure Slovakia into a Moscow-oriented entente because the pull of the West is simply too strong and close. Slovak political, economic, and military links with the West are too valuable for Slovak leaders to forgo. Joining a Russian camp would certainly prejudice and possibly destroy the chances of Slovakia taking its place with its neighbors in the West, a position to which Slovak leaders, starting with President Kovac, and including, perhaps, Meciar, are committed.[63] Slovakia could hardly wait to join the Council of Europe in 1993 and continued to seek membership in the EU and NATO. SNC Chairman Gasparovic told the Russians during his visit to Moscow at the end of November 1996 that the Slovak decision to enter European structures was "unchangeable," though he also spoke in favor of balanced relations with Russia because "we need each other."[64] Moreover, developing an intimacy with Russia at the expense of the West would in fact compromise Slovakia's overall strategy of serving as a bridge between East and West.[65]

Furthermore, Slovak leaders worry about Russia's aggrandistic impulses. They watched with anxiety Russia's aggressive behavior in Chechnya in 1995 and 1996, as well as the ongoing expansion of Russian political and military influence in the Near Abroad. In his meeting with

Russian Army Chief Kolesnikov at the end of September 1996, Kovac pointedly said that European security arrangements "preclude any possibility of re-erecting the Iron Curtain."[66]

In addition, the Slovak leadership has been extremely sensitive to the few occasions when the Russians did seem to have stepped out of line to prevent former allies becoming full members of NATO. For example, in November 1996, Ambassador Yastrzembsky criticized remarks by U.S. Ambassador to Slovakia Ralph Johnson that Slovak democratic reforms were too slow in coming. The Slovak government promptly responded with a warning to the Russians to mind their own business. A Slovak Foreign Ministry spokesman also criticized Yastrzembsky for his "regret" that NATO was pressuring governments and peoples to accept this or that decision without giving them the opportunity to express their own views. This too, the Slovak Minister said, was none of Russia's business.[67]

The Slovak leadership also worried about the appearance of "big power collusion" in which the Kremlin sometimes seemed, at least to Bratislava, to be involved for the sake of furthering Russia's strategic or economic interests at Slovakia's expense. For example, in April 1997 the Meciar government accused Russia of reaching a secret agreement with the United States to exclude Slovakia from participating in the first wave of countries to be invited to join NATO. Russian prime minister Viktor Chernomyrdin vehemently denied such a deal, despite the logic of it from the point of view of both Washington and Moscow and told the Slovaks that Russia had never discussed Slovak exclusion with the Americans.[68] Whether Chernomyrdin's denial is true or not is impossible to determine. The possibility that he might have raised this issue with Washington is not totally out of the question.

In any event, tensions surrounding the NATO question seemed to ease somewhat when on May 14, 1997, Russia agreed to accept NATO's eastward expansion in the so-called "Founding Act" the Kremlin signed with NATO in return for membership in a new council consisting of NATO representatives. This council was to convene at regular intervals to discuss matters of common concern to NATO members and Russia. Slovakia was pleased by this arrangement because it believed that in its new role, however limited and informal, in NATO deliberations, Russia would feel less threatened by NATO and more neutral about Slovak membership.

Russia and the May 1997 NATO Referendum. At the same time, there seemed to be no problems with Russia over the holding of the NATO referendum on May 24 and 25, 1997. Meciar took care to minimize Russian sensitivity to the possibility that a majority of Slovak voters say yes to NATO and to the prospect of an upgrading of Slovak military facilities to bring them in line with existing NATO countries by including questions on deployment of NATO weapons on Slovak soil. If voters said no to questions on deployment of NATO weapons in Slovakia, as Meciar surmised might be the case, Slovak-Russian relations would not suffer in the event Slovakia became a member of NATO. If Slovak voters said yes to these questions, the Slovak government could simply tell the Russians it was acting in accordance with the national will, which it could not ignore.

While Russia carefully monitored the Slovak referendum, its reaction to the preparations for the referendum was at all times correct and cautious, despite concern that Slovakia might well join NATO soon. Sergei Zlotov, the Russian Ambassador to Slovakia in 1997, said that while his country would never change its negative attitude toward NATO enlargement, if Slovak citizens voted in a referendum for memberships in the alliance, that did not mean that the two countries would be enemies.[69] He said, "We Russians and Slovaks have never been enemies. The feeling of Slavic solidarity, the common fight against foes . . . are factors strong enough not to be erased by any hostile influences."[70] On the other hand, Zlotov suggested Russia's willingness to help with a campaign against a "yes" vote. He said there were experts in Russia in the fields of television, the press, and radio as well as political scientists who could come to Slovakia, if requested, to manage a campaign against NATO enlargement. Zlotov said, "We have a right to explain our national interests in every possible way."[71] At the same time, however, Zlotov went out of his way to assure the Slovak government that Russia had no intention of trying to interfere to influence the Slovak position on NATO membership, saying, "We recognize that Slovakia must decide its own political line and we do not wish to force our opinion on her."[72]

Nevertheless, the Kremlin certainly must have taken comfort from the Slovak government's mishandling of the NATO referendum and must have been gratified by its outcome, in particular by the fact that only 10 percent of Slovak voters went to the polls and that a majority of those voters said no to NATO membership. To Moscow's satisfaction the referendum somewhat tarnished Slovakia's relations with the West and compromised its chances of gaining early membership in NATO at its July 1997 conference in Madrid, and increased the likelihood of further Slovak efforts to cultivate Russian friendship.

Trade

While the security questions with Russia are gradually working themselves out, trade issues remain difficult. Slovakia wants to increase exports to Russia to offset the purchases of Russian oil and natural gas on which its industrial sector has become dependent. By late 1996, Slovakia had a huge trade gap with a deficit to Russia of 32.23 billion crowns, in contrast to the trade surplus it had with most other central European, African, and Asian countries.[73]

Obstacles to Trade Expansion. "Cracking the Russian market" for Slovak exports has been difficult. When the Council for Mutual Economic Assistance broke down along with the collapse of Communist rule in Central Europe in the Early 1990s, Slovakia lost a significant trading relationship. Between 30 percent and 40 percent of Slovak economic capacity had been devoted to Russian exports.[74] Furthermore, Moscow did not make it easy for Slovakia and other former Communist countries to sell in its market. The Kremlin imposed very high customs duties, ranging from 200 percent to 300 percent, which it has since reduced somewhat. With Russia's planned Jumal-Europe gas pipeline, stretching through Belarus and Poland to Germany, Russia no longer needed Slovak help to transport its energy exports westward. The Kremlin rejected Bratislava's request for a special southern route for the Jumal-Europe pipeline from Poland to southern Europe because the Russian oil corporation GAZPROM did not consider it economically viable.[75]

Also, as Slovakia's dependence on Russia gas and oil exports increased, the benefits of Russian imports declined, primarily because the Kremlin had been under intense pressure from the International Monetary Fund in early 1996 to raise the prices of its energy exports. The impact of higher energy costs for Slovakia was immediate. The price of gasoline to consumers and of electricity to business and households increased suddenly and rapidly, straining an already fragile economy. Higher energy costs also threatened political instability and the course of Slovakia's foreign policy toward the West.[76]

Meciar was not optimistic about an improvement in Slovak-Russian trade. He worried that Slovakia would continue to buy more than it sells. On September 6, 1996, Meciar reportedly told the newspaper *Hospodarske Noviny* that the volume of imported crude oil and natural gas, for which prices had been steadily rising, was not going to decline because diversifying Slovakia's energy sources was difficult. Moreover, he did not think Slovakia could find an economically more advantageous supplier of energy than Russia because transport to the West had not been built and because prices for energy from other sources were even higher than those charged by the Russians.[77]

Meciar continued to lobby with the Russians to open their market to Slovak exports, making a special pitch to the Kremlin to expand trade with Slovakia in September 1996.[78] The Slovak government proposed a free trade zone agreement between the two countries, though Meciar did not push this idea aggressively to avoid the appearance of tilting toward Russia. Nevertheless, Slovak trade officials continued discussion of a free trade agreement with their Russian counterparts and called for joint ventures.[79] In mid-December 1996, Slovak foreign minister Hamzik told the Russians that "the pillars of Slovak-Russian cooperation are...mainly economic cooperation."[80]

Russia Makes Concessions. Certainly the Kremlin could not ignore persistent Slovak demands for more trade between the two countries if it hoped to encourage Slovak independence in dealing with the West, in particular the EU. At the most, the Kremlin wanted to use the trade issue to strengthen its relations with Bratislava in the strategic area. In March 1993, with the aim of pulling Slovakia into its orbit and away from the West and perhaps offsetting a perceived expansion of Western influence in central Europe, the Kremlin granted Bratislava observer status at the conference of ex-Soviet republics hosted by Russia at Surgut in western Siberia that set up a natural gas and oil cooperation council under the auspices of the Commonwealth of Independent States (CIS). Slovakia was the first country not part of the former Soviet Union to be involved in CIS activities. The conferees agreed at Surgut to provide for a bilateral pricing system for Russian energy exports, making it possible for Russia to charge discount prices to preferred customers. Russia allowed Slovakia to benefit substantially by purchasing energy from Russia at below world market prices. Indeed, between 1993 and 1995 approximately 80 percent of Slovakia's oil needs and all of its gas needs were met by Russia.[81]

In the spring of 1997, when it was apparent that NATO intended to invite Poland, Hungary, and the Czech Republic to enter the alliance at its summit meeting scheduled for July in Madrid and that it would not invite Slovakia, the Kremlin offered Slovakia a substantial package of trade concessions. Russian prime minister Viktor Chernomyrdin went to Bratislava on April 27, 1997, for a two-day meeting with Slovak leaders. On the agenda was the signing of agreements providing for a liberalization of trade, cooperation between the central banks of both countries, the establishment of a committee for cooperation in science and technology, cooperation in arms production, and ways of reducing Russia's still-enormous debt to Slovakia, now valued at about $1.8 billion.[82] Chernomyrdin also concluded agreements involving Russian sales of natural gas and the creation of a joint company between Russia's GAZPROM and the Slovak state gas company to assure a long-term supply of Russian gas to Slovakia.

The Russian prime minister went out of his way to emphasize how much of a concession this deal was to the Slovaks, saying, "We do not usually sign such agreements for such long periods. We have done it for this first time with Slovakia. By 2008 it will fully safeguard the needs of Slovakia."[83]

Prospects of a Slovak-Russian Free Trade Zone. If Chernomyrdin and the Kremlin were looking for a positive Slovak response to their conciliatory gestures in Bratislava, they were not disappointed. Meciar raised the possibility of revisiting the idea of a Slovak-Russian free trade zone, despite EU warnings that the establishment of Slovak-Russian free trade leading to expanded economic links between the two countries could prejudice Slovakia's chances of joining the EU in the near future. He implied to Chernomyrdin that Slovak interest in concluding a free trade zone agreement with Russia might be more likely, given the little likelihood that Slovakia would be among the first countries in central and Eastern Europe to receive an invitation to join NATO at its Madrid summit meeting in July.[84] Chernomyrdin reciprocated by raising the possibility of Russian-Slovak cooperation in space. He said, "Our governments agreed that it was not enough for others to fly into space. It is time for a Slovak to go."[85]

The creation of a Slovak-Russian free trade zone, however, to say the least was problematical. Slovak government experts believed that a free trade zone had more liabilities than assets because of strong and persistent EU opposition. In October 1996, Meciar told a meeting of leading Slovak industrialists that "the countries of the EU have pointed out to us that any steps toward liberalization of trade with Russia...no matter how advantageous [to Slovakia]...would have negative political signals of Slovakia's foreign political orientation." He said also that another reason for the negative EU attitude on closer Slovak economic ties to Russia was that if Slovakia joined the EU, Bratislava would have to break free of the agreement. He suggested, however, that Slovakia could get around EU objections by concluding an agreement with the Russians limiting the free trade zone for a period of one or two years. EU concerns, he said, need not be an obstacle.[86] Slovak experts disagreed, saying that a free trade zone would mean a loss of customs revenue, given the likelihood of increased Russian imports resulting from the lifting of trade barriers. The experts believed that another way must be found to resolve the problem of the country's chronic trade deficit with Russia.[87]

Strong EU opposition to a Slovak-Russian free trade zone was decisive in prompting Meciar to back off, although he continued to believe the free trade zone was a good idea, given the existing trade deficit and

Slovakia's dependence on Russian energy sources and raw materials.[88] At the end of March 1997, Meciar's spokeswoman, Magda Pospisilova, however, assured vice president of the European Commission Leon Brittan that Slovakia would make no agreements with Russia regarding a free trade zone without prior agreement with the EU. Pospisilova insisted that Slovakia intended no action without EU agreement.[89]

On the other hand, the deal with GAZPROM has been favorable to the Slovak side and a real gesture of help from the Russians, who agreed to lower prices for their energy exports until 2008. Slovakia, it was estimated, stood to save tens of millions of dollars when compared to prices the Russians were charging Poland, Hungary, and the Czech Republic. This meant lower prices for natural gas for Slovak consumers. At the same time the Russians weren't doing so badly themselves, because they were to be paid in Slovak goods that otherwise they could not afford.[90]

In the long run, however, profitable economic relations with Russia could work to the disadvantage of Slovakia's policy toward the West, in particular its efforts to obtain full membership in the EU, which opposes a strengthening of Slovakia's economic ties to Russia. Bratislava is likely to conclude that Slovakia's economic growth will be better served by working to cultivate the Western market instead of trying to gain short-term advantage from the Russian market, which is likely to remain in turmoil.

Still, a modest improvement in Slovak-Russian trade did occur throughout 1996, according to the Russian Ministry for Foreign Economic Relations, which reported that Russian exports to Slovakia grew by 28 percent in 1996 compared with the previous year. If the Russian market becomes more stable, as Chernomyrdin predicted, the Slovak-Russian trade picture will brighten.[91] With the failure of Slovakia to gain early admission to NATO and the EU in the summer of 1997, Bratislava worked hard at expanding trade with Russia and probably continued to do so throughout 1998.

The Future of Slovak-Russian Relations

By the end of 1997, Slovak leaders were disappointed and a bit disillusioned with Slovak-Russian relations. They complained that Russia had failed to implement a wide range of treaties and agreements concluded with Slovakia in the preceding two years. Political leaders in Bratislava could barely conceal their annoyance over comments by GAZPROM officials comparing them to "little children" and accusing Slovaks of paying for Russian imports with worthless goods. The Slovak government also lodged a formal complaint when Russian television aired a news story emphasizing Slovakia's growing dependence on Moscow.[92]

CONCLUSIONS

Slovakia continues to seek a balance of initiatives toward both Russia and the West, but the Slovaks are caught in the region's complex web of international relations. While the West welcomes the Slovak interest in strengthening ties after a long period of isolation, given the country's strategic location in the heart of Europe, its demands on Bratislava, which must be met if Slovakia really wants to have close ties to the transatlantic democracies, frequently include limitations on Slovakia's range of options vis-à-vis Russia. For its part Russia can be a jealous friend, to put it charitably. The Kremlin has strong feelings about the westward orientation of its former allies in central Europe. The Kremlin views with suspicion, frustration, and even some hostility the effort of these countries to join NATO. As it still considers NATO a threat to Russian security, it frequently tries to limit Slovakia's choice of action. Nevertheless, the government in Bratislava needs Russia's cooperation in areas like trade and security, given the absence of permanent and strong links to the West.

Working to the advantage of Meciar's policy of drawing Slovakia closer to Russia, ironically, is the West, through its difficult-to-meet demands in both the foreign policy and the domestic areas. For example, the West insists that Slovakia make concessions to its minorities that may be quite impossible at the moment given the country's psychological insecurity, which helps explain the authoritarian undertone of its government. In this respect the minorities often are seen as a potential threat to Slovak cultural identity, and in the mind of some leaders and voters they are also a threat to Slovak territorial integrity and political sovereignty.

At the same time, the pull of Russia is especially strong given shared perspectives on political, economic, and sociocultural development. Like Slovakia, Russia has assertive minorities whose drive for autonomy threatens its internal stability and territorial integrity. Like Slovakia, its movement toward free enterprise has been difficult and dangerous.

Balanced against this pull of Russia is an undeniable lure of the West, with its capacity to provide Slovakia much-needed economic help and much-wanted security. Moreover, there is support in the Slovak parliament and in the voting public for orienting Slovakia westward, even if that means a weakening of relations with Russia. Many in Slovakia believe their country belongs to the West culturally, historically, economically, and psychologically and that the split from Czechoslovakia did not automatically mean a split from the West.

Finally, much of the Slovak political establishment believes that the future of Slovakia's well-being and, indeed, its survivability may be determined more by its relations with the West, which in the foreseeable future can do more good for Slovakia, than with Russia, which continues in a state of political and economic turmoil.

NOTES

1. "Opinion Poll Indicates That Slovaks Will Support NATO Membership in Referendum," *CTK News Agency* (Prague, February 15, 1997), *Lexis-Nexis/European Library*, BBC Monitoring Service: Eastern Europe (February 17, 1997); "Slovak Support for EU Membership Falling—Poll," Reuters (Bratislava, February 20, 1997), Reuters Textline, Reuters News Service—CIS and Eastern Europe (February 20, 1997); see also Sharon Fisher, "Slovak Foreign Policy since Independence," *Radio Free Europe/Radio Liberty Research Report* (hereafter cited as *RFE/RL Research Report*), vol. 2, no. 49 (December 10, 1993), pp. 29–30, 33–34.

2. The Economist Intelligence Unit, "Country Report: Slovakia," 3rd Quarter, 1997 (London: The Unit, 1997) on CD-ROM.

3. Carol Skalnik Leff, *The Czech and Slovak Republics: Nation versus State* (Boulder, Colo.: Westview Press, 1997), pp. 256–257.

4. Peter Laca, "US, EU Warns Slovakia on Democratic Reforms," Reuters (Bratislava, October 21, 1996), *LN/EL*, Reuters Textline, Reuters News Service—CIS and Eastern Europe (October 22, 1996).

5. The Economist Intelligence Unit, "Country Report: Slovakia," 3rd Quarter, 1997 (London: The Unit, 1997) on CD-ROM; *LN/EL* Eastern Europe, "Hilfe Country Report-Slovakia," Comment, Analyses, Statistics, Tables, Forcasts (December 1997), Quest Economic Database: Janet Mathews Information Services, 1997).

6. "Ruling Coalition Party against Joining 'European Structures,'" *CTK News Agency* (Prague, March 20, 1997), *LN/EL*, Eastern Europe TXTEE, BBC Monitoring Service: Eastern Europe (March 22, 1997).

7. Leff, *Czech and Slovak Republics*, p. 261.

8. Sharon Fisher, "Domestic Policies Cause Conflict with the West," *Transition*, vol. 2, no. 19 (September 20, 1996), pp. 56–57.

9. "Slovak Army Commander Supports NATO Membership," Reuters (Bratislava, March 18, 1997), *LN/EL*, Reuters Textline, Reuters News Service—CIS and Eastern Europe (March 18, 1997).

10. Peter Laca, "Slovak Coalition Party Warns against Entry into NATO," Reuters (Bratislava, March 2, 1997), *LN/EL*, Reuters Textline, Reuters News Service—CIS and Eastern Europe (March 2, 1997).

11. "Ruling Coalition Party against Joining 'European Structures,'" *CTK News Agency* (Prague, March 20, 1997), *LN/EL*, Eastern Europe TXTEE, BBC Monitoring Service: Eastern Europe (March 22, 1997).

12. Jiri Pehe, "Opinion—Czech Slovak Tensions" (Prague, April 15, 1997), *LN/EL*, Reuters Textline, Reuters News Service—CIS and Eastern Europe (April 15, 1997).

13. "Foreign Minister Defends NATO Referendum Questions"; Fisher, "Domestic Policies Cause Conflict with the West," p. 58; Leff, *Czech and Slovak Republics*, p. 247.

14. Leff, *Czech and Slovak Republics*, p. 247.

15. Ibid.; Stephen Kinzer, "West Says Slovakia Falls Short of Democracy," *NYT* (December 26, 1995); Fisher, "Domestic Politics Cause Conflict with the West," p. 247.

16. Kinzer, "West Says Slovakia Falls Short of Democracy."

17. Fisher, "Domestic Politics Cause Conflict with the West," pp. 56–57.

18. Ibid., p. 58.

19. Ibid.

20. "Premier...Discusses Ties with Germany," *BBC Summary of World Broadcasts* (hereafter cited as *BBC-SWB*), EE/D2712/C (September 9, 1996).

21. Ibid.

22. Fisher, "Domestic Politics Cause Conflict with the West," pp. 56–57.

23. *Narodna Obroda* (May 3, 1997), *Lexis-Nexis*, Europe Library, File (hereafter cited as *LN/EL*) Reuters Textline, Reuters News Service—CIS and Eastern Europe (May 2, 1997).

24. "Too Early for Details on Meciar-Kohl Talks," "From the Press, Bratislava," cited in *CTK National News Wire* (August 6, 1996, September 5, 1996, respectively).

25. "From the Slovak Press" (Bratislava) cited by *CTK National News Wire* (September 9, 1996).

26. U.S. Department of State, *Country Reports on Human Rights Practices for 1995: Report Submitted to the Committee on International Relations, U.S. House of Representatives and the Committee on Foreign Relations, U.S. Senate, April 1995*, "Slovakia" (Washington, D.C.: U.S. Government Printing Office, 1996), p. 1023.

27. Laca, "US, EU Warns Slovakia on Democratic Reforms."

28. "U.S. Report Critical of Slovakia's Human Rights Record," *CTK News Agency* (Prague, March 7, 1996), *LN/EL*, Eastern Europe, TXTEE, BBC Monitoring Service: Eastern Europe (March 8, 1996).

29. Jan Krcmar, "Western Pressure Mounts before Slovak Treaty Vote," Reuters (Bratislava, March 21, 1996), *LN/EL*, Reuters Textline, Reuters News Service—CIS and Eastern Europe (March 21, 1996).

30. United States Department of State, *Country Reports on Human Rights Practices for 1996: Report Submitted to the Committee on International Relations, U.S. House of Representatives and the Committee on Foreign Relations U.S. Senate February 1997*, "Slovakia" (Washington, D.C.: U.S. Government Printing Office, 1997), p. 1118.

31. "Deputy Premier Rejects U.S. Criticisms," *Sme* (Bratislava, March 8, 1996), *LN/EL*, Eastern Europe, TXTEE, BBC Monitoring Service: Eastern Europe (March 13, 1996); "U.S. Criticism Damages Slovakia's Image Abroad," *Slovenska Republica* (Bratislava, May 2, 1997) *LN/EL*, Reuters Textline, BBC Monitoring Service: Eastern Europe (May 5, 1997).

32. Jan Krcmar, "US Again Questions Slovakia's Democracy," Reuters (Bratislava, October 23, 1996), *LN/EL*, Reuters Textline, Reuters News Agency—CIS and Eastern Europe (October 24, 1996).

33. "U.S.A. to Continue to Support Slovakia's Integration," *TASR News Agency* (Bratislava, March 20, 1996), *LN/EL*, Eastern Europe TXTEE, BBC Monitoring Service: Eastern Europe (March 21, 1996).

34. "Foreign Minister Explains U.S. Definition of World Security," *Radio 1* (Bratislava, March 21, 1996), *LN/EL*, Eastern Europe TXTEE, BBC Monitoring Service: Eastern Europe (March 23, 1996).

35. "Delegation 'Disappointed' by NATO Talks in Washington," *Slovenska Republica* (Bratislava, November 21, 1996), *LN/EL*, Eastern Europe TXTEE, BBC Monitoring Service: Eastern Europe (November 23, 1996).

36. "Foreign Minister Comments on Talks with US Secretary of State," *Radio 1* (Bratislava, April 24, 1997), *LN/EL*, Eastern Europe TXTEE, BBC Monitoring Service: Eastern Europe (April 26, 1997).

37. "US Report on Human Rights Criticizes Slovakia," *Slovak Radio 1* (Bratislava, January 31, 1997), *LN/EL*, Eastern Europe, TXTEE, BBC Monitoring Service: Eastern Europe (February 1, 1997).

38. Jan Krcmar, "U.S. Report on Slovakia Facile—Slovak Diplomat," Reuters (Bratislava, March 12, 1997), *LN/EL*, Reuters Textline, Reuters News Agency—CIS and Eastern Europe (March 12, 1997).

39. Jan Krcmar, "Slovak Official Attacks Critical U.S. Report," Reuters (Bratislava, March 12, 1997), *LN/EL*, Reuters Textline, Reuters News Service—CIS and Eastern Europe (March 12, 1997); "Statement Submitted by Ambassador of the Slovak Republic, H.E. Branislav Lichardus," in CSCE, *Report on Human Rights and the Process of NATO Enlargement* (Washington, D.C.; CSCE, June 1997), pp. 117-119.

40. Peter Javurek, "Clinton Voices Concern on Slovak Democratic Reform," Reuters (Bratislava, May 22, 1997), *LN/EL*, Reuters Textline, Reuters News Service—CIS and Eastern Europe (May 22, 1997).

41. Ibid.; Peter Javurek, "Slovak PM Blames US for Expected NATO Failure," Reuters (Bratislava, April 29, 1997), *LN/EL*, Reuters Textline, Reuters News Service—CIS and Eastern Europe (April 29, 1997); James Morrison, "A New Slovakia?," *Washington Times* (October 27, 1997).

42. Javurek, "Slovak PM Blames U.S. for Expected NATO Failure."

43. "Ruling Coalition Partner Asks Washington for Neutrality," *CTK News Agency* (Prague, May 19, 1997), *LN/EL*, Eastern Europe TXTEE, BBC Monitoring Service: Eastern Europe (May 21, 1997); Peter Javurek, "U.S. Rejects Call to Protect Slovakia if Neutral," Reuters (Bratislava, May 20, 1997), Reuters Textlines, Reuters News Service—CIS and Eastern Europe (May 20, 1997).

44. "Referendum Turnout under 10%," *CTK News Agency* (Prague May 25, 1997), *LN/EL*, Eastern Europe TXTEE, BBC Monitoring Service: Eastern Europe (May 27, 1997).

45. "Foreign Minister Defends NATO Referendum Questions," Pravda (Bratislava, February 18, 1997), *LN/EL*, Eastern Europe TXTEE, BBC Monitoring Service: Eastern Europe (February 20, 1997); Peter Javurek, "Meciar Policies Cost Slovakia NATO Place," Reuters (Bratislava, March 24, 1997), Reuters Textline, Reuters News Service—CIS and Eastern Europe (March 24, 1997).

46. "Opinion Poll Indicates That Slovaks Will Support NATO Membership in Referendum," *CTK News Agency* (Prague, February 15, 1997), *LN/EL*, Eastern Europe TXTEE, BBC Monitoring Service: Eastern Europe (February 17, 1997).

47. "Opposition Calls on Premier to Resign," *CTK News Agency* (Prague, May 24, 1997), *LN/EL*, Eastern Europe TXTEE, BBC Monitoring Service: Eastern Europe (May 26, 1997).

48. Peter Javurek, "Slovak Opposition Calls for Yes on NATO" (Bratislava, May 7, 1997), *LN/EL*, Reuters Textline, Reuters News Service—CIS and Eastern Europe (May 7, 1997).

49. "Government Halts Distribution of Referendum Ballots on Presidential Election," *Pravda* (Bratislava, April 23, 1997), *LN/EL*, Eastern Europe TXTEE, BBC Monitoring Service: Eastern Europe (April 25, 1997).

50. Peter Javurek, "Slovak President Refuses to Vote in Own Referendum," Reuters (Bratislava, May 23, 1997), *LN/EL*, Reuters Textline, Reuters News Agency (May 24, 1997); Jan Krcmar, "Slovak Prospects Bleak after Poll Chaos (Say) Diplomats," Reuters (Bratislava, May 27, 1977), *LN/EL*, Reuters Textline, Reuters News Service—CIS and Eastern Europe (May 27, 1997).

51. Jan Krcmar, "Van Den Broek Has Tough Message over Slovak Vote," Reuters (Bratislava, May 28, 1997), *LN/EL*, Reuters News Service–CIS and Eastern Europe (May 28, 1997).

52. "EU Appeals to Government 'to Respect Rule of Law,'" *TASR News Agency* (Bratislava, May 29, 1997), *LN/EL*, BBC Monitoring Service: Eastern Europe (May 31, 1997).

53. "President and Premier Hold Talks with Russian Army Chief," *TASR News Agency* (Bratislava, September 30, 1996), *LN/EL*, Eastern Europe TXTEE, BBC Monitoring Service—CIS and Eastern Europe (October 2, 1996).

54. Jan Obrman, "Uncertain Prospects for Independent Slovakia," *RFE/RL Research Report*, vol. 1, no. 49 (December 11, 1992), p. 45.

55. Obrman, "Uncertain Prospects for Independent Slovakia," p. 45.

56. "Departing Russian Ambassador Holds Press Conference," *BBC-SWB*, Central Europe, Slovakia EE/2709C/C (September 5, 1996).

57. Pyotr Yudin, "Russia Barters Down Debt, Sends...MiG 29s to Slovakia," *Defense News*, (September 30, 1995).

58. "President and Premier Hold Talks with Russian Army Chief."

59. David Stamp, "Moscow Discards NATO Megaphone in Eastern Europe," Reuters (Prague, October 24, 1996), *LN/EL*, Eastern Europe TXTEE, Reuters News Service—CIS and Eastern Europe (October 24, 1996).

60. "Russian-Slovak Defense Ministries' Cooperation Plan Signed in Moscow," *TASR News Agency* (Bratislava, November 23, 1996), *LN/EL*, Eastern Europe TXTEE, BBC Monitoring Service: Eastern Europe (November 25, 1996).

61. "Speaker Denies Russian Economic Pressure over NATO," *Slovakia 1 Radio* (Bratislava, November 28, 1996), *LN/EL*, Eastern Europe TXTEE, BBC Monitoring Service: Eastern Europe (November 30, 1997).

62. Jane Perlez, "Abduction Casts New Doubts on Slovakia Chief," *NYT* (December 17, 1996).

63. "Foreign Minister Sees No Scope for Neutrality," *BBC-SWB* Central Europe, Slovakia, EE/D2720/C (September 18, 1996).

64. "Speaker Discusses NATO and EU with Moscow," *TASR News Agency* (Bratislava, November 28, 1996), *LN/EL*, Eastern Europe TXTEE, BBC Monitoring Service: Eastern Europe (November 30, 1996).

65. "Foreign Minister Sees No Scope for Neutrality."

66. "President and Premier Hold Talks with Russian Army Chief."

67. "Slovaks Rebuff Russia for Internal Interference," Reuters (Bratislava, November 12, 1996), *LN/EL*, Eastern Europe TXTEE, Reuters News Service—CIS and Eastern Europe (November 12, 1996).

68. "Chernomyrdin Denies US-Russian Agreement on Slovakia," *CTK News Agency* (Prague, April 29, 1997), *LN/EL*, Eastern Europe TXTEE, BBC Monitoring Service: Eastern Europe (May 1, 1997).

69. *Narodna Obrada* (February 24, 1997), *LN/EL*, Reuters News Service—CIS and Eastern Europe (February 24, 1997).

70. "Russia to Continue Opposing NATO Expansion Despite Referendum," *TASR News Agency* (Bratislava, February 23, 1997), *LN/EL*, Eastern Europe TXTEE, BBC Monitoring Service: Eastern Europe (February 25, 1997).

71. Ibid.

72. Jan Krcmar, "Russia, Slovakia to Intensify Economic Ties," Reuters (Bratislava, April 27, 1997), *LN/EL*, Reuters News Service (April 27, 1997).

73. Peter Juvarek, "Slovaks Seek to Increase Exports to Russia," Reuters (Bratislava, October 10, 1996), *LN/EL*, Eastern Europe TXTEE Reuters News Service—CIS and Eastern Europe (October 10, 1996).

74. Alexander Duleba, "Pursuing an Eastern Agenda," *Transition*, vol. 2, no. 19 (September 20, 1996), p. 52.

75. Ibid., p. 53.

76. Ibid., p. 55.

77. "Premier on Interest in Negotiating Free trade Agreement with Russia," *LEXIS-NEXIS, BBC-SWB* (September 12, 1996), Part 2, Central Europe, Slovakia, Foreign Economic Relations, EE/WO 452/WC.

78. "Foreign Minister Sees Great Potential in Relations with Russia," *TASR News Agency* (Bratislava, December 16, 1996), *LN/EL*, Eastern Europe TXTEE, BBC Monitoring Service: Eastern Europe (December 18, 1996).

79. "Premier on Interest in Negotiating Free Trade Agreement with Russia," (September 12, 1996), *BBC-SWB*, Central Europe, Slovakia, Foreign Economic Relations, EE WO 452 WC.

80. "Meciar Says Move onto Russian Market Strategic Aim for Slovakia," *CTK* (Bratislava, November 22, 1996), *LN/EL*, Reuters Textline CSTK Ecoservice (November 22, 1996).

81. Duleba, "Pursuing an Eastern Agenda," p. 53.

82. Jan Krcmar, "Russia, Slovakia to Intensify Economic Ties," Reuters (Bratislava, April 27, 1997), *LN/EL*, Reuters Textline, Reuters News Service—CIS and Eastern Europe (April 27, 1997); "Russian-Slovak Talks Confirm Interest in Developing Cooperation in All Spheres," *ITAR-TASS* News Agency—World Service (Moscow, April 28, 1997), *LN/EL*, BBC Monitoring Service: CIS (April 30, 1997).

83. "Chernomyrdin and Meciar Report on Agreements Signed in Bratislava," *Slovakia Radio 1* (Bratislava, April 29, 1997), *LN/EL*, Eastern Europe TXTEE, BBC Monitoring Service: Eastern Europe (May 1, 1997).

84. Ibid.

85. Ibid.

86. "Report to Government Cautious about Free Trade Zone with Russia," *Sme* (Bratislava, January 29, 1997), *LN/EL*, Eastern Europe TXTEE, BBC Monitoring Service: Eastern Europe (February 6, 1997).

87. "EU Opposes Slovak-Russian Free Trade Area," Reuters (Bratislava, October 17, 1996), *LN/EL*, Reuters Textline, Reuters News Service—CIS and Eastern Europe (October 17, 1996).

88. Ibid.

89. "Meciar and Brittan Discuss Trade with Russia," *CTK* (Prague, March 21, 1997), *LN/EL* Eastern Europe TXTEE, BBC Monitoring Service: Eastern Europe (March 25, 1997).

90. Slovakia Pays Less Than Before for Russian Gas," *CTK* (Bratislava, June 9, 1997), *LN/EL*, Eastern Europe TXTEE, CSTK Ecoservice (June 9, 1997).

91. "Russian-Slovak Talks Confirm Interest in Developing Cooperation in All Spheres," *ITAR-TASS* News Agency (Moscow, April 28, 1997), *LN/EL*, Eastern Europe TXTEE, BBC Monitoring Service: CIS (April 30, 1997); "Trade between Russia and Slovakia Growing," *ITAR-TASS* News Agency (Moscow, April 28, 1997), *LN/EL*, Eastern Europe TXTEE, BBC Monitoring Service: CIS (May 2, 1997).

92. The Economist Intelligence Unit, *Country Report: Slovakia*, Third Quarter, 1997 (London: The Unit, 1997).

7

Slovak Relations with Hungary, Romania, the Czech Republic, and Poland

Post-independence Slovakia's policy toward central and Eastern Europe has focused primarily on Hungary, the Czech Republic, and Poland, its nearest neighbors, and also on Romania. While Slovakia has had some serious problems with Hungary and the Czech Republic, inherited from the past, its relations with Romania and Poland for the most part have been friendly and cooperative. Romania was always a logical friend of Slovakia because of shared difficulties with Hungary regarding treatment of Hungarian minorities. Poland has been consistently sympathetic to Slovak efforts to join NATO and participate as an equal partner in the so-called Visegrad grouping of central European countries that has been meeting periodically since the early 1990s to discuss and address problems of concern to the northern area of Eastern Europe. All four countries are eager to discourage Slovakia from seeking intimacy with post-Communist Russia, which appears bent on trying to restore some of the influence it had in central and Eastern Europe in the Soviet era.

Underlying Slovakia's policy toward its neighbors in central and Eastern Europe are considerations of security, trade, and political legitimacy. Slovakia wants friends in the region with which it can cooperate to assure the permanence of its independence. It also wants to continue and expand the extensive trade links it had developed with its neighbors during the Communist era and on which its economic growth and well-being depend. Moreover, the Slovak government's legitimacy at home is strengthened by good relations with its well-established, influential, and comparatively well-off neighbors in Central Europe.

Slovak relations with its neighbors, especially with Hungary, are influenced also by Slovakia's desire to strengthen ties with the West and obtain full membership in NATO and the European Union (EU). But the West has made it clear to Bratislava that its relations with its neighbors must be peaceful and productive, saying in effect that not only Slovakia but all other countries in the region must resolve whatever squabbles they have had before joining Western military and economic institutions.

Slovakia wants to demonstrate to the West that it is doing just that and has tried to resolve differences, promote friendship, and cooperate with neighbors in bilateral and multilateral ways. Pursuing this conciliatory diplomacy, however, has been difficult for the Meciar government, especially toward Hungary and the Czech Republic. At times Slovakia has had abrasive relations with these countries, with the possibility of confrontation.

HUNGARY

Independent Slovakia's relations with Hungary must be looked at in light of a pervasive prejudice against Hungarians born of the long history of oppressive Hungarian control of Slovak lands before World War I. Moreover, Slovak leaders today, especially nationalists like Prime Minister Vladimir Meciar, suspect that the Hungarian leadership, as in the past, has not really accepted the permanent loss of Hungarian control over Slovak territory ceded to the new state of Czechoslovakia in the Treaty of Trianon of March 1920. Rightly or wrongly, many Slovak politicians suspect that post-Communist governments in Budapest have been waiting for an opportunity to regain control of this territory, now inhabited by a Hungarian community of about 600,000 people.

These beliefs, suspicions, and anxieties have had a major influence on how Slovakia has handled the two most contentious issues in its relations with Hungary. One of these issue concerns Hungarian opposition to the building of the Nagymoros-Gabcikovo Dam. The other issue is Hungary's perceived role as protector of the political and cultural interests of the Hungarian minority living in southeastern Slovakia. In the late 1980s, Czechoslovak and Hungarian Communist leaders tried to keep these issues from provoking a major confrontation between the two countries. The Soviet Union encouraged this restraint to avoid dividing and weakening the Warsaw Pact. With the collapse of Communist rule, the end of Soviet satellization, and the democratization of the domestic political environment, these issues have been raised anew and pursued aggressively by Slovak and Hungarian governments under nationalist leaders.

The Dam Project

In a 1977 treaty the Communist governments of Czechoslovakia and Hungary agreed to build the Nagymoros-Gabcikovo dam to provide the region with a reliable and cheap supply of energy. The Kremlin encouraged the project, which was to consist of a complex system of canals and dams on the Danube to introduce water management, resolve energy problems, and facilitate shipping. Plans for construction of the dam excluded environmental experts and ignored the interests of the affected population, a predictable omission given the ignorance of and indifference toward the environment of Communist political leaders.[1]

From the outset, Hungary had misgivings about the project, centering on concern about environmental pollution. By the end of the 1980s, Hungarian leaders regretted the original decision to build the dam. Hungary's last Communist prime minister, Miklos Nemeth, had no sympathy for the project and wanted to get Hungary out from under it. Anti-dam environmentalists lobbied against the project with Nemeth and other Hungarian Communist Party reform leaders. The environmental argument was compelling. The 144-kilometer stretch of the Danube affected by the Gabcikovo hydroelectric system provides about 45 percent of Hungary's drinking water. Hungarian environmentalists claimed that since the Gabcikovo canal was envisaged as a straight insulated, cemented canal, in some places rising 18 meters above the ground, the groundwater levels in the area would sink by 4 to 5 meters, and consequently there would be a shortage of drinking water. In addition, a projected reduction of the water flow in the Danube from an average of 2200 cubic meters to a fraction of this amount would cause drastic changes in the plant and animal life in the Danube and its tributaries and severe sewerage problems for the large Hungarian city of Gyor.[2]

Sympathetic to the environmental argument and eager to have the support of its advocates, on May 13, 1989, Nemeth canceled the Hungarian part of the project. With only 30 percent of the construction of the dam completed, the Hungarian leadership tried to get the Czechoslovak government to agree to terminate the project. Failing that, the Hungarian parliament favored renegotiating the 1977 treaty with the Czechoslovak government to make changes in the construction of the dam to make it less menacing to the environment.[3]

Following the collapse of Communist rule and Soviet power in central Europe at the end of 1989, the Hungarian parliament affirmed its decision to pull out of the unfinished project, but the Czechoslovak government would not go along. While sympathetic to the Hungarian case, the leadership in Prague was under pressure from Slovak leaders to continue work on the Czechoslovak section of the dam and power plant at Gabcikovo and in particular to divert the Danube's waters into an artificial channel 25 kilometers long on its own territory.[4]

Although the Hungarians took strong exception to the Czechoslovak decision to move forward with the project, continuing to insist it was dangerous for the environment, in particular the wildlife living off the Danube, the Czechoslovak government was determined to finish construction of the dam. Indeed, Slovak politicians told Czech leaders that they wanted no major deviation from the plans outlined in the 1977 treaty, especially with regard to diversion of the Danube waters. They saw the project in nationalistic terms and were convinced that cancellation of the project because of Hungarian opposition would be an intolerable humiliation. Moreover, popular support for the project in Slovakia undoubtedly was influenced by the fact that Slovak voters knew little about the environmental hazards of the project, since the Meciar government suppressed such information. The Slovak government also argued that substantial money already had been spent on the Slovak side of the project, notably the dam works at Gabcikovo, and their part of the project was nearly complete.[5] Hungarian Prime Minister Jozef Antall, however, was equally determined to end Hungary's participation in the project. On May 7, 1992, his government announced that on May 25 it would annul the 1977 treaty between Hungary and Czechoslovakia on the ground that completion of it would cause irreversible environmental damage to the Danube and surrounding region.[6]

At this point the European Community (EC), now known as the European Union (EU), offered to mediate. Within a few days both sides agreed to halt temporarily further work and reverse the diversion of Danube waters. The two sides also agreed to submit the dispute to the International Court of Justice for adjudication. However, Slovakia went back on its promise and refused to complete the reversal of the diversion of Danube waters, returning only about 20 percent of the water to the original riverbed. Budapest was furious, complaining that the diversion was causing an ecological disaster on the Hungarian side. The EC then told Slovakia in February 1993 to give back two-thirds of the water that had been diverted. Bratislava agreed, and for a moment the dispute seemed to ease.[7]

But the controversy flared up again in October 1993, when Budapest decided to dismantle the part of the dam it had built. The Hungarian parliament voted a substantial amount of money to proceed with this task, which was intended to restore the coastal environment on the Hungarian side of the river. This move in turn provoked a Slovak charge that Hungary had no right to dismantle its part of the dam because the whole project had been a joint undertaking and decisions regarding it

had to be taken by both sides. Angry at Hungarian readiness to dismantle the dam before the World Court had gotten round to giving a
decision, Meciar decided to complete the diversion as the Slovak side
had planned and to put its part of the dam in operation regardless of
the environmental liabilities for the whole area.[8]

When it made its case before the World Court, the Slovak government
rejected the environmental pleas, saying that the Hungarian
government's real concerns were commercial. According to the Slovaks,
the Hungarians wanted the dam torn down so that Hungary could
benefit from increased international shipping. At the end of September
1997, the World Court finally rendered a decision, but it was inconclu-
sive. The court said that both Hungary and Slovakia had broken the
1977 treaty and that Hungary had been wrong to suspend and abandon
its obligations to help build the dam. It also ruled that Czechoslovakia
had proceeded illegally when it diverted the river through the dam in
1992. The Court ordered both Hungary and Slovakia to negotiate in
good faith to insure the achievement of the 1977 treaty. The Court also
ordered that each side compensate the other for damages.[9]

The Hungarian government promised that it would form a negotiating team to address the environmental and economic interests in the
controversy. But, the sharp differences among the two states over the
project continued and complicated their relations. Moreover, the loser
all around, according to Philip Weller, director of World Wide Fund for
Nature's Green Danube Program, was the Danube River, because the
Court's decision said practically nothing about the environment. Weller
argued that the best settlement would be for the majority of the water
to be returned to the Danube.[10]

The Hungarian Minority in Slovakia

The dispute over the dam, however sharp it occasionally was, paled
in the shadow of the Hungarian minority issue, which severely strained
Slovak-Hungarian relations throughout most of the 1990s. Slovak leaders thought that the Hungarians were behind a campaign by the political leadership of Slovakia's Hungarian minority of 600,000 for cultural
recognition and administrative autonomy. They believed that eventually the Hungarian minority in Slovakia would seek independence and
annexation to Hungary.[11]

Scope of Hungarian Interference. In the early and mid-1990s, Hungarian
leaders in Budapest argued that they had a right to be concerned about
the interests of Hungarian minorities living abroad. For example,
shortly after the March 1990 parliamentary elections in Hungary, the

country's new non-Communist prime minister, Jozef Antall, declared that he was prime minister of "all" Hungarians. He meant that he had a right to be concerned about the well-being of not only Hungarians living in the Republic of Hungary, but also Hungarian minority communities living in neighboring countries, such as Slovakia, Romania, and Serbia. Antall's statement provoked an angry response from Meciar, who declared:

> Never in my life would I dare declare that I am the premier of all Slovaks in the world. . . . I therefore reject out of principle the claim of the Premier of the Hungarian republic that he is the premier of all 15 million Hungarians. . . . Our Hungarians have their own government in Bratislava and Prague. . . . To this, we reply that our state border is inviolable...this is our country and it will never again be Upper Hungary.[12]

Then, in 1992, the Hungarian government established an agency called the Office for the Affairs of Hungarians Living Abroad to monitor the conditions of ethnic Hungarians living in other countries, a gesture that aroused resentment and anxiety in Slovakia, Romania, and Serbia. When Slovakia became an independent state on January 1, 1993, Hungary refused to sign a bilateral treaty declaring the inviolability of the two states' boundaries. Slovak anxiety about possible Hungarian expansionism was not lessened by claims of Budapest that it had no intention of seeking changes in borders established after World War I.

Hungary also maintained ties with the main political parties representing Hungarian interests in the Slovak parliament in Bratislava, the Slovak National Council (SNC). These parties are the Hungarian Christian Democratic Movement (HCDM), the Hungarian Civic Party, the Hungarian People's Party, and the Coexistence Political Movement. But Hungary's policy had been to let these groups more or less fend for themselves in lobbying for autonomy with the Slovak government. After Slovak independence, Budapest paid increased attention to these organizations as it became clear that the Meciar leadership had little intention of accommodating the demands of the Hungarian community for autonomy. Budapest wanted not only to reassure the small parties of the Hungarian community that they were not alone in campaigning for minority rights but also to assuage a sensitive public opinion in Hungary critical of perceived discrimination against Hungarians in Slovakia.

The Hungarian government argued that the best way for Bratislava to discourage separatism among Slovakia's Hungarian minority was to protect minority rights, starting with a grant of autonomy in local administrative matters that would allow Hungarian to be the language of both instruction and grade reporting in the schools. This would be consistent with the political democracy Slovak politicians said they supported.[13]

Hungarian officials also reputedly have raised in a very oblique way the possibility of seeking the recovery of some Slovak territory where Hungarian-speaking people outnumber Slovaks. This territory was ceded to the Republic of Czechoslovak in the Treaty of Trianon of 1920; now that Czechoslovakia no longer existed, the Hungarians have hinted, this territory should go back to Hungary.[14] In an interview published by *Le Monde* on July 7, 1992, Meciar contended that Hungary's advocacy of first cultural and then territorial autonomy for Hungarian minorities abroad was an "ill-concealed scenario" for their subsequent annexation.[15]

In response to pressure from popular Hungarian nationalist politicians like Izstvan Csurka, who called for more aggressive statements of Hungarian concern about minorities abroad, the Hungarian government also threatened to block Slovak membership in the Council of Europe if Meciar did not act more sympathetically toward the Hungarian community. Budapest told the council that Slovakia had not met its standards for democratic treatment of minorities. But, eager to get the newly independent Slovakia into the Council as quickly as possible, the Czech Republic torpedoed this strategy. With support from other Council members, the Czech Republic persuaded the Hungarian government to back off, following Slovak acceptance of a Council demand that Bratislava allow a biennial monitoring of the minority situation and allow the use of bilingual road signs and Hungarian family names.[16]

Liabilities of Hungarian Policy. In the mid-1990s, Budapest's policy toward the Hungarian minority in Slovakia carried substantial risks. It severely strained relations with Slovakia, it aroused the concern of the West, and it jeopardized Hungary's campaign to join Western institutions such as NATO and the EU.

Meciar and other Slovak nationalist politicians were furious over Hungarian efforts, however diplomatically put, to help and encourage the Hungarian minority. Meciar considered problems with the Hungarian community a matter of domestic concern. In September 1992, he contended that Hungary's emphasis on ethnic issues, meaning its perceived interference in the internal affairs of other countries with Hungarian-speaking minorities, not only made conditions worse for those minorities but also threatened to cause the kind of internal political destabilization then going on in the former Yugoslavia.[17]

If in its dealings with Slovakia Hungary were shrill and hypernationalist, it could appear to be a potentially troublesome European citizen, and its applications for admission to the EU and NATO would be prejudiced. Western governments made clear they had little interest in welcoming countries into NATO and the EU that were squabbling with neighbors. Furthermore, while Council of Europe members were ready to encourage Slovakia to observe international rules governing the treatment of minorities, they were not prepared to endorse Hungary's demands regarding the government in Bratislava.[18]

Given the Western position, in the latter half of 1992, Hungary tried to diminish Slovak anxieties. The Hungarian leadership in Budapest said it was willing to discuss anything, any time, anywhere, about Hungarian-Slovak relations with a view to resolving differences. It also expressed willingness to give its Slovak minority all the rights it was asking for, without reciprocity for Hungarians living under Slovak rule.[19]

The 1995 Slovak-Hungarian State Treaty. In response to Western pressures the two countries agreed to conclude a state treaty pledging their governments to fair and equitable treatment of their minorities. From the outset, Meciar had misgivings about such a treaty, fearing that it might somehow oblige his government to make concessions to the Hungarian minority on the issue of autonomy that he and his nationalist supporters had always resisted. Determined to avoid antagonizing the West and prejudicing Slovakia's chances of gaining Council of Europe membership, however, he signed the state treaty with Hungary in the spring of 1995. In the treaty, both signatories agreed to respect the Council of Europe's Convention for the Protection of Minorities, a prerequisite for membership in that organization.

While Hungary promptly ratified the treaty in June 1995, considering it something of a diplomatic success in the sense of getting the Slovak government to pledge a liberalization of its treatment of minorities, the SNC dragged its feet and did not complete its ratification until the end of March 1996, largely because of nationalist opposition coming mainly from an ultranationalist faction within the MDS. Radical Slovak nationalists saw the treaty as a potentially dangerous concession to the Hungarian minority and demanded in return for their agreement to it a tightening of Bratislava's grip on the Hungarians. What they sought was a stronger language law, a redrawing of local boundaries that would diminish the political influence of the Hungarian minority, and an official disclaimer that nothing in the new treaty obliged Bratislava to grant the Hungarian community in Slovakia the "collective rights" it had been demanding.[20]

At the same time, the 17 Hungarian deputies inside the SNC also opposed ratification, arguing in effect that "Slovakia has already violated the treaty before it was even ratified" with its passage in November 1995 of a law making Slovak the sole official language.[21] The Hungarian deputies had some sympathy from other segments of the opposition in the SNC, in particular the Christian Democratic Movement (CDM) leader Jan Carnogursky, who thought the treaty was "legally inadequate" and badly negotiated by Meciar, presumably because the prime minister deliberately agreed to as little as he could.[22]

To hasten Slovak ratification, the EC and the United States pressured Meciar to obtain prompt parliamentary ratification of the treaty. They virtually threatened Meciar with the exclusion of Slovakia from Western institutions. Their message to Bratislava was clear enough: Without the State Treaty, Slovakia had no chance of joining the EU and NATO.[23] The United States in particular exhorted the Meciar government to move forward with ratification. In late March 1996, Secretary of State Warren Christopher made no secret of the Clinton Administration's impatience with Slovak footdragging on ratification, telling a meeting of central and East European foreign ministers in Prague, "The United States and every NATO Ally looks forward to Slovakia's ratification of its treaty with Hungary."[24]

The denouement of the ratification controversy occurred on March 26 when the SNC formally approved the 1995 treaty by a vote of 119 to 1 with 19 abstentions. The government at the same time accommodated nationalists skeptical of the treaty by ramming through the parliament the Law on the Defense of the Republic. This law imposed a severe limitation on freedom of speech in its criminalization of the spread of "false information damaging to the Republic of Slovakia." Opposition deputies as well as church leaders strongly criticized this law and compared it to a similar law passed in 1948 that the Communists had used to carry out Stalinist-style purges. Members of the opposition in the SNC said they had accepted the controversial law as the price of treaty ratification, which required Meciar to keep his nationalist colleagues in line. President Kovac, however, vetoed the Law on the Defense of the Republic.[25]

SNC ratification of the treaty was qualified also by two accompanying resolutions rejecting any possible interpretation of the treaty either to encompass the principle of collective administrative and cultural rights for the Hungarian minority or to grant any minority the right to create autonomous structures or statutes on an ethnic basis.[26] According to Slovak Foreign Ministry spokesman Juraj Matejovsky, the intent of the resolutions was to make sure that "the treaty provisions do not lay a foundation for the conception of collective rights for minorities." He went on to tell Slovak Radio that "now after the treaty has been approved no manoeuvering space for extremist [Hungarian] demands is left."[27]

At the same time, the Meciar government did not want the treaty in any way to encourage Hungary "to extend a protective hand over the citizens of another country." In early May 1996, Meciar quite pointedly told Budapest:

> If we do not respect the fact that minorities are first and foremost citizens of other countries; if we do not respect the fact that a state's sovereignty applies on its territory to each and every person; and if Hungary aims in its policy to be a guarantor of minorities, providing guarantees going beyond the powers of the bodies of sovereign countries, nobody will benefit.[28]

The Hungarian parties in the SNC took exception to the resolutions, saying that they would harm Slovakia's Hungarian-speaking citizens. The Hungarian government also was critical of them, saying that "they reflect some intentions that are not favorable (to the treaty)." The government in Budapest insisted that the resolutions "do not change the basic treaty itself." On the other hand, analyst Ivan Scipiades, writing in the daily *Magyar Hirlap,* said that if Hungary accepted the treaty it could be seen as accepting the Slovak resolutions.[29] The Hungarian government accepted Scipiades's view and warned that the final exchange of documents could not take place if they included the resolutions.[30]

Under pressure from the opposition and President Kovac, as well as from the West and from Hungary, Meciar eventually backed away from both the resolutions as well as from the Law on the Protection of the Republic. Meciar agreed to send the ratified treaty to Budapest without the two resolutions and accepted President Kovac's veto of the Law on the Protection of the Republic.[31]

The July 1996 Budapest Conference. An especially provocative incident in Slovak-Hungarian relations was the decision of the Hungarian ministry of foreign affairs to host a conference in Budapest in July 1996 on Hungarian minorities living in Slovakia, Romania, and Serbia. Attending the conference were representatives of the Hungarian Foreign Ministry, the Office of Hungarians beyond the Borders, and eleven delegates of Hungarian minority parties abroad. The conference issued a declaration of concern about the living conditions of Hungarians in neighboring countries, saying that "the establishment of local governments and autonomy—in line with the current European practice and the spirit of international norms—is vital to preserving the identity of Hungarians beyond the borders, their survival, and development."[32] It also spoke of Budapest's constitutional responsibility to those minorities and pledged coordinated support in the form of money to be set aside in the Hungarian state budget.[33]

The Hungarian Foreign Ministry's involvement in this conference reflected a growing concern on the part of its own nationalistically minded politicians about the rights of the Hungarian minorities in southeastern Slovakia and the Transylvanian region of Romania. Hungarian nationalists pointed to the fact that Budapest had done little beyond protesting the November 1995 Slovak language law, which in their view was intended to undermine the cultural identity of Slovakia's Hungarian minority. They believed that the government in Budapest was obsessed with speeding up Hungary's admission to the EU and NATO, to the extent that it would not involve itself enough in the minority question with which many Hungarian voters, especially those with relatives abroad, were concerned. Indeed, Prime Minister Gyula Horn seemed to betray these fears when, immediately after becoming prime minister in May 1994, he declared that "everything will be subordinated to the Euro-Atlantic integration of the country."[34] The unusually explicit character of this statement was no doubt influenced by Horn's desire to reassure the West that he intended to work, as his predecessors had done and despite his Communist background, for Hungarian membership in the Western community.

The Slovak leadership was infuriated by the Budapest conference declaration, which did seem to confirm its long-standing belief that Budapest was seeking to use the autonomy issue as a means of expanding Hungarian influence in southeastern Slovakia and eventually, perhaps, in the name of protecting kinsmen abroad, to raise claims to territory inhabited by Hungarians in neighboring countries. The Slovak government called the declaration "a step against the trend of positive development of mutual relations" and accused Hungary of trying to destabilize the region.[35] President Kovac, not usually on Meciar's side, supported him on this issue, saying that the declaration "arouses mistrust." He was especially upset over the connection the declaration made between the expression of Hungarian identity and the possession of special legal rights. At the same time Meciar complained in a radio address on July 12 that the declaration violated Slovak sovereignty.[36]

There followed a heated exchange between the two governments, with Bratislava accusing Hungary of having violated the pledge both countries had taken in the 1995 State Treaty to respect each others' boundaries and to disavow any territorial claims against each other. Some Slovak officials called for a unilateral abrogation of the treaty, saying that Hungary had violated it.[37]

Lazlo Lobody, head of the Hungarian government's Office for Hungarians Living Abroad, suggested that the Slovaks were reacting with unjustifiable vehemence because the declaration was really only a "recommendation" by the Council on Europe regarding treatment of minorities. He said that the word "autonomy" did not refer to administrative autonomy or even collective rights, as the Slovaks insisted, but only to a right of democratic expression. Budapest attributed Bratislava's emotional outburst to distrust, to domestic political considerations, and to wilfull misunderstanding.[38]

More Hungarian Interference. Within two months of the flap over the Budapest conference, the Hungarian government again provoked the Slovaks by what seemed at least to Bratislava a gratuitous gesture of interference. In mid-September 1996, Hungarian Culture and Education Minister Belint Magyar told his Slovak counterpart Ivan Hudec about an alleged worsening of the situation of Hungarians living in Slovakia. He was referring to the results of a recent poll among ethnic Hungarians in Slovakia showing that their situation had not improved since the early 1990s; in fact, it had deteriorated. Magyar blamed these results on the discriminatory effects of the 1995 language law and also on the administrative arrangement of the country, which in effect gerrymandered the districts so that Hungarian inhabitants would not exceed 27 percent in any region, a situation that would affect them negatively in elections by lowering the number of Hungarian representatives in local government in the SNC in Bratislava.[39]

In late April of 1997, Hungarian Deputy Prime Minister and Interior Minister Gabor Kuncze asked Meciar to allow Slovakia's Hungarian parties to send representatives to a newly created Slovak-Hungarian intergovernmental commission. The commission was to be made up of delegates from Slovak and Hungarian governments. They were to address minority problems. Kuncze believed representatives of Slovakia's Hungarian parties should attend commission meetings since their interests were directly involved and since they deserved an opportunity to present their views. Meciar refused to authorize their attendance. After the meeting, Magda Pospisilova, Meciar's spokesperson, said that the prime minister saw no reason for the participation of ethnic Hungarian parties in an intergovernmental commission. According to Pospisilova, since the Hungarian parties were not members of the government coalition, they had no business participating in the commission. In the Slovak view, Kuncze's position in support of the Hungarian parties' right to lobby for their interests in the commission was more evidence of the intrusive nature of Hungarian foreign policy when it came to dealing with Hungarian minorities living abroad.[40]

Confrontation over the Minority Language Law. Another bone of contention in Slovak relations with Hungary concerned the Slovak government's promise in the State Treaty to adjust the 1995 language law to ease its application to the Hungarian minority. In early November 1995 Hungarian Foreign Minister Laszlo Kovac in a meeting in Graz, Austria, with Slovak Foreign Minister Pavol Hamzik asked when Bratislava intended to pass such a law.[41]

With no evidence that passage of the law by the NCS was imminent, the Hungarian government in early February 1997 accused Bratislava of contravening its international commitments to the ethnic Hungarian community, arguing that failure to enact the amendment of the 1995 law repeatedly promised by Slovak politicians up to the highest levels violated the 1995 State Treaty.[42]

The Slovak government rejected Hungarian charges. Slovak Foreign Ministry spokesman Ivan Korcok complained that "misleading statements such as this, which place Slovakia in a negative position before the international public, are unfounded and counter-productive."[43] Meciar told Budapest that minority languages were sufficiently protected by the constitution and national laws.[44]

Hungarian Foreign Minister Kovac swiftly replied that "if you have in Slovakia some dozens of laws on the use of the minority language, what is the argument against having just one bill which would incorporate all this legislation into one?"[45] Kovacs said Hungary would continue to pressure Bratislava for the law on minority languages. In the early months of 1997, he promised to raise the issue at meetings with Slovak leaders in Slovakia and abroad.[46]

In response, the Slovak Foreign Ministry issued a long formal statement on February 15, 1997, summing up official Slovak frustration over what the Bratislava government perceived as Hungary's persistent interference on behalf of the Hungarian community in Slovakia. The statement accused the Hungarian government of exploiting the Hungarian minority issue for narrow political considerations, calling it "a wedge to be used whenever the internal political situation calls for it." It was deplorable, the statement alleged, that Hungarian official representatives were abusing the Slovak-Hungarian Basic Treaty to cast a shadow on Slovak minority policy and to create the impression that this document related exclusively to minorities. Furthermore, the Slovak statement went on, remarks of Hungarian Foreign Minister Kovac to the Hungarian parliament on February 10, 1997, to the effect that the treaty will be used to "make (Slovakia) responsible" for alleged violations of Hungarian minority citizens were absolutely unacceptable as communication between two sovereign countries. The statement ended with the observation that the real problem at issue in relations between Slovakia and Hungary was not the living conditions of the Hungarian minority in Slovakia but the Hungarian government's policy toward Hungarian minorities abroad. It seemed to be telling the Hungarian government to mind its own business and that its interference was spoiling relations between the two countries.[47]

A New Source of Tension: Meciar's "Modest Proposal." In August 1997, Meciar made a bizarre and, as it turned out, extremely provocative proposal to Hungarian Prime Minister Gyula Horn at a meeting in Gyor, in northwest Hungary. He proposed that the two countries exchange their Slovak and Hungarian minorities, with Slovaks living in Hungary returning to Slovakia and the Hungarian community in Slovakia moving permanently to Hungary. Hungarian leaders were flabbergasted by this proposal, not the least because it presaged pose a threat to the Hungarian community in Slovakia. Horn said at the time: "I was furious that he could make such a proposal. I suggested he forget about it."[48]

Meciar defended the proposal during an MDS political rally in September, saying that the exchange was necessary to assure the preservation of Slovakia's territorial integrity endangered by the presence of the large Hungarian community on Slovak soil adjacent to Hungary and vulnerable to what Slovaks perceived to be a secret Hungarian agenda of expansion into countries inhabited by Hungarian minorities. At the very least, some SNP leaders believed there was in fact a secessionist movement afoot among Hungarians living in southeastern Slovakia with the appearance of an organization called the Upper Land Civic Movement, which had some ties to the Hungarian government in Budapest.[49] Meciar's comments, incidentally, seemed timed to coincide with the 50th anniversary of the post–World War II Czechoslovak government's deportation of 70,000 Hungarians to Hungary as punishment for that government's cooperation with the Nazis in the destruction of the Czechoslovak state in 1938 and 1939.[50]

Meciar's proposal may have been inspired also by a campaign to increase voter support of his leadership in 1998, when Slovakia was to have a new round of presidential and parliamentary elections. Meciar wanted to revive popular sensitivity to the minorities issue and play on latent Slovak prejudice toward the Hungarians, which many Slovak citizens seemed to have put aside. Indeed, the opposition parties, which had little sympathy for his provocative tactics, refused to denounce Meciar's proposed population exchange, fearing a loss of votes. Another reason for the population exchange proposal probably was Meciar's interest in stirring up Slovak prejudice in the towns and villages in southeastern Slovakia, with a Hungarian majority where relations between Hungarian and Slovak neighbors had been friendly

and cooperative and where bilingualism prevailed and schools oper-
ated smoothly, except when the Slovak national government in
Bratislava intervened, as in the case of making the Slovak language
mandatory for student report cards.[51]

Hungarian officials believed Meciar had another motive, namely, to
derail Hungary's admission to NATO by provoking a confrontation
with Budapest, which was trying hard to meet NATO's admission
prerequisites of stable borders.[52] "The most serious danger in all this is
that it will get out of control," said Peter Huncik, chairman of the
Sandor Marai Foundation, a nongovernmental agency in Budapest that
monitored day-to-day relationships between Hungarians and Slovaks
in Slovakia. Huncik's agency had determined that only 33.3 percent of
Slovaks were strongly anti-Hungarian, and he feared that Meciar, by
arousing anti-Hungarian prejudice among the Slovaks, was bound to
make trouble between the two countries just as Hungary's admission
to NATO was being debated in NATO capitals.[53]

The Future. The minorities issue continues to burden Slovakia's relations with Hungary, both because Bratislava does not accommodate the
demands of the Hungarian minority for increased recognition of their
cultural and political aspirations and because Hungarian politicians
want those aspirations fulfilled. On the other hand, the strong interest
of both countries in joining the EU and NATO provides a powerful
incentive to the Slovak government to end the controversy. As former
Slovak president Michal Kovac put it, "We both know that neither the
European Community nor NATO are ready to welcome any new members who would be incapable of putting an end to quarrels."[54]

ROMANIA

In the mid-1990s, shared concerns about their Hungarian minorities
brought Slovakia closer to Romania. Both had difficulties with Hungary
in dealing with their Hungarian population, which they believe posed
a threat to their unity and stability. Both had been willing also to play
the nationalist card in dealing with their Hungarian minority, especially
when Hungarian groups agitate for administrative autonomy.

In the early 1990s, Meciar sought a common front with Romania
regarding treatment of their Hungarian minority. For example, in the
fall of 1992, Slovak foreign minister Knazko and his Romanian counterpart, Adrian Nastase, denied the need for collective minority rights.
They agreed that their respective minority policies were fair and that
they would continue to consult on minority affairs.[55]

In June 1993 in Bucharest, Meciar and Romanian president Ion Iliescu agreed in principle that minorities should be loyal to the state in which they lived and should not become a source of social tension or a cause of intervention by an outside power claiming a special concern. In September 1993, Iliescu on a state visit to Bratislava spoke to the NCS of Hungarian revisionism and of the danger of singling out minority rights from human rights. Ethnic Hungarian deputies in the parliament walked out before Iliescu finished his speech.[56]

A final incentive of Slovakia to strengthen ties with Romania was a perceived Hungarian military buildup. In mid-1993, Meciar voiced concern about Hungary's acquisition of 28 Russian-built MiG-29 fighter planes in partial repayment of Russia's foreign debt to Hungary. That the number of Hungary's combat aircraft was still under the limit imposed by the Conventional Forces Europe Treaty and that Slovakia in fact already had ten MiG-29s did not seem to console Meciar. Indeed, in October 1993, Meciar publicly accused Hungary of an arms buildup despite a lack of evidence. Probably Meciar wanted to alarm the Romanians who seemed less disturbed than Bratislava with Hungarian arms acquisition, having just concluded an agreement without Hungary on military cooperation and on "open skies."[57]

Needless to say, the Hungarian government was uncomfortable with this Slovak-Romanian alignment in the making. Budapest correctly saw it as anti-Hungarian and reminiscent of the pre–World War II "Little Entente" of Czechoslovakia, Romania, and Yugoslavia. A revival of some version of the Little Entente is not out of the question. Although in the mid-1990s the new rump state of Yugoslavia, dominated by the Republic of Serbia, has been preoccupied by the civil war in Bosnia-Herzegovina, in the near future a Serb-led Yugoslavia in fact would be sympathetic to a strengthening of ties with Slovakia and Romania in light of its own large, though very peaceful, Hungarian minority in the Vojvodina. President Slobodan Milosevic, who was elected president of Yugoslavia in the summer of 1997, has much in common with Meciar in terms of his nationalist orientation and his authoritarian style of leadership.

Nevertheless, a Slovak-Romanian entente has its limits. The pull toward the West with membership in NATO forms a strong counterweight to Slovak policies in the Balkans. Furthermore, when Slovak difficulties with Hungary escalated in 1996–1997, mainly as a result of Bratislava's restrictive policies toward the Hungarian community, Hungary's relations with Romania improved. Determined to meet conditions laid down for entry into the EU and NATO, Hungarian prime minister Gyula Horn went out of his way to improve relations with Romania. He was in large part successful. On September 16, 1996, Horn and Romanian prime minister Nicolae Vacaroiu signed a treaty designed to reduce tensions between the two countries and promote cooperation in areas of shared interest, in particular the treatment of minorities. The Hungarian-Romanian treaty provides for an expansion of cooperation in economic, environmental, and cultural areas. Most significantly, Romania pledged to respect the rights of its two million ethnic Hungarians. It was also made clear, however, that nothing in the agreement obligated the government in Bucharest to allow the Hungarian community in Transylvania the right to set up autonomous structures. At the same time, Hungary renounced any claim to the Transylvanian region of northwest Romania, where most of Romania's Hungarian community reside and which had belonged to Hungary before World War I. In seeking parliamentary approval of this treaty, Iliescu overcame the opposition of rabid nationalists like Gheorge Funar, who called this new treaty an act of national treason. Dominated by Iliescu's political party, the National Salvation Front, the lower house of the Romanian parliament ratified the Hungarian-Romanian treaty with only one dissenting vote.[58]

Romanian parliamentary and presidential elections held in late October and early November 1996 changed the political dynamics of the Slovak-Romanian relationship in a major way. The opposition Democratic Convention and its allies won a majority of seats; and in the presidential election several weeks later, Emil Constantinescu, a geology professor, a liberal, and a reformer, defeated incumbent President Iliescu by 54 percent to 46 percent. Constantinescu is a far different kind of politician from Slovakia's Meciar and, unlike his predecessor, Iliescu, does not have much sympathy for either the Slovak leader's authoritarian behavior or his intolerance of ethnocultural minorities.[59]

In early May 1997, the Hungarian Foreign Ministry affirmed a new era in Hungarian relations with Romania with regard to the Hungarian minority. State Secretary Matyas Eoersi pointed out to Janos T. Barabas of *Magyar Hirlap* that representatives of the Hungarian Democratic Union of Romania had become members of the Romanian government, punctuating a truly positive change in the situation of ethnic Hungarians living in Romania. He said that the Romanian foreign minister himself had declared that it might be possible for the Romanian government to exceed the stipulation on minority rights contained in the Hungarian-Romanian state treaty, say by increased responsiveness to the complaints and aspirations of the Hungarian regulation in Transylvania.[60]

By the end of 1997, the basis of a Slovak-Romanian entente had eroded further as a result of Constantinescu's determination to draw closer to the West. Constantinescu received encouragement from President Clinton during Clinton's visit to Bucharest in July 1997, when he assured Romania that it was headed eventually for membership in NATO. To the chagrin of the Slovak leadership, especially the advocates of NATO membership, Slovakia received no such assurances from the West. Thus, as Romania strengthened ties with the West under Constantinescu, Slovakia under Meciar seemed headed in the opposite direction and therefore seemed to be of declining interest to Bucharest as a friend and ally. This tendency may be reversed, but only in the event of a change of leadership in Bratislava in which Meciar is replaced by someone more committed than he has been to friendship and cooperation with the West.

THE CZECH REPUBLIC

Problems with Hungary and the uncertain nature of relations with Romania make Slovakia's relations with the Czech Republic extremely important to the future well-being of Slovakia. For most of the post-independence period, on balance, Czech-Slovak relations have generally been friendly and cooperative.

Both countries are eager to integrate with Western regional institutions like the EU and NATO and have cooperated with one another and with their neighbors, Poland and Hungary. For example, in the summer of 1993, the Czech Republic exerted pressure on Budapest to agree to the prompt admission of Slovakia to the Council of Europe. Despite some sympathy for Hungarian complaints about Bratislava's unwillingness to be more forthcoming in granting cultural rights to the country's Hungarian minority, as requested by the Council, the Czech side was working for Slovakia. Indeed, in the summer of 1993, former Czech prime minister Vaclav Klaus did not take Hungary's side in its dispute with Slovakia and helped Slovakia to gain admission to the Council of Europe before, not after, as Budapest wanted, the Slovak government had implemented recommendations by the Council on equitable treatment of minorities.[61]

Slovakia and the Czech Republic cooperated in other areas. The Czech Republic supported Slovakia's bid for membership in NATO. Bratislava reciprocated by supporting the Czech Republic's campaign for one of the nonpermanent seats on the UN Security Council, which it received on October 30, 1993.[62]

Other evidence of good working relations between the two countries has been the regular, frequent, and very busy bilateral meetings of both leaders and lower-level technicians. Bilateral summit meetings between Kovac and Havel provide an arena for the discussion of border problems, cultural ties, and foreign policy issues, such as how to respond to the "partnership for peace" proposed by the United States as an alternative to immediate admission of the two countries to NATO. On this issue the two countries agreed to accept the American proposal and view it as a first step on a path that eventually would lead to their full membership in NATO. Other meetings between lower-level diplomatic officials in 1993 took care of a variety of technical problems arising out of the separation of the two republics. On balance, the two countries have gotten along rather well considering the sharpness of differences that led them to separate after 75 years of living together.

Problems between Bratislava and Prague

At the same time, however, Slovakia and the Czech Republic continued to have problems as a result of their existence as two independent sovereign countries. These problems involved the division of federal property, border control, trade, citizenship, and minorities.

Division of Federation Property. The division of federal property was complicated, involving the distinction between fixed and moveable property, the proceeds from the nationalization of state enterprises prior to the split, the special drawing rights granted by the IMF to the unified Czechoslovak state, and the assets of national banks. At first, Czech Republic prime minister Klaus took a hard line, saying that the Slovaks owed the Czech Republic about $882 million in bank assets. He delayed the division of those assets. In addition, Prague refused to turn over to Bratislava the 22.6 billion crowns' worth of shares in Czech firms that Slovaks held from the voucher privatization scheme. Under pressure from Czech voters, who disliked what they perceived as bullying tactics by Prague, Prime Minister Klaus eventually came forward with what was due the Slovaks from the proceeds of the first wave of privatization in Slovakia. Eventually most of the property of the former Czechoslovakia was divided to the satisfaction of both sides; but the Czech Republic government, in refusing to consider a proposal simply to split what was left equally between the two, came off looking mean-spirited and cheap, given the strength of its economy when compared with Slovakia's. By late 1994, however, the sharing out of federal property was no longer a serious problem in Slovak-Czech relations.[63]

The Border. According to an agreement made in October 1992, just before the completion of the split, the Czech-Slovak border between the Slovak and Czech republics was to remain open, allowing Slovak and Czech citizens to travel freely between the two republics without visas and without being required to use special border crossings. The border was to remain as it had been at the time of the split until a Czech-Slovak border commission should determine otherwise in the form of a new treaty.[64]

In mid-1993, the Czechs sought a formal border involving restrictions on transit across it. The Slovaks opposed this, viewing it as a way of isolating them from the West. Meciar said such a border would be tantamount to creating an "iron curtain" against Slovakia. The Czech side proceeded to impose border controls anyway, primarily to monitor the transit of people going through the Czech Republic to or from third countries. Prague seemed to be under some pressure from Germany to do something to discourage illegal immigrants from Slovakia from crossing Czech territory to reach Germany. Indeed, Germany offered to help pay for setting up a formal border with booths and personnel to monitor the flow of traffic. The border control problem, however, was soon resolved with an agreement signed on July 17, 1993, stipulating that Czech and Slovak citizens would not be checked at the border, leaving them freedom to go back and forth as they wished without special travel documents.[65]

One especially acrimonious dispute concerned jurisdiction over several border villages. Throughout 1993 and early 1994, esoteric circumstances peculiar to each of the places complicated efforts to settle the dispute. Some villages were assigned to Slovakia and others to the Czech Republic, based on the willingness of each side to pay compensation to the other for this or that village exchanged. Determining which side got what village involved exquisite detail that took months of on-site examination and discussion. Eventually, a mutually acceptable set of exchanges was agreed upon, but not before Meciar had declared that Slovakia would not give up "even a square centimeter of Slovak soil" without compensation from the Czechs. The Czech side did pay some compensation, and the agreement was formally concluded after the Moravcik government came to power in March 1994.[66]

Trade. Following the split, the Czech Republic and Slovakia established a customs union with the goal of maintaining the already substantial trade between them, but the union ran into problems. Slovakia was limiting imports from the Czech Republic that had to be paid off in hard currency after a certain amount of indebtedness had been incurred. Slovakia simply could not afford to purchase an unlimited amount of Czech consumer products. One way out of this trade dilemma was currency devaluation, to encourage an expansion of Slovak exports. In July 1993, the Slovak government announced a 10 percent devaluation. By the end of the month the devaluation had had a positive effect on Slovakia's balance of trade with the Czech Republic. This effect was short-lived, however; and by December, Slovakia had run up a substantial deficit in its balance of trade with the Czech Republic, evidence of continuing Slovak economic weakness.[67]

In early 1994, Bratislava was called upon to settle its account with Prague in scarce hard currency. In response the Slovak government did some belt tightening. It limited Czech imports, and in February 1994 it began inspecting all foodstuffs imported from the Czech Republic. This move was quickly followed in March by the imposition of a 10 percent surcharge on consumer goods imported from the Czech Republic. The immediate effect of these limits on trade were positive for Slovakia, as its indebtedness to the Czech Republic substantially diminished, and by May 1994 Slovakia actually had a trade surplus.[68]

Slovak industry continued to have difficulty exporting to the Czech Republic, however, and a trade imbalance built up in the mid-1990s. In 1997, the Meciar government again tried to restrict trade with the Czech Republic by imposing limits on a range of food imports including sugar, potatoes, spirits, soft drinks, cigarettes, margarine, and beer. In mid-1997, Meciar declared that the level of economic interdependence between the two countries still was too high and ought to be reduced in the near future. The Slovak government established a new quota for alcoholic spirits and ordered stricter enforcement of what were called "quality certificates" for all imports from the Czech Republic, with the hope of reducing the Slovak import of Czech goods by 7 percent.[69]

Slovak restrictions on trade with the Czech Republic antagonized Prague, so much so that Czech officials wondered out loud about the future of the customs union between the two countries. In the summer of 1997, Trade and Industry Minister Karel Kuhn suggested that Slovak behavior violate the spirit if not the letter of the customs union, raising the possibility of abandoning it if Bratislava imposed further restrictions on Czech imports into Slovakia.[70] While the Czech Republic remains Slovakia's chief trade partner, it can no longer be said that Slovakia is the Czech Republic's chief trade partner, a distinction that now belongs to Germany.

Citizenship. The issue of citizenship was complicated and emotion-laden; hence, at the end of October 1992 Klaus and Meciar assigned the resolution of citizenship problems to the independent republics. As an operating principle in the determination of citizenship, the Czech side wanted an "alien regime" under which Slovaks would be considered foreigners in the Czech Republic. The Czech side also said that citizens of both republics should be barred from holding dual Slovak and Czech citizenship. Initially, the Slovak side took an alternative position, known as the "union regime," under which there would be one common citizenship for the people of both republics. The Czech side firmly rejected the "union regime," arguing that very few countries tolerated it and insisting that the Czech Republic would recognize only one citizenship, Czech. The Czech government proposed that after two years Slovaks residing permanently in the Czech Republic could obtain Czech citizenship, provided they renounced their Slovak citizenship, with the corollary that Czechs living in Slovakia after two years could become Slovak citizens but they would lose their Czech citizenship.[71]

After the split the status of Czechs living permanently in Slovakia and Slovaks living permanently in the Czech Republic became a serious issue. At least 12 percent of all marriages in Czechoslovakia were between Czechs and Slovaks and over a half million Slovaks resided in the Czech Republic at the time of the split and wanted to know the status of their citizenship. The Slovak government was sympathetic to the idea of dual citizenship sought by the Czech minority in Slovakia; but the Czech government would not hear of it, even though it did allow dual citizenship for other groups. The two countries eventually agreed that Slovaks in the Czech Republic could opt for Czech citizenship and Czechs in Slovakia could opt for Slovak citizenship and that no work or resident permits would be needed for the citizens of one republic to live and work in the other. This arrangement seemed to satisfy both sides. According to a poll in the spring of 1993, most Czech and Slovak citizens expressed no qualms about being "next-door neighbors."[72]

The Hungarian Minority in Slovakia. Bratislava's policies toward the Hungarian minority in southeastern Slovakia was and remains an issue in Slovak-Czech relations. The problem for the Slovak government is the occasionally schizophrenic reactions of Prague to Bratislava's handling of relations with the Hungarian minority. On the one hand, the Czech leadership has shown some sympathy for Slovak anxieties about the security of the country's territory in the face of oblique but continuing suggestions by Budapest of a legitimate concern on its part with Slovak treatment of the Hungarian minority. To the satisfaction of the Slovak leadership, the Czech Republic stood by it in the summer of 1993, when Hungary was trying to use Slovak eagerness to join the Council of Europe as leverage to induce a softening of Bratislava's policy toward the Hungarian community.

On the other hand, the Slovak government has not been pleased by occasional Czech Republic complaints about its failure to respect the minority rights of its Hungarian-speaking citizens. The Slovak leadership sees much of Czech criticism of its policies regarding minorities as being motivated primarily by a Czech effort to score

points with the West. Moreover, Slovak nationalists, including Prime
Minister Meciar, are also aware of the disdain many Czech liberals
have toward Slovakia and which they believe makes the Czechs
especially "righteous" when commenting on Slovakia's minority problems. This perceived undercurrent of Czech prejudice is likely to
continue, at least as long as Meciar is leading Slovakia and diverging
from well-established principles of democracy such as respect for
political freedoms and minority rights.

"A War of Words" in 1997. In early 1997, Slovak-Czech relations
were especially strained by an increase in hostile Czech rhetoric
toward the Meciar government. While many Czech politicians could
barely conceal their contempt for the Meciar government's authoritarian style of leadership, a war of words, so to speak, got started in
March 1997, when Czech president Havel described Meciar as "paranoid." Havel was responding to Meciar's allegations that Russia and
the United States had colluded to keep Slovakia out of NATO and
that the Czech Republic and Hungary were trying to compromise
Slovakia's chances of being admitted to NATO. After years of poor
Czech understanding of Slovak national aspirations when both had
a common state, Meciar had no trouble using Havel's comments to
create the feeling among Slovak citizens that their country was a
victim of an international conspiracy in which Czechs played an
important role.[73]

The hypersensitive Meciar was infuriated by the "paranoid" remark,
coinciding as it did with frequent complaints by Western officials,
and from American leaders in particular, that Slovakia's problems
with democracy were a major stumbling block to Slovak admission
to NATO. Meciar abruptly canceled a visit to Prague scheduled in
March 1997. It was a bizarre gesture because the meeting was
unrelated to the NATO issue and was called to satisfy a Slovak
complaint that the Czech Republic was illegally holding about 4.5
tons of Slovak gold, the remnants of assets of the former Czechoslovakia. Although this gold, on deposit in the National Bank of
Czechoslovakia since the end of World War II, was being held by the
Czech Republic government to cover a Slovak debt, officials in Prague
had been willing to discuss the issue with the Slovak leaders. Meciar
feared, however, that the Czechs would use the meeting for further
attempts to lecture him on Slovak governance. The Czech press was
suggesting that if Meciar came to Prague, he would be in for a lesson
from Havel on how to govern Slovakia in a democratic manner. Havel
allegedly said, "Meciar is welcome to come but he will not like what

he hears." Meciar decided that he would not meet with the Czechs, at least not until they had offered him a public apology.[74]

The Future of Slovak-Czech Relations

Despite these problems, Slovak leaders, starting with Meciar himself, want good relations between the two countries. In early September 1996, Slovak foreign minister Hamzik said that the time had come to start a new chapter in Slovak-Czech relations. He said the two countries needed each other now more than at any other time since their split, given their shared foreign policy goals, in particular the desire for integration with European and transatlantic communities. He called for frequent meetings with his Czech counterpart, Jozef Zieleniec, to take advantage of opportunities to enhance bilateral cooperation.[75]

Policy alone, however, will not make the difference. A major obstacle to improved Slovak-Czech relations is the Slovak perception of a patronizing tone of Czech leaders and journalists in their comments about Slovakia. For Meciar it is too much to hear Czech officials echoing the complaints of NATO and EU officials about his undemocratic practices. Other Slovak leaders share his sensitivity. Moreover, Slovak leaders are annoyed by what they also perceive as indifference on the part of both Czech politicians and ordinary Czech citizens toward developments in Slovakia. For example, Slovak leaders of all ideological persuasions were annoyed by the fact that Czech Republic prime minister Vaclav Klaus had shown little interest in visiting Slovakia. Even when the democratic reformer Jozef Moravcik was prime minister, in the summer of 1994, and tried to steer Slovakia away from violations of democratic rules, Klaus had refused to meet with him officially and lend him support.[76]

POLAND

While relations between post-independence Slovakia and Poland have been comparatively smooth and uneventful, the two countries do have divergent strategic interests in the region, especially regarding Russia. Both Bratislava and Warsaw have strong incentives, however, to keep their relations on an even keel and to cooperate with one another in areas of shared interest, such as membership in NATO and the EU.

Divergent Interests

Initially, Slovak-Polish relations were lukewarm. Polish political leaders never have had a high regard for Slovakia, which they considered politically and economically underdeveloped. Moreover, Poland had mixed feelings about the split of Czechoslovakia and the emergence of an independent Slovak state under the leadership of Prime Minister Meciar who was an ex-Communist, highly nationalistic, and conservative on issues of political and economic democratization. The former Czechoslovakia, whatever differences it had with Poland, had strong democratic credentials; was eager to move as quickly as possible, though not as quickly as Poland, to a free market economy; and shared with Poland an unequivocal commitment to integration with the West.

Furthermore, it was apparent that Slovakia and Poland had different approaches to relations with both Russia and Western Europe, given the peculiar versions of distrust each had of Russian power in the region. Warsaw was somewhat ill at ease over Meciar's perceived interest in developing extensive political and economic ties to Russia. Polish leaders also were suspicious of the interest that Meciar and other Slovak nationalists had in the notion of neutrality, especially as it pertained to Russia, which involved among other things a careful Slovak diplomacy to avoid antagonizing Russia in strategic matters like NATO's eastward expansion, even if that meant at times annoying Western Europe and the United States.

Slovak leaders have never shared the deep-seated fear of and hostility to Russia that Poland has always had, largely because Slovakia never felt threatened by Kremlin policies. In fact, more than any other former satellite of the Kremlin, Slovakia actually benefitted economically from Soviet Communist rule, which facilitated expansion of Slovak industry, especially in the area of weapons production. In the 1990s, Slovak leaders had a friendly eye to Russia, a view the Yeltsin Kremlin has worked very hard to encourage. Moreover, unlike Poland, the post-Communist Slovak leadership of Meciar, the MDS, and its coalition partners, the Slovak National Party and the Association of Slovak Workers, viewed good Slovak-Russian relations as an important means of enhancing Slovak security in central Europe and of dealing confidently with an overcritical West.

Thus, Slovakia diverged somewhat from Poland in its attitude toward membership in NATO. While Polish leaders in the mid- and late 1990s lobbied aggressively for Polish membership in NATO, Slovak leaders, while also committed to membership in the alliance, displayed some ambivalence. They saw the disadvantages of allowing the deployment of Western military personnel and equipment on Slovak soil; of risking the loss of foreign policy independence, particularly in regard to relations with Russia; and of the prospect of straining relations with Russia because of its well-known and unrelenting opposition to NATO's eastward expansion. These disadvantages outweigh whatever advantages for Slovak security NATO membership and integration with Western Europe would bring. Polish leaders, to the contrary, were convinced that membership in NATO would have a salutary impact on Polish-Russian relations by discouraging Russian thoughts of restoring influence in Eastern Europe and in particular in Poland.

A New Bratislava-Warsaw Axis?

Slovak-Polish relations grew stronger with the defeat of President Walesa and the victory of Aleksandr Kwasniewski, a former Communist and an advocate of a moderate pace of change to the free market, in the Polish presidential elections of October 1995. Unlike Walesa, an aggressive reformer and vehement anti-Communist, Kwasniewski, like Meciar, was skeptical of shock therapy. Kwasniewski understood and had some sympathy for Meciar's populism, his cautious approach to free market reform, and his interest in developing good relations with Russia. In addition, by the mid-1990s Slovakia had developed a modest but nonetheless profitable trade relationship with Poland. By 1995, 2.6 percent of Slovak imports came from Poland, which purchased 2.4 percent of Slovak exports. In both instances the value of Slovak-Polish trade exceeded that of Slovak trade with Hungary.

Poland had other reasons, as well, for bringing Slovakia into its orbit. A neutral Slovakia is a liability for Polish security in central Europe. It encourages Russia in a strategy of resistance to NATO's eastward expansion, and it encourages the Kremlin's hope that it can persuade other countries, notably Belarus, Ukraine, and the Caucasus republics of the former Soviet Union, to join a group of countries that eventually would be oriented eastward to Moscow rather than westward to Brussels. In sum, from Warsaw's vantage point, Slovakia's ambivalence toward NATO and its inclination to strengthen ties with Russia tended to undermine the value of NATO membership as a security shield for Poland. Thus, Warsaw has been an unequivocal supporter of Slovakia's bid to join NATO.[77]

Polish leaders have carefully refrained from the kind of criticism of Slovak internal behavior frequently made by Western countries such as Germany and the United States. While Warsaw certainly does not approve of Meciar's authoritarian style of leadership and has very gently chided the Slovak government, urging it to reflect on Western criticisms of its internal policies from NATO leaders, it is unwilling itself to criticize Bratislava. For Polish leaders, the strategic importance of Slovakia's westward orientation is far more important than the alleged undemocratic behavior of its conservative leadership, which may well change as a result of parliamentary elections scheduled in the fall of 1998. This Polish diplomacy has increased Warsaw's influence in Bratislava, especially among Slovak political leaders who may succeed to power in the not-too-distant future.

Slovak-Polish relations were strengthened when President Kwasniewski visited Bratislava in August 1997 and stated warmly that "Poland has excellent relations with all its neighbors and countries of central and Eastern Europe regardless of whether they are members of NATO or not."[78] Slovak and Polish leaders also discussed further expansion of trade, which at the time of the visit topped $200 million. Marian Servatka, Slovakia's ambassador to Poland, predicted that the value of trade between the two countries could soon exceed a billion dollars.[79]

Slovak leaders were gratified by the summit meeting with their Polish counterparts, coming as it did in the aftermath of Slovakia's failure to receive an invitation along with Poland, Hungary, and the Czech Republic to join NATO at its July 1997 summit in Madrid. Slovak President Kovac described Kwasniewski's visit as an extremely important moment in the history of his country and recalled that the Polish government was the first to support publicly Slovakia's pro-Western aspirations.[80] Kovac presented Kwasniewski with Slovakia's "White Cross," its highest medal for "his merits in developing good neighborly relations."[81]

For its part, the Meciar government wanted to promote military cooperation with Poland, not only for reasons of regional defense strategy but also to increase by as much as possible Slovakia's links with its neighbors on the threshold of becoming full members of NATO, in the belief that such ties would bring Slovakia a bit closer to joining them in the Western alliance. At the end of October 1997, Slovak defense minister Jan Sitek and Slovak Army chief of staff Lieutenant General Jozef Tuchnya met Polish Army chief of staff General Henryk Szumski in Bratislava to discuss European security, Slovak-Polish military cooperation, especially between the defense ministries of both countries, and weapons modernization.[82]

The Slovak-Polish relationship is important to Slovakia, and the Meciar government can be expected to do what it can to keep it intact. As long as Slovakia remains outside of NATO, it will need the friendship of Poland to help its campaign to join the alliance, given Poland's credibility with the Western powers. Good relations with Poland also can strengthen Slovakia's hand in dealing with the Czech Republic and Hungary since throughout the 1990s Poland has developed close cooperative relations with these countries through their membership in the Visegrad Group.

SLOVAKIA AND THE VISEGRAD GROUP

Slovakia and her central European neighbors—Poland, Hungary, and the Czech Republic—belong to the Visegrad Group formed shortly after the collapse in the early 1990s of the Warsaw Pact and the Council for Economic Mutual Assistance. The Visegrad Group meets periodically to consult on problems of common concern and in particular to expand trade relations and discuss environmental problems that cut across state lines. The Visegrad Group, however, played no role in helping Slovakia and Hungary to resolve their controversy over minorities, and the group certainly has no commitments in the areas of defense and security.

Nevertheless, membership in the Visegrad Group is of some importance to Slovakia. Membership strengthens Slovakia's image and credibility abroad and in that respect is important for Slovakia's legitimacy as a participant in international politics, given the newness of its independence. Moreover, with considerably dimmer prospects for early EU admission on its own, Slovakia sees some benefits in belonging to the Visegrad Group and in encouraging its regular meetings at a time when the group's other members seem to be on the threshold of integration into Western Europe.

Indeed, in the latter part of 1996, the Visegrad countries acted together in supporting Slovak membership in NATO. Meeting at the end of September 1996 in Warsaw, Visegrad defense ministers agreed to lobby with NATO leaders, especially the Clinton Administration, to include Slovakia in the group of countries slated to receive an invitation to join NATO. They obviously were concerned about the strategic liabilities of leaving Slovakia isolated from the West and vulnerable to Russian pressures to induce a stronger Slovak eastward orientation. Vile Halcyon, chairman of the Czech parliament's foreign affairs committee, said, "A new political issue is arising in connection with NATO enlargement—the issue of Slovakia." He went on to say, with the agreement of Polish defense minister Stanislaw Dobrzanski, that Slovak membership in NATO was supremely important to both the Czech Republic and Poland. He also noted the concern of NATO countries with Slovakia's internal policies and let it be known that the Czech Republic thought that "it is damaging to Slovakia that it is not steering clear of arms supplies from Russia."[83]

On the eve of the NATO summit in Madrid in July 1997, Slovakia's Visegrad neighbors seemed united in their support of its membership in NATO, whatever differences existed between them and the Slovak government. That support was sincere, the occasionally sharp differences of these countries with Bratislava notwithstanding, because both Prague and Budapest, as well as Warsaw, of course, saw Slovakia's early entry into NATO to be important for European security. At the same time, they recognized that Visegrad support of Slovakia would not be enough to persuade the West to approve Slovak membership. At the very least, however, the Visegrad entente provided Slovakia with mainly psychological and moral support, especially for those Slovak leaders and voters who favored their country's integration with the West.

CONCLUSIONS

Since independence, Slovakia has had a difficult time improving relations with its central and East European neighbors. The most important problem for Slovak policy in the region is strategic. Slovakia seems less committed than its Visegrad neighbors and Romania today to integration with the West. More than its neighbors, it seems determined to maintain substantial political and economic links with Russia, despite the Kremlin's harsh policies toward the region in the post–World War II era.

Slovakia's relations with Hungary and the Czech Republic have been especially problematical because of divisive issues that have grown out of Slovak domestic policy. With Hungary, of course, the main issue has centered around Meciar's allegedly discriminatory policies toward the Hungarian minority, which the Slovak prime minister adamantly refuses to alter in any significant way to accommodate the concerns of Budapest. With the Czech Republic a host of problems that individually are not profoundly important but when taken together as whole have contributed to misunderstanding and frustration in both Prague and Bratislava. These problems in the aggregate have prevented the development of the close and harmonious relationship between the two former partners that many Slovak voters and political leaders would prefer and consider essential to Slovak stability and prosperity.

Still, the record of Slovak diplomacy toward its neighbors since independence suggests Bratislava's abiding interest in promoting friendship and cooperation with them. In its own way the Meciar government has tried not only to keep its political fences mended with neighbors but also to keep some of the more intractable problems, in particular the treatment of the Hungarian minority, open to negotiation. Given the strong will of these neighbors to pull Slovakia into the Western orbit, these underlying attitudes and goals suggest that Slovakia's relations with its neighbors will improve over the long term.

NOTES

1. Karolyi Okolicsanyi, "Hungary Cancels Treaty on Danube Dam Construction," *Radio Free Europe/Radio Liberty Research Report*, (hereafter cited as *RFE/RL Research Report*), vol. 1, no. 26 (June 26, 1992), p. 46.

2. Ibid., p. 49.

3. Ibid., p. 46.

4. Alfred A. Reisch, "Hungarian-Slovak Relations: A Difficult First Year," *RFE/RL Research Report*, vol. 2, no. 50 (December 17, 1993), pp. 16–17; see also Sharon Fisher, "Slovak Foreign Policy since Independence," *RFE/RL Research Report*, vol. 2, no. 49 (December 10, 1993), pp. 28–34.

5. Ibid.; Okolicsanyi, "Hungary Cancels Treaty on Danube Dam Construction," pp. 47–48.

6. Okolicsanyi, "Hungary Cancels Treaty on Danube Dam Construction," p. 46.

7. Ibid., pp. 47–48; see also Sharon Fisher, "The Gabcikovo-Nagymoros Dam Controversy Continues," *RFE/RL Research Report*, vol. 2, no. 30 (July 23, 1993), pp. 42–48.

8. Reisch, "Hungarian-Slovak Relations," pp. 17–18.

9. Jane Perlez, "World Court Leaves Fight over the Danube Unresolved," *New York Times* (hereinafter cited as *NYT*) (September 26, 1997).

10. Ibid.

11. Carol Skalnik Leff, *The Czech and Slovak Republics: Nation versus State* (Boulder, Colo.: Westview Press, 1997), p. 247; see also Fisher, "Slovak Foreign Policy since Independence," pp. 28–34.

12. Ibid., p. 249.

13. Alfred A. Reisch, "The Difficult Search for a Hungarian-Slovak Accord," *RFE/RL Research Report*, vol. 1, no. 42 (October 23, 1992), p. 26.

14. J. F. Brown, *Hopes and Shadows: Eastern Europe after Communism* (Durham, N.C.: Duke University Press, 1995), p. 202; see also Bennett Kovrig, "Hungarian Minorities in East Central Europe," *Occasional Paper Series: The Atlantic Council of the United States* (March 1994), p. 19.

15. Reisch, "Difficult Search for a Hungarian-Slovak Accord," p. 26.

16. Leff, *Czech and Slovak Republics*, pp. 249–250.

17. Reisch, "Difficult Search for a Hungarian-Slovak Accord," p. 30.

18. Leff, *Czech and Slovak Republics*, p. 250.

19. Reisch, "Difficult Search for a Hungarian-Slovak Accord," p. 26.

20. Leff, *Czech and Slovak Republics*, p. 250; see also Duncan Shiels, "Slovakia Will Ratify Treaty with Hungary—Minister," Reuters (Budapest, March 21, 1996), *LN/EL*, Reuters Textline, Reuters News Service—CIS and Eastern Europe (March 21, 1996); Jan Krcmar, "Western Pressure Mounts before Slovak Treaty Vote," Reuters (Bratislava, March 21, 1996), Reuters Textline, Reuters News Service—CIS and Eastern Europe (March 21, 1996).

21. Krcmar, "Western Pressure Mounts before Slovak Treaty Vote."

22. Jan Krcmar, "Slovakia Approves Hungarian Friendship Treaty," Reuters (Bratislava, March 26, 1997), *LN/EL*, Reuters Textline, Reuter News Service (March 26, 1996).

23. Shiels, "Slovakia Will Ratify Treaty with Hungary—Minister."

24. Ibid.

25. "Slovaks Approve Hungarian Friendship Treaty," Reuters (Bratislava, March 26, 1996), *LN/EL*, Reuters Textline, Reuters News Service—CIS and Eastern Europe (March 26, 1997).

26. Ibid.

27. "No Collective Rights for Hungarian Minority in Slovakia," *CTK New Agency—Prague* (Bratislava, March 28, 1996), *LN/EL*, Eastern Europe TXTEE, BBC Monitoring Service: Eastern Europe (March 30, 1996).

28. "Premier Interviewed on Relations with Hungary, NATO Entry," *Slovak 1 Radio* (Bratislava, May 3, 1996), *LN/EL*, Eastern Europe TXTEE, BBC Monitoring Service: Eastern Europe (May 6, 1996).

29. Sandor Peto, "Hungarian Parties Slam Slovak Treaty Riders," Reuters (Budapest, March 27, 1996), *LN/EL*, Reuters Textline, Reuters News Service—CIS and Eastern Europe (March 28, 1996).

30. Jan Krcmar, "Slovakia Soothes Hungary, Western Fears on Treaty," Reuters (Bratislava, May 9, 1996), *LN/EL*, Reuters Textline, Reuters News Agency (May 9, 1996).

31. Ibid.

32. Zsofia Szilagyi, "Hungarian Minority Summit Causes Uproar in the Region," *Transition*, vol. 2, no. 18 (September 6, 1996), p. 45.

33. Ibid., pp. 45–46; see also "Conference Declaration," ibid., p. 49.

34. Ibid., p. 45.

35. Ibid., p. 46.

36. *Facts on File*, vol. 56, no. 2906 (August 15, 1996), p. 584.

37. Reisch, "Hungarian-Slovak Relations," pp. 46–47; see also *Facts on File*, vol. 56, no. 2906 (August 15, 1996), p. 584.

38. Ibid.

39. "Ministry Polls Ethnic Hungarians in Slovakia," *TASR News Agency Bratislava* (Budapest, September 19, 1996), *LN/EL*, Eastern Europe TXTEE, BBC Monitoring Service: Eastern Europe (September 20, 1996).

40. "Premier Rejects Hungarian Minister's Plea over Minorities," *TASR News Agency* (Bratislava, April 21, 1997), *LN/EL*, Eastern Europe TXTEE, BBC Monitoring Service: Eastern Europe (April 23, 1997).

41. "Hungarian and Slovak Foreign Ministers Discuss Situation of Minorities," *MTI* Hungarian News Agency (Graz, November 8, 1996), *LN/EL*, Eastern Europe TXTEE, BBC Monitoring Service: Eastern Europe (November 11, 1996).

42. Duncan Shiels, "Hungary Presses Slovakia on Language Law Delay," Reuters (Budapest, February 3, 1997), *LN/EL*, Reuters Textline, Reuters News Service—CIS and Eastern Europe (February 3, 1997).

43. Jan Krcmar, "Slovakia Rejects Hungarian Language Concerns," Reuters (Bratislava, February 5, 1997), *LN/EL*, Reuters Textline, Reuters News Service—CIS and Eastern Europe (February 5, 1997).

44. Ibid.

45. Shiels, "Hungary Says Slovak Language Law Delay Breaks Treaty."

46. "Foreign Minister on Minority Language Law Delay in Slovakia," *Duna TV Satellite Service* (Budapest, February 2, 1997), *LN/EL*, Eastern Europe TXTEE, BBC Monitoring Service: Eastern Europe (February 5, 1997).

47. "Foreign Ministry Criticizes Hungarian Statements on Minority Situation," *TASR News Agency* (Bratislava, February 13, 1997), *LN/EL*, Eastern Europe TXTEE, BBC Monitoring Service: Eastern Europe (February 15, 1997).

48. Jane Perlez, "Slovak Leader Fans a Region's Old Ethnic Flames," *NYT* (October 12, 1997).

49. "Slovak National Party Tells Hungarian Diplomat About Secessionist Moves," *TASR News Agency* (Bratislava, June 3, 1997), *LN/EL*, Eastern Europe TXTEE, BBC Monitoring Service: Eastern Europe (June 6, 1997).

50. Perlez, "Slovak Leader Fans a Region's Old Ethnic Flames."

51. Ibid.

52. "Meciar Seeking to Thwart Hungary's NATO Ambitions?" *Die Welt* (October 2, 1996), cited in *CTK National News Wire* (October 2, 1996).

53. Perlez, "Slovak Leader Fans a Region's Old Ethnic Flames."

54. Leff, *Czech and Slovak Republics*, p. 250.

55. Reisch, "Difficult Search for a Hungarian-Slovak Accord," p. 30.

56. Reisch, "Hungarian-Slovak Relations," pp. 21–22.

57. Reisch, "Hungarian-Slovak Relations: A Difficult First Year," p. 23.

58. *Facts on File* (October 31, 1996), p. 803; "A Blow to European Nationalism," *NYT* (October 14, 1996).

59. Jane Perlez, "Incumbent in Romania, a Leftist, Faces Run-Off," "Non-Communist Elected Romania's Leader," "Romania's Anti-Communist Revolutionary: Emil Constantinescu," *NYT* (November 5, 18, 19, 1996, respectively).

60. "New Foreign Affairs Official Promises Continuity in Policy," *Magyar Hirlap* (Budapest, May 7, 1997), *LN/EL*, Eastern Europe TXTEE, BBC Monitoring Service: Eastern Europe (May 9, 1997).

61. Sharon Fisher, "Czech-Slovak Relations Two Years after the Elections," *RFE/RL Research Report*, vol. 3, no. 27 (July 8, 1994), p. 10.

62. Ibid.

63. Ibid., pp. 11-12; see also Jiri Pehe, "Czech-Slovak Relations Deteriorate," *RFE/RL Research Report*, vol. 2, no. 18 (April 30, 1993), pp. 1–3.

64. Fisher, "Czech-Slovak Relations Two Years after the Elections," pp. 12–13.

65. Ibid.

66. Ibid., p. 13.

67. Ibid., pp. 14–15; see also Pehe, "Czech-Slovak Relations Deteriorate," pp. 3–4.

68. Ibid.

69. The Economist Intelligence Unit, *Country Report: Slovakia*, Third Quarter, 1997 (London: The Unit, 1997).

70. Ibid.

71. Jiri Pehe, "Czechs and Slovaks Define Post-divorce Relations, *RFE/RL Research Report*, vol. 1, no. 45 (November 13, 1992), pp. 9–10.

72. Fisher, "Czech-Slovak Relations Two Years after the Elections," p. 17.

73. Jiri Pehe, "Opinion—Czech-Slovak Tensions" (Prague, April 15, 1997), Reuters News Service—CIS and Eastern Europe (April 15, 1997).

74. Ibid.

75. "Hamzik Wants to Start New Chapter in Czech-Slovak Relations," *CTK National News Wire* (September 10, 1996).

76. Pehe, "Opinion—Czech-Slovak Tensions."

77. "Slovakia Seeking Support from Visegrad States for NATO Membership," *CTK News Agency* (Prague, August 19, 1996), *LN/EL*, Reuters Textline, BBC Monitoring Service: Eastern Europe (August 21, 1996).

78. "Kwasniewski in Poland," *Polish News Bulletin* (Warsaw, August 20, 1997), based on August 21 issue of *Rzeczpospolita*, no. 194, p. 5, and *Dziennik Prawa i Gospodarki*, no. 194, p. 2, *LN/EL*, Eastern Europe TXTEE, Polish News Bulletin (August 21, 1997).

79. Ibid.

80. Ibid.

81. Ibid.

82. "Defense Minister Meets Polish Chief of Staff," "Chief of Staff Discusses Military Cooperation with Polish Counterpart," *TASR News Agency* (Bratislava, October 22, 23, 1997, respectively), *LN/EL*, Eastern Europe TXTEE, BBC Summary of World Broadcasts (October 24, 25, 1997, respectively).

83. "Prague and Warsaw Back Slovakia's Entry into NATO," *Mlada Fronta DNES* (Prague, October 8, 1996), *LN/EL*, Reuters Textline, BBC Monitoring Service: Eastern Europe (October 10, 1996).

Conclusions

Since it gained independence in the beginning of 1993, Slovakia has made slow but steady progress away from the Communist dictatorship that ruled the country for 40 years toward something resembling a West European style of parliamentary democracy with political pluralism and respect for fundamental freedoms of speech, press, and assembly. There are no formal restrictions on what people can say politically, there is no official censorship, and a multiplicity of political parties are free to compete for voter support in local and national elections without fear of government restrictions and prohibitions. In the economic sphere, post-independence Slovakia has made extraordinary strides toward the free market. By late 1997, 79 percent of gross domestic product came from the free sector of the country's economic life. In the sociocultural sphere the Slovak government has tried to promote social peace and harmony among its minorities by some concessions designed to accommodate demands for cultural recognition. It also has diminished gender-based discrimination, at least in the public sphere, where women hold high positions in both the legislative and the executive branches of the national government. Finally, post-independence Slovakia gradually has strengthened ties with the West. Leaders of most of the major political parties look forward to the day when Slovakia will become a full member of the European Union (EU) and the North Atlantic Treaty Organization (NATO), though they also want to maintain friendly and cooperative relations with Russia and Slovakia's nearest neighbors in central and Eastern Europe, notably Poland, Hungary, the Czech Republic, and Romania. In sum, there is little question about its survival as an independent state and its capacity to achieve a stable, prosperous, and durable democratic polity.

PROBLEMS

Slovakia's overall development since independence also has been problem ridden. The severity of these problems at times has raised questions in Slovakia as well as abroad about the vitality of its commitment to democratic reform in the political, economic, and sociocultural spheres. These problems also have disturbed Slovakia's friends in the West and complicated its relations with regional neighbors.

Most important has been the persistence of authoritarian tendencies in the day-to-day functioning of the national government in Bratislava, involving harassment of journalists critical of government behavior and politically motivated dismissals of public officials. Slovakia has moved more slowly than its neighbors in Central Europe in the halting and far from complete movement away from the Communist command economy to some variant of Western-style free enterprise, especially in the areas of defense production, transportation, and public utilities; and the persistence of deeply rooted interethnic cleavages productive of social disharmony, confrontation, and conflict, especially with respect to the Hungarian community and the Roma people, have burdened Slovak society, threatening its unity and stability.

Slovakia also has had difficulties getting along with the West and fulfilling the expectation of most Slovak leaders and voters that someday soon Slovakia will be integrated with the West, politically, economically, culturally, and in terms of security and defense. In particular the West has been critical, at times quite severely so, of Slovakia's perceived disregard of Western liberal values and its perceived readiness to strengthen ties with Russia, which undercut the protestations by Slovak leaders of their determination to integrate with the West. Finally, Slovakia has had serious problems with Hungary that have contributed to abrasive relations dangerous to the peace and stability of central Europe and therefore of great concern to the West.

Certainly one reason for these problems, arguably the most important, is the singular role of Prime Minister Vladimir Meciar, who has held power for almost five and a half years, with the exception of a seven-month period between March and October 1994. Because of his leadership and perhaps as a result of it, Slovakia's political opposition has been weak, vulnerable, and consequently unable to unseat him, except in the middle of 1994, when an opposition government briefly ruled the country. One must also blame the problems of Slovak development, especially in the socioeconomic sphere, on the weaknesses of the political opposition, in particular its failure to offer Slovak voters alternative leadership and policies. Finally, outsiders must take some blame for the problems of development for which they have criticized Slovakia. Outside countries have behaved somewhat perversely toward Slovakia—notably the West, Russia, and two of its neighbors, Hungary and the Czech Republic, with which the Slovak people historically have had close ties.

Meciar's Leadership

Meciar's leadership of Slovakia has been something of an anomaly. He has been very conservative in a period marked by profound change in all areas of Slovak national life. As Slovakia embraced Western-style democratic processes, Meciar displayed a distinctly authoritarian bent, showing in particular a hypersensitivity to criticism of his policies. In governing the country he engaged in a kind of cronyism and personal corruption characteristic of dictatorial regimes in less developed countries. In leading Slovakia he was obsessed with national unity and the preservation of the Slovak national identity at the expense of minority groups of non-Slovak ethnic background. Underpinning much of what he said and did as the political head of post-independence Slovakia was an occasionally aggressive nationalism that he used to enhance popular support of his policies, despite skepticism and misgivings about them throughout the electorate.

What magnified Meciar's influence and buttressed his political authority was his personification of the burdens of the past, in particular the long history of Slovak subservience and hostility to Czechs in the Czechoslovak state established in 1918. In the Slovak view, the Czechs had deprived Slovakia of the equality and autonomy promised in the agreement between the two peoples to live in a single state after World War I. By the time Slovakia achieved full independence and sovereignty on January 1, 1993, most Slovaks, like Meciar himself, had become extremely sensitive to their cultural identity and determined to protect and preserve it—in a reformed Czechoslovakia, if possible, or alone outside it, if necessary. Meciar seemed to fulfil the dream of many Slovaks of being in control of their own destiny. And Meciar encouraged Slovaks to believe that self-rule in whatever form it took would mean an automatic improvement in their level of material well-being, which had been comprised along with their cultural identity by their close association with and perceived subordination to the Czechs.

Furthermore, Meciar's leadership was a response to the newness of the Slovakia state, which confronted severe, "state-threatening" problems of survival and transformation. His authoritarian bent, in particular his sensitivity to the protest and dissent that are normal in a democratic environment, seemed justified to many Slovaks. Indeed, he seemed to cater to a popular yearning for a strong directive, paternalistic leadership to which Slovaks had become accustomed during most of their recent political history. In addition, Meciar's skepticism about radical change resonated with much of the Slovak countryside, which was conservative and superstitious. At the same time, his sensitivity to popular expectations about the role of the state, honed fine in the Communist era, in assuring at least a minimum level of material well-being and personal security was shared by a large plurality of Slovaks, who were loyal supporters of his Movement for a Democratic Slovakia (MDS) in parliamentary elections. Finally, his leadership, especially his policies toward ethnic minorities, reflected cultural prejudices throughout Slovak society against non-Slovak peoples and were seen as a legitimate response to perceived threats to the country's cultural identity and administrative unity posed by demands of the Hungarians for "collective rights."

Weaknesses of the Opposition

For most of the post-independence period of Slovak development, the opposition parties have been unable to challenge Meciar's commanding position. When Meciar received a vote of no confidence from the Slovak National Council (SNC) in March 1994, it was due as much to disgruntled members of Meciar's own MDS as to the opposition parties. The opposition has been consistently weak and almost ineffectual in providing an alternative to Meciar's leadership, thus inadvertently strengthening it and contributing to its longevity.

Of the many reasons for the opposition's weakness the most important, arguably, is its failure to come up with either a program congenial to a large plurality of Slovak voters or an appealing leadership that could effectively compete with Meciar for public support. The opposition remains divided, lacking direction and cohesion. Sharing some of the prejudices of Meciar —and, for that matter, the whole country—regarding the ethnic minorities, opposition parties that drew their support from the ethnic Slovak majority, during much of the 1990s refused to cooperate with them in a common front against behavior of Meciar they criticised. The Slovak opposition suffered also from some aspects of the constitutional system in place since September 1992. The parliamentary structure with its emphasis on rule by a majority, despite its democratic character, actually tended to undermine democracy by making it difficult for opposition parties to challenge and confront the majority and wrest power from it. President Michal Kovac, one of the most prominent critics of Meciar, has tried to resist and reverse some of the Prime Minister's anti-democratic behavior without much permanent effect because the presidential office is weak. The president is supposed to be primarily a symbol and not a decision-maker, and certainly not an adversary of the Cabinet. And a strengthening of the presidency as a means of resisting an imperious Prime Minister and Cabinet is controversial and unlikely in the near future. An influential president would compete with the Prime Minister and provoke dualism within the national leadership of the country, inevitably weakening it. Moreover, a powerful presidency could itself become a focal point of dictatorship.

The Behavior of Outsiders

The highly critical behavior of the West regarding Meciar's leadership not only has strengthened him and encouraged him to continue policies perceived as conservative and sometimes antidemocratic but also weakened the opposition. It not only has increased Slovakia's defensiveness toward the West, it also invigorated Slovak nationalism and provided Meciar with a justification for the strong and occasionally illiberal leadership for which he is being criticized.

Russian behavior, on the other hand, pays little attention to antidemocratic aspects of Meciar's leadership and in fact exploits the sensitivity of all Slovak leaders to Western criticism. Indeed, the Yeltsin Kremlin understood and probably sympathized with Meciar's toughness toward critics and opponents in the media and elsewhere. The Russian government certainly did not share the Western concern about a perceived Slovak neglect of minority rights in its policies toward the Hungarian and Roma communities. Russia's nonideological, pragmatic approach to Slovakia may well have helped encourage Meciar to rule his country as he wished without having to worry, as he did in the case of relations with the West, about negative internal fallout.

PROSPECTS

Several circumstances, however, suggest a positive prognosis for democratic development in the political, economic, and sociocultural spheres of Slovak national life. The opposition has been persistent and durable in its criticism of Meciar and shows no signs of erosion, never mind disappearance from the parliamentary scene. It takes comfort, perhaps even encouragement, from the fact that Meciar has shown no willingness to try destroying it after the fashion of his Communist predecessors, perhaps because there is little support in Slovak society for a return to the repressive Communist dictatorship of the past. Slovak voters enjoy their freedom to select leaders and policy alternatives, and there is no evidence of a popular willingness to trade political freedom, say for economic security. At the same time, the democratic rules by which Meciar has been willing to play, as seen in his resignation in response to the vote of no confidence in 1994, can and very well may lead to a change of leadership and policies in the presidential and parliamentary elections scheduled in 1998. Voters certainly will have the opportunity to vote the MDS and Meciar out of power. Meanwhile, the steady improvement in economic growth has contributed to a modest but steady improvement in the well-being of wage earners; as this trend continues, voters eventually will feel more confident about the new pluralistic political order and its commitment to the establishment of the free market economy and, perhaps, give it the credit due it by supporting parties and leaders critical of Meciar's authoritarian style. The apparent loyalty of the Hungarian community, by now quite evident in its leadership's rejection of separatism and annexation to Hungary, further strengthens the democratic system by lessening the justification for harsh, antidemocratic policies to preserve the country's unity, integrity, and cultural identity.

Slovak democracy can also benefit from the sympathy Western nations do have for Slovakia's statehood, despite their occasional criticism of Slovak development. The West is committed to the full democratization of Slovakia, and institutions like the EU and OSCE monitor Slovak development very closely and are quick to remind the leadership in Bratislava when it veers from the straight and narrow path of liberal rule. Moreover, the West wants Slovakia to be oriented westward, not only to assure the integrity of its transformation to democracy but also because of its strategically significant location adjacent to the former Soviet republics, where the transition to democracy has not been as promising as it is in central Europe. Although the West has kept Slovakia at arm's length regarding its application for membership in the EU and NATO, no Western country has closed the door to Slovak membership. Indeed, the West has held out the prospect of membership as soon as Slovakia's "problems with democracy" have been resolved.

Bibliography

GOVERNMENT DOCUMENTS AND PUBLICATIONS

National Council of the Slovak Republic. *The Constitution of the Slovak Republic.* Privatpress Presov, Slovakia.

U.S. Department of State. *Country Reports on Human Rights Practices for 1995: Report Submitted to the Committee on International Relations, U.S. House of Representatives and the Committee on Foreign Relations U.S. Senate April 1996,* "Slovakia." Washington D.C.: U.S. Government Printing Office, 1996, pp. 1021–1028.

U.S. Department of State. *Country Reports on Human Rights Practices for 1996: Report Submitted to the Committee on International Relations, U.S. House of Representatives and the Committee on Foreign Relations U.S. Senate April 1997,* "Slovakia" (Washington, D.C.: U.S. Government Printing Office, 1997), pp. 1114–1123.

U.S. Department of State. *Foreign Broadcast Information Service Daily Report: Eastern Europe.* 1992-1997.

ON-LINE ELECTRONIC SOURCES

The Economist Intelligence Unit. *Country Report: Slovakia,* Third Quarter, 1997. London: The Unit, 1997). On CD-ROM.

The Economist Intelligence Unit. *Country Report: Slovakia 1997-1998 Prospect.* (London: The Unit, 1998).

Lexis-Nexis. Library: Europe, File, Eastern Europe, BBC Summary of World Broadcasts EE/D2712/C.

Lexis-Nexis. Library: Europe, File, Eastern Europe, BBC Monitoring Service: Eastern Europe (1996, 1997).

Lexis-Nexis. Library: Europe, File, Eastern Europe, CSTK Ecoservice (1997).

Lexis-Nexis. Library: Europe, File, Eastern Europe, "Hilfe Country Report—Slovakia," Comment, Analyses, Statistics, Tables, Forecasts (July 1996, December 1997), Quest Economy Database: Janet Mathews Information Services (1996, 1997 respectively).

Lexis-Nexis. Library: Europe, File, Eastern Europe, Reuters News Service—CIS and Eastern Europe (1996, 1997).

Radio Free Europe/Radio Liberty Newsline (January, March, May 1998)(Prague: Paul Goble Publisher, 1998) ON LINE @ http://www.rferl.org/newsline

NEWSPAPERS

The New York Times (1991–1997)
Chicago Tribune (1997)
The Washington Times (1997)

BOOKS

Judy Batt. *East Central Europe: From Reform to Transformation.* New York: Council on Foreign Relations, 1991.

Sten Berglund and Jan Ake Dellenbrant (eds.). *The New Democracies in Eastern Europe: Party Systems and Political Cleavages,* 2nd ed. Brookfield, Vt.: Edward Elgar, 1994.

J. F. Brown. *Hopes and Shadows: Eastern Europe After Communism.* Durham, N.C.: Duke University Press, 1994.

Zbigniew Brzezinski. *The Soviet Bloc: Unity and Conflict,* revised and enlarged ed. Cambridge, Mass.: Harvard University Press, 1971.

Janusz Bugajski. *Nations in Turmoil: Conflict and Cooperation in Eastern Europe.* Boulder, Colo.: Westview Press, 1993.

Commission on Security and Cooperation in Europe (CSCE). *Human Rights and Democratization in Slovakia.* Washington, D.C.: CSCE, September 1997.

CSCE. *Report on Human Rights and the Process of NATO Enlargement.* Washington, D.C.: CSCE, June 1997.

Karen Dawisha and Bruce Parrott (eds.) *The Consolidation of Democracy in East-Central Europe.* Cambridge, U.K.: Cambridge University Press, 1997.

The Europa World Yearbook 1995. Rochester, Kent, U.K.: Europa Publications, Ltd., 1995.

Daniel S. Fogel (ed.). *Managing in Emerging Market Economies: Cases from the Czech and Slovak Republics.* Boulder, Colo.: Westview Press, 1993.

Jeffrey Goldfarb. *After the Fall: The Pursuit of Democracy in Central Europe.* New York: Basic Books, 1992.

Ted Robert Gurr and Barbara Harff. *Ethnic Conflict in World Politics.* Boulder, Colo.: Westview Press, 1994.

Joseph Held (ed.). *Democracy and Right Wing Politics in Eastern Europe in the 1990s.* New York: Columbia University Press, 1993.

Frederick G. Heymann. *Poland and Czechoslovakia.* Englewood Cliffs, N.J.: Prentice Hall, 1966.

Owen V. Johnson. *Slovakia 1918–1938: Education and the Making of a Nation.* New York: Columbia University Press, 1985.

Stanislaw Kirschbaum. *A History of Slovakia: The Struggle for Survival.* New York: St. Martin's Press, 1995.

Paul Latawski (ed.). *Contemporary Nationalism in East-Central Europe.* New York: St. Martin's Press, 1995.

Carol Skalnik Leff. *The Czech and Slovak Republics: Nation versus State.* Boulder, Colo.: Westview Press, 1997.

———. *National Conflict in Czechoslovakia: The Making and Remaking of a State 1918–1987.* Princeton, N.J.: Princeton University Press, 1988.

Lyman H. Legters (ed.). *Eastern Europe Transformation and Revolution 1945–1991.* Lexington, Mass: D. C. Heath, 1991.

Jozef Lettrich. *History of Modern Slovakia.* New York: Praeger, 1955.

Victor S. Mamatey and Radmir Luza (eds.). *A History of the Czechoslovak Republic 1918–1948.* Princeton, N.J.: Princeton University Press, 1975.

Thomas G. Masaryk. *The Making of a State: Memories and Observations 1914–1918.* New York: Frederick A. Stokes, 1927.

Jaroslaw Piekalkiewicz, *Public Opinion Polling in Czechoslovakia 1968–1969.* New York: Praeger, 1972.

Sabrina P. Ramet. *Whose Democracy? Nationalism, Religion, and the Doctrine of Collective Rights in Post 1989 Eastern Europe.* Lanaham, Md.: Rowman and Littlefield, 1997.

Thomas F. Remington (ed.). *Parliaments in Transition: The New Legislative Politics in the Former USSR and Eastern Europe.* Boulder, Colo.: Westview Press, 1994.

Hugh Seton-Watson. *The East European Revolution.* New York: Frederick A. Praeger, 1956.

R. W. Seton-Watson. *A History of the Czechs and Slovaks.* London: Hutchinson, 1943.

H. Gordon Skilling. *Czechoslovakia's Interrupted Revolution.* Princeton, N.J.: Princeton University Press, 1976.

Eric Stein. *Czecho/Slovakia: Ethnic Conflict, Constitutional Fissure, Negotiated Breakup.* Ann Arbor: University of Michigan Press, 1997.

Gale Stokes. *The Walls Came Tumbling Down: The Collapse of Communism in Eastern Europe.* New York: Oxford University Press, 1993.

Zdenek Suda. *The Czechoslovak Socialist Republic.* Baltimore: Johns Hopkins Press, 1969.

Tad Szulc. *Czechoslovakia since World War II.* New York: Grosset and Dunlap, 1971.

Edward Taborsky. *Czechoslovak Democracy at Work.* London: George Allen and Unwin, 1945.

Samuel Harrison Thompson. *Czechoslovakia in European History.* Princeton, N.J.: Princeton University Press, 1953.

Bernard Wheaton and Zdenek Kavan. *The Velvet Revolution.* Boulder, Colo.: Westview, 1992.

Stephen White, Judy Batt, and Paul G. Lewis (eds.). *Developments in East European Politics*. Durham, N.C.: Duke University Press, 1995.

Sharon Wolchik. *Czechoslovakia in Transition*. London: Pinter, 1991.

Yearbook of International Communist Affairs 1991. Stanford, Calif.: Hoover Institution, 1992.

BOOK CHAPTERS

Vaclav Benes. "Czechoslovak Democracy and Its Problems 1918–1920." In Mamatey and Luza (eds.), *The Czechoslovak Republic 1918–1948*, pp. 39–88.

Dusan Hendrych. "Constitutional Transition and Preparation of the New Constitution in Czechoslovakia after 1989." In Joachim Jens Hesse and Neville Johnson (eds.), *Constitutional Policy and Change in Europe* (New York: Oxford University Press, 1995).

Jorg K. Hoensch. "The Slovak Republic 1939–1945." In Mamatey and Luza (eds.), *A History of the Czechoslovak Republic 1918–1948*, pp. 271–295.

Anna Josko, "The Slovak Resistance Movement." In Mamatey and Luza (eds.), *A History of the Czechoslovak Republic 1918–1948*, pp. 362–386.

Tony R. Judt. "Metamorphoses: The Democratic Revolution in Czechoslovakia." In Ivo Banac (ed.), *Eastern Europe in Revolution* (Ithaca, N.Y.: Cornell University Press, 1992), pp. 96–116.

Radomir Luza. "Czechoslovakia between Democracy and Communism." In Mamatey and Luza (eds.), *A History of the Czechoslovak Republic 1918–1948*, pp. 387–415.

Victor S. Mamatey. "The Establishment of the Republic." In Mamatey and Luza (eds.), *A History of the Czechoslovak Republic 1918–1948* pp. 3–38.

Peter Martin. "Relations between the Czechs and the Slovaks." In Legters (ed.), *Eastern Europe Transformation and Revolution 1945–1991*, pp. 382–383

John Morison. "The Road to Separation: Nationalism in Czechoslovakia." In Latawski (ed.), *Contemporary Nationalism in East–Central Europe*, pp. 73–81.

David M. Olson. "Federalism and Parliament in Czechoslovakia." In Remington (ed.), *Parliaments in Transition: The New Legislative Politics in the Former USSR and Eastern Europe*, pp. 97–123.

Theodor Prochazka. "The Second Republic 1938–1939." In Mamatey and Luza (eds.), *A History of the Czechoslovak Republic*, pp. 255–270.

Otto Ulc. "The Right in Post-Communist Czechoslovakia." In Held (ed.), *Democracy and Right Wing Politics in Eastern Europe*, pp. 89–103.

Gordon Wightman. "The Czech and Slovak Republics." In White, Batt, and Lewis (eds.), *Developments in East European Politics*, pp. 51–65.

Sharon Wolchik, "Democratization and Political Participation in Slovakia." In Karen Dawish and Bruce Parrott (eds.), *The Consolidation of Democracy in East Central Europe*, pp. 197–243.

PERIODICALS

"Another Constitutional Issue in Slovakia," *CSCE Digest*, vol. 20, no. 8 (August 1997), p. 85.

Paulina Brett. "The Status of Women in Post 1989 Czechoslovakia." *Radio Free Europe/Radio Liberty Research Report* (hereafter cited as *RFE/RL Research Report*), vol. 1, no. 42 (October 16, 1992), pp. 58–63.

Dean Calbreath. "While Slovakia Grows, Its Companies Don't." *Central and Eastern Europe Report*, vol. 5, no. 6 (July–August 1997), p. 18.

Milos Dokulil. "Ethnic Unity and Diversity in Czechoslovakia." *International Social Science Review*, vol. 67 (Spring 1992), pp. 76–86.

Alexander Duleba. "Pursuing an Eastern Agenda." *Transition*, vol. 2, no. 19 (September 20, 1996), pp. 52–55.

Sharon Fisher. "Church Restitution Law Passed in Slovakia." *RFE/RL Research Report*, vol. 2, no. 46 (November 19, 1993), pp. 51–55.

———. "Czech–Slovak Relations Two Years after the Elections." *RFE/RL Research Report*, vol. 3, no. 27 (July 8, 1994), p. 9–17.

———. "Domestic Policies Cause Conflict with the West." *Transition*, vol. 2, no. 19 (September 20, 1996), pp. 56–57.

———. "Economic Developments in the Newly Independent Slovakia," *RFE/RL Research Report*, vol. 2, no. 30 (July 23, 1993), pp. 42–48.

———. "The Gabcikovo–Nagymoros Dam Controversy Continues." *RFE/RL Research Report*, vol. 2, no. 37 (September 17, 1993), pp. 7–12.

———. "Is Slovakia Headed for New Elections?" *RFE/RL Research Report*. vol. 2, no. 32 (August 13, 1993), pp. 34–41.

———. "Kidnapping Case Continues to Complicate Political Scene." *Transition*, vol. 2, no. 13 (June 28, 1996), pp. 40–43.

———. "Making Slovakia More Slovak." *Transition*, vol. 2, no. 24 (November 29, 1996), pp. 14–17.

———. "Meciar Retains Control of the Political Scene." *Transition*, vol. 2, no. 16 (August 9, 1996), pp. 32–36.

———. "Meeting of Slovakia's Hungarians Causes Stir." *RFE/RL Research Report*, vol. 3, no. 4 (January 28, 1994), pp. 35–42.

———. "New Slovak Government Formed after Meciar's Fall." *RFE/RL Research Report*, vol. 3, no. 13 (April 1, 1994), pp. 7–13.

———. "Political Crisis in Slovakia." *RFE/RL Research Report*, vol. 3, no. 10 (March 11, 1994), pp. 20–26.

———. "Romanies in Slovakia." *RFE/RL Research Report*, vol. 2, no. 42 (October 22, 1993), pp. 54–59.

———. "The Slovak Arms Industry." *RFE/RL Research Report*, vol. 2, no. 38 (September 24, 1993), pp. 34–39.

———. "The Slovak Economy: Signs of Recovery." *RFE/RL Research Report*, vol. 3, no. 33 (August 26, 1994), pp. 58–65.

———. "Slovak Foreign Policy since Independence." *RFE/RL Research Report*, vol. 2, no. 49 (December 10, 1993), pp. 28–34.

———. "Slovak Government's Personnel Changes Cause Controversy." *RFE/RL Research Report*, vol. 3, no. 21 (May 27, 1994), pp. 10–15.

————. "Slovak Television in Disarrray." *RFE/RL Research Report*, vol. 3, no. 27 (February 18, 1994), pp. 29–33.

————. "Slovakia," *RFE/RL Research Report*, vol. 3, no. 16 (April 22, 1994), pp. 68–71.

————. "Slovakia: The First Year of Independence." *RFE/RL Research Report*, vol. 3, no. 1 (January 7, 1994), pp. 87–91.

————. "Slovakia Heads toward International Isolation." *Transition*, vol. 3, no. 2 (February 7, 1997), pp. 11–13.

————. "Slovakia's Troubled Print Media." *Transition*, vol. 2, no. 21 (October 18, 1996), pp. 46–48.

————. "Unraveling the Enigma of SIS Director Ivan Lexa." *Transition*, vol. 2, no. 13 (June 28, 1996), pp. 44–47.

Sharon Fisher and Stefan Hrib. "Political Crisis in Slovakia." *RFE/RL Research Report*, vol. 3, no. 10 (March 11, 1994), pp. 20–26.

Pavol Fric. "Slovakia on Its Way toward Another Misunderstanding?" *Sisyphus*, vol. 8, no. 2 (1992), pp. 115–120.

John Gould and Sona Szomolanyi. "Bridging the Chasm in Slovakia." *Transition*, vol. 4, no. 6 (November 1997), pp. 70–76.

Adele Kalniczky. "The Slovak Government's First Six Months in Office." *RFE/RL Research Report*, vol. 2, no. 6 (February 5, 1993), pp. 18–25.

Steve Kettle. "Slovakia's One Man Band: Profile of Prime Minister Vladimir Meciar." *Transition*, vol. 2, no. 17 (August 23, 1996), pp. 12–15.

William Kieran. "The Magyar Minority in Slovakia." *Regional and Federal Studies*, vol. 6 (Spring 1996), pp. 1–20.

Bennett Kovrig. "Hungarian Minorities in East Central Europe." *Occasional Paper Series: The Atlantic Council of the United States* (March 1994), pp. 17–20.

Eve Marikova Leeds. "Voucher Privatization in Czechoslovakia." *Comparative Economic Studies*, vol. 35 (Fall 1993), pp. 19–23.

Carol Skalnik Leff. "Could This Marriage Have Been Saved? The Czechoslovak Divorce." *Current History* (March 1996), pp. 129–134.

William H. Luers. "Czechoslovakia: Road to Revolution." *Foreign Affairs* (Spring 1990), pp. 77–98.

Peter Martin. "Calculating the Cost of Independence." *RFE/RL Research Report* (March 20, 1992), pp. 33–38.

Pavel Mates. "The New Slovak Constitution." *RFE/RL Research Report*, vol. 1, no. 43 (October 30, 1992), pp. 39–42.

Jiri Musil. "Czech and Slovak Society." *Government and Opposition*, vol. 28 (Autumn 1993), pp. 479–495.

Milan Nic, Jan Obrman, and Sharon Fisher. "New Slovak Government? More Stability?" *RFE/RL Research Report*, vol. 2, no. 47 (November 26, 1993), pp. 24–30.

Anne Nivat. "Slovak Media under Government Fire." *Transition*, vol. 2, no. 9 (May 6, 1996), p. 60.

Jan Obrman. "The Czechoslovak Elections." *RFE/RL Research Report*, vol. 1, no. 26 (June 26, 1992), pp. 12–19.

————. "The Czechoslovak Elections (1992): A Guide to the Parties." *RFE/RL Research Report*, vol. 1, no. 22 (May 29, 1992), pp. 10–16.

——. "Czechoslovakia: A Messy Divorce after All." *RFE/RL Research Report*, vol. 1, no. 41 (October 16, 1992), pp. 1–5.

——. "Czechoslovakia: Stage Set for Disintegration." *RFE/RL Research Report*, vol. 1, no. 28 (July 10, 1992), p. 26–32.

——. "Internal Disputes Shake Slovak Government." *RFE/RL Research Report*, vol. 2, no. 14 (April 2, 1993), pp. 13–17.

——. "The Slovak Government *versus* the Media." *RFE/RL Research Report*, vol. 2, no. 6 (February 1993), pp. 26–30.

——. "Slovak Politician Accused of Secret Police Ties." *RFE/RL Research Report*, vol. 1, no. 15 (April 12, 1992), pp. 13–17.

——. "Slovakia Declares Sovereignty; President Havel Resigns." *RFE/RL Research Report*, vol. 1, no. 31 (July 31, 1992), pp. 25–29.

——. "Uncertain Prospects for Independent Slovakia." *RFE/RL Research Report*, vol. 1, no. 49 (December 11, 1992), pp. 43–48.

Karolyi Okolicsanyi. "Hungary Cancels Treaty on Danube Dam Construction." *RFE/RL Research Report*, vol. 1, no. 26 (June 26, 1992), pp. 46–50.

——. "Slovak–Hungarian Tension: Bratislava Diverts the Danube." *RFE/RL Research Report*, vol. 1, no. 49 (December 11, 1992), pp. 49–54.

——. "Uncertain Prospects for Independent Slovakia." *RFE/RL Research Report*, vol. 1, no. 49 (December 11, 1992), pp. 43–48.

David M. Olson. "Dissolution of the State Political Parties and the 1992 Elections in Czechoslovakia." *Communist and Post–Communist Studies*, vol. 26, no. 3 (1993), pp. 301–314.

Jiri Pehe. "Controversy over the Referendum on the Future of Czechoslovakia." *RFE/RL Research Report*, vol. 1, no. 35 (August 30, 1991), pp. 27–30.

——. "Czechoslovak Parliament Votes to Dissolve Federation." *RFE/RL Research Report*, vol. 1, no. 48 (December 4, 1992), pp. 1–5.

——. "Czechoslovakia: Parties Register for Elections." *RFE/RL Research Report*, vol. 1, no. 18 (May 1, 1992), pp. 20–25.

——. "Czechoslovakia: Stage Set for Disintegration." *RFE/RL Research Report*, vol. 1, no. 28 (July 10, 1992), pp. 26–31.

——. "Czechs and Slovaks Define Post-divorce Relations." *RFE/RL Research Report*, vol. 1, no. 45 (November 13, 1992), pp. 7–11.

——. "Czechs and Slovaks Prepare to Part." *RFE/RL Research Report*, vol. 1, no. 37 (September 18, 1992), pp. 12–15.

——. "Czech-Slovak Conflict Threatens State Unity." *RFE/RL Research Report*, vol. 1, No. 1 (January 3, 1992), pp. 83-86.

——. "Czech–Slovak Relations Deteriorate." *RFE/RL Research Report*, vol. 2, no. 18 (April 30, 1993), pp. 1–5.

——. "Growing Slovak Demands Seen as Threat to Federation." *RFE/RL Research Report*, vol. 1, no. 12 (March 22, 1991), pp. 1–6.

——. "The Referendum Controversy in Czechoslovakia." *RFE/RL Research Report*, vol. 1, no. 43 (October 30, 1992), pp. 35–38.

——. "The State Treaty between the Czech and Slovak Republics." *RFE/RL Research Report*, vol. 1, no. 23 (June 7, 1991), pp. 11–15.

Jan S. Prybyla. "The Road from Socialism: Why, Where, What, and How." *Problems of Communism* (January–February 1991), pp. 1–17.

Alfred A. Reisch. "The Difficult Search for a Hungarian–Slovak Accord." *RFE/RL Research Report*, vol. 1, no. 42 (October 23, 1992), pp. 26–30.

———. "Hungarian Coalition Succeeds in Czech Elections." *RFE/RL Research Report*, vol. 1, no. 26 (June 16, 1992), pp. 20–22.

———. "Hungarian–Slovak Relations: A Difficult First Year." *RFE/RL Research Report*, vol. 2, no. 50 (December 17, 1993), pp. 16–23.

———. "Meciar and Slovakia's Hungarian Minority." *RFE/RL Research Report*, vol. 1, no. 43 (October 30, 1992), pp. 13–20.

Mathew Rhodes. "National Identity and Minority Rights in the Constitutions of the Czech Republic and Slovakia." *East European Quarterly*, vol. 29, no. 3 (Fall 1995), pp. 347–359.

Andrej Skolkay. "Slovak Government Tightens Its Grip on the Airwaves." *Transition*, vol. 2, no. 8 (April 19, 1996), pp. 18–21.

Zsofia Szilagyi, "Hungarian Minority Summit Causes Uproar in the Region." *Transition*, vol. 2, no. 18 (September 6, 1996), pp. 45–49.

Otto Ulc. "The Bumpy Road of Czechoslovakia's Velvet Revolution." *Problems of Communism* (May–June 1992), pp. 19–33.

———. "Czechoslovakia's Velvet Divorce." *East European Quarterly*, vol. 30, no. 3 (Fall 1996), pp. 331–352.

Leah D. Wedmore. "The Political Costs of Mochovce." *Transition*, vol. 1, no. 10 (June 23, 1995), pp. 46–50.

Michael Wyzan and Ben Slay. "Central, Eastern and Southeastern Europe's Year of Recovery." *Transition*, vol. 3, no. 2 (February 7, 1997), pp. 58–63.

Paul Wilson. "Czechoslovakia: The Pain of Divorce." *New York Review of Books* (December 17, 1992), pp. 69–75.

Pyotr Yudin. "Russia Barters Down Debt, Sends...MiG 29s to Slovakia." *Defense News*, September 30, 1995.

Index

ABOUT THE AUTHOR

MINTON F. GOLDMAN is Professor of Political Science at Northeastern University. A specialist in Russian and East European politics, he has published extensively, including *Revolution and Change in Central and Eastern Europe* (1997) and *Russia, The Eurasian Republics, and Central/Eastern Europe* (1998).